Fortune Telling
FOR FUN AND POPULARITY

Fortune Telling

FOR FUN

By Paul Showers

Distributed by:
THORSONS PUBLISHERS LIMITED,
Denington Estate, Wellingborough,
Northamptonshire, England.

NEWCASTLE PUBLISHING COMPANY, INC.

Printed in the United States of America.

NEWCASTLE PUBLISHING COMPANY, INC.

EDITION 1971

ISBN 0—87877—007—

Introduction

YOU ARE soon going to come into a lot of money, and . . .

You will meet someone you will marry, and . . .

You are going to make new friends who will greatly influence your life, and . . .

Yes, it's in the cards! And if you don't play cards, you can lift the veil into the future via your palm or your birthday.

Perhaps you're good at figures. Then "What Your Numbers Tell" is just your dish. By this process you can pry into the unknown and claim a good big share of all the health, happiness, and prosperity that is coming your way.

That dream you had last night. What does it mean? Your answer is in this book.

And don't miss "Your Fate in Magic Tables." You will be fascinated by its revelations.

For those who prefer other means of forecasting the future, this book shows you how to tell fortunes by tea leaves, handwriting, dice, dominoes, fire, moles, lucky charms, the Ouija Board, table tipping, and crystal gazing.

If you want to give your predictions that "professional touch," there is a chapter on "The Psychology of Fortune Telling."

Use this book when friends drop in for an evening. Let it entertain everybody at your next party.

Ladies and gentlemen, we give you—FORTUNE TELLING FOR FUN AND POPULARITY!

P. S.

Contents

CONTENTS

Fortune Telling
FOR FUN AND POPULARITY

What Your Palm Predicts

THE SHAPE OF THE FINGERS

THERE ARE four types of fingers, classified chiefly according to the shape of their tips. (See Fig. 1) These types are: rectangular, wedge-shaped, pointed, and tapering.

1—THE RECTANGULAR FINGER. The tip and the nail are practically square. The finger itself is substantial and almost appears to have four sides rather than to be rounded.

This indicates an individual whose sincerity and honesty will never be questioned. A conventional, law-abiding citizen, who will always command the respect of his acquaintances, he will, nevertheless, have to be on his guard against a lack of imagination which may lead him to overlook the truth in new ideas because he is too satisfied with his own knowledge. He would do well to remember the warning against being "the last to lay the old aside," for he will tend to forget that the world is constantly changing. Thirty years ago he probably never would have thought that the automobile would replace the horse, and today he will have to beware lest he fail to see the advantages in new inventions and new and untried ways of doing things.

2—THE WEDGE-SHAPED FINGER. The tip is wider at the end than it is at the first joint.

A sign that the individual is to have a life filled with activity and accomplishment. Marked creative ability will make itself evident here, though not along artistic lines. The owner may become a research chemist, a designer of bridges and buildings, or an engineer—he will be connected with something that has to do with the practical aspects of science. He will not hesitate to pursue aggressively whatever goal is before him, and since he

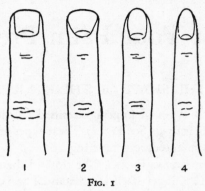

FIG. 1

has a pioneering strain, no obstacles will be too overwhelming for him. A problem he will have to contend with is a tendency to grow impatient, not only with others who may be less capable than he, but also with himself when he feels he is not progressing as rapidly as he should. This trait may make him restless and disagreeable at times, for all his life he will be driven by the relentless ambition of the go-getter, and unless he understands his own nature he may be lacking in consideration for the feelings of others.

3—THE POINTED FINGER. The tip alone—above the first joint—is pointed or rounded. The rest of the finger, below the first joint, is uniform in size throughout its length.

When a hand bears fingers of this type, together with a slender thumb and a palm that is not overly large, we have the sign of the artist, with all the characteristics of the sensitive temperament. This person will have to face throughout his life fully to the suggestion of less exacting minds to avoid being considered too strict and puritanical.

SMOOTH FINGERS. A lack of knots at the joints emphasizes the poetical, reflective nature. Here we can expect to find the budding poet—if he has not already "arrived," the author, the composer, the actor on the legitimate stage. These careers beckon to this type of individual, and it is possible that if this sign is combined with others which show initiative and alertness, he will follow his inclination even if it means changing his present mode of life.

THE FINGERS AS A GROUP

THE SPACES. The presence of a space between the first and second fingers indicates a person who is not going to have anybody make up his mind for him except himself, although this does not mean that he is necessarily stubborn or willful. He will be well fitted for an executive position which requires prompt decision.

Between the second and third fingers a space signifies that the owner of the hand may encounter some bitter obstacles but he will never allow himself to be defeated and in the end he will be amply rewarded for his courage.

If there is a space between the third and last finger, the individual may expect an attractive business offer, possibly a partnership in some going concern where his special capacity for direct action is particularly desired.

THE SIZE. Fingers that are extremely short are a sign that the owner may some day be amazed to discover that his fortunes have suddenly taken a turn for the worse. He may lose his job when he had no idea that the boss was not satisfied with his work; or he may discover that investments he has made are no longer worth anything. All this will happen because he is so inclined to take things for granted, instead of investigating carefully. There is hope for him, however, for if he can remember this failing and take care to overcome it, he will be able to avoid much trouble.

If the fingers are very long, almost the reverse is true. Here the individual spends entirely too much time fretting about matters of no consequence, and if he doesn't look out, he may bring on misfortune entirely through his own worrying. The best advice to him is: Take it easy; things aren't half as bad as you think they are.

When the fingers bend backward readily, watch out for a nosey, prying disposition, or extravagance with money.

THE NAILS

White or black specks or markings frequently appear on the nails. If they lie generally on the side of the nail which is toward the thumb, they are favorable and indicate either that a wish is coming true or that a gift may be expected.

However, if one of these spots occurs on that half of the nail which is farther away from the thumb, it may mean one of several things as follows:

BLACK SPOTS. *On the little finger* (See Fig. 3 A)—You are going to fail in some undertaking.

On the ring finger—You are in danger of doing something dishonorable.

On the middle finger—Something you value is going to be wrecked or destroyed.

On the index finger (See Fig. 3 B)—You are going to mislay something; possibly you will never find it again.

WHITE SPOTS. *On the little finger*—You are going to have a success in some business transaction that you had not anticipated.

On the ring finger—You are going to receive some money.

On the middle finger—You will make a journey soon, possibly by air.

On the index finger—Your ship will come in within the next year.

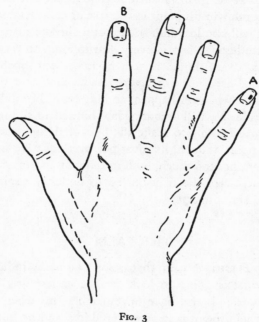

Fig. 3

THE THUMB

SMALL. If the thumb is small in relation to the rest of the hand, we may expect a person who may arrive at his goal largely through the efforts of others. In moments of crisis he will not be very reliable, since his emotions and not his intellect will dominate him.

LARGE. If the thumb is large, there is an indication of unsuspected coolness in the face of danger, hence we may have here someone who will perform some heroic deed some day that will win the attention of the entire nation.

RIGID. If the thumb bends back only with difficulty, the owner will have to be on guard against a stubborn streak. It will help him at times to win his point in the face of considerable opposition, but it will also lose him friends and alienate many persons who might otherwise become very dear to him and very helpful.

MOVEABLE. If the thumb is bent back without much trouble, the individual need not worry very much about what the future will bring; for whatever happens to him, he will be able to take it in his stride. He will accommodate himself to strangers with ease, and will be able to make the best of things wherever he goes. One point, though, he must not overlook: He inclines to exaggerate things too much, both in thought and in action; and if he is not careful he may be led to undertake some rather foolish and silly projects.

THE PALM

SOFT AND FLESHY. A palm that is soft and fleshy indicates that the individual is going to look for the easiest way of doing things. His friends will have to remember this when they call on him to help them in some undertaking, and he himself will have to be careful not to overindulge a fondness for fine foods and wines, expensive clothes, and other luxury items.

FIRM. A firm palm indicates a sense of responsibility that will bring rewards in the form of promotions and advancement in the chosen profession.

HARD AND THIN. The owner of a hard, thin palm should be advised to stop pinching pennies. With his type excessive thrift will not bring him satisfaction, for if he persists in his ways, he is going to lose friends, which in the long run really mean much more to him, for he is not by nature a miserly person.

HOLLOW. When a palm is very hollow the owner should be warned against risking much of his money in business, for he is bound to fail when he tries to start some enterprise in this field. He has no talents for commercial affairs, and should remember this in the conduct of his life.

THE SEVEN MOUNTS

The little swellings or mounds which are found around the edge of the palm are known as the Mounts. They are named after the planets, and their location is indicated in the diagram (Fig. 4).

THE MOUNT OF MERCURY. A normal development here indicates that the individual is going to do a certain amount of traveling during his lifetime. It also means that he is going to prosper in business life; and if the Mount is placed close to the edge of the hand, he can expect to have a decided success and to make a lot of money. He will deservedly acquire a reputation as a wit, and his quick and agile mind will also bring him considerable fame, possibly as an inventor, a scientist or a lawyer. He will be a noted conversationalist and will usually be lucky at cards, which will be due largely to his skill in playing. If this Mount is placed close to the Mount of the Sun, he will frequently be called upon to speak in public, and his brilliant eloquence will make him extremely popular as a toastmaster, after-dinner speaker or political orator.

Lack of this Mount is a sign the possessor will never get anywhere in business. All the gifts and talents which ordinarily go with the Mount will be denied him.

Overdevelopment of this Mount is a danger signal. Instead of merely being bright and clever, the owner is likely to use his quick brain to take advantage of those about him, devising crooked schemes and other disreputable ventures. Consequently he will have to be very alert to curb the impulses of his over-active mind, otherwise he may end up in the toils of the law where even his glibness and eloquence will not be able to save him from punishment.

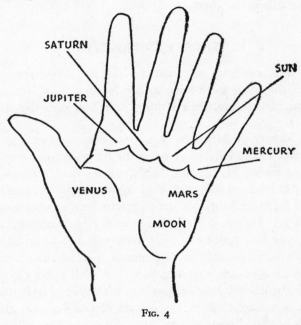

Fig. 4

With Mount of Venus. If Venus is also well developed, the individual will never have any trouble making friends, provided the lines in the palm are generally favorable. If they are un-favorable, the two Mounts warn the individual to guard against being fickle and to take care not to give up too readily when confronted by obstacles.

With Mount of the Moon. This combination signifies that the owner is likely to become a research scientist or professor, provided the lines of the palm are favorable. If they are not, he probably will lose a considerable amount of money through illegal conniving.

THE MOUNT OF THE SUN (APOLLO). Normal development indicates a bright future in many respects. To you who possess this Mount belong fame and wealth. Your instinctive love of beauty and splendor will lead you to success in the arts. If you have a more commercial turn of mind and reach the pinnacle of fortune in business, then your business will have something to do with the beautiful. You will be greatly admired because of your poise, your generosity, your graciousness. A truly sunny and golden personality, you will be able to see the bright side of things no matter what troubles beset you, and your natural optimism will be transmitted to all those about you, inspiring them when they are melancholy. Though your temper flares up easily, you will seldom make permanent enemies, for you will not be one to harbor grudges or to "stay mad" for very long. There is an unfavorable side to all this. Though you will have hosts of acquaintances it is probable that you will never have very many true friends. You may be affectionate but you will not be very persistent either in friendship or in love. For this reason your marital life may never be very happy, and your circle of friends will constantly be changing.

Lack of this Mount promises a future as dull as a cloudy day. Since there will be few intellectual interests in life, one cannot expect any sort of fame or brilliant success in anything. What interests there are will never lead to anything worthy of note.

Overdevelopment of the Sun means a serious danger of self-deception. Excessive vanity in matters of dress and conduct will lead you to reckless spending and general extravagance. Beware of overestimating talents which may not be at all remarkable. This is a sign of the "butterfly" type, careless, spendthrift, lacking in true wisdom. This type is a ready victim for flatterers, who may lead him into very serious difficulties because he is unwilling to face the stern realities about him.

With Mount of Mercury. With normal development of both you may expect advancement in professions calling for insight and resolute decision. A legal career will inevitably lead to the appointment to a judge's post. If scholarship and learning are chosen as a life work, you may expect some day to head a department in some important institution of learning.

With Mount of Venus. You would be wise to take up a career as an actor, a singer, or a dancer if you have a reasonable amount of talent, for you will always be happy in a profession in which you are giving pleasure to other people. You are naturally intended to be an entertainer.

With Mount of the Moon. You will make an excellent teacher, for you combine a sound common sense with a lively imagination which should help you to inspire your pupils while at the same time you give them the very best training possible.

With Mount of Mars. In the realm of the arts you will not be deterred by a belated success. If critics and the public do not recognize your talent at first, you will continue your work with undiminished enthusiasm, for you will be sure of your ultimate recognition.

THE MOUNT OF SATURN. Normal development indicates the hermit temperament—the love of solitude, the grave and philosophic mind. It is very possible that you will never marry, and you probably will not have many friends. All this is because Saturn casts a baleful influence, endowing the personality with a pessimistic, fatalistic streak. There is a certain amount of timidity here, a cautiousness which will prevent you from ever making much of a show in life. Because of a natural inclination toward profound thought and study, you may become very learned, but few in the world will ever be aware of this. Nor will you care, for you will show independence—almost contempt

—for the opinions of others. It is useless to struggle against this nature with which you have been endowed. You can only accept it for what it is.

Slight development of this Mount is a bit more favorable. The gloomy nature is modified a trifle and the cynicism and doubt are supplanted by a healthy skepticism and self-reliance. The timidity which plagues the possessor of a normally developed Mount is in this case prudence.

Lack of this Mount means an unspectacular life, void of any significance.

Overdevelopment is most unfavorable. The life of a recluse is indicated, for the individual's company is avoided by everyone who knows him. His pessimism will be a damper on the enthusiasm of people with whom he comes in contact. The dread of death will be constantly in his thoughts, and his morbid reflections may become so intense that they will interfere with whatever work he may be undertaking. This is a solemn sign, a warning of serious things to come. There is here, however, a ray of hope. If this Mount leans in the direction of the Mount of the Sun all of these morbid traits may be successfully combated and overcome.

With Mount of Mercury. If lines in the palm are favorable, this is a sign of happiness to come. There will be a keen delight in study, especially in scientific investigations. The individual will probably develop some scientific hobby at which he will spend many enjoyable hours, and if there is the sign of wealth elsewhere in the hand, it may come in connection with this hobby, possibly as a discovery in chemistry or physics leading to a new commercial process of some sort. If, however, the lines in the palm are generally unfavorable, Mercury with Saturn indicates a future filled with deception. The individual may become a salesman of fake securities or of quack nostrums.

With Mount of Moon. This combination shows a great gift

for occult lore. You will win reknown as an astrologer or an interpreter of hidden and mystic knowledge.

With Mount of Venus. If the lines of the palm are favorable, you should be successful as a comedian with a large dance orchestra or in vaudeville, for you have the natural inclination to be an entertainer. If the lines are not favorable, you should be warned that your greatest difficulty will be in controlling an unreasonably jealous nature.

With Mount of the Sun. If the palm's lines are favorable, you will often be consulted when people want advice on matters of taste and behavior. For this reason you might make a success as a confidential adviser or possibly a decorator—anything where you can capitalize upon this talent. If the lines are unfavorable, the reverse is the truth and you should always follow the advice of others in matters of dress and etiquette.

With Mount of Mars. A tactless, combative spirit may cost you dearly some day, and your cynical disregard of other people's rights may break a very dear friendship.

THE MOUNT OF JUPITER. Normal development shows that a natural inclination to dominate (though not necessarily to domineer) over others will probably result in a career in politics or military life. One other possibility is that a religious nature will lead the subject into the church, where he will rise as a minister or priest. Whatever he does, however, he will never allow his career to interfere with a love for the out-of-doors; and if he should have to spend a certain amount of time cooped up in an office, he will see to it that he is allowed generous vacation periods when he can get away from the noise and bustle of the city.

Lack of the Mount indicates a gradual loss of faith in religion, leading to agnosticism or atheism, even in defiance of the entreaties of parents and older friends. This may lead to much sorrow and even tragedy in the individual's immediate family.

Overdevelopment indicates coming cruelty to loved ones and friends as a result of a proud, tyrannical disposition. Jealousy is another trait the individual will have to guard against, or the intensity of this passion may lead him into trouble. A haughty, vain manner is not going to win him many friends, and it may lose him the ones he has already won.

With Mount of Mercury. A favorable sign, counteracting some of the less desirable Jupiter traits. Success as a surgeon or doctor is indicated; also, strange as it may seem, a talent for writing verse which may flower into a considerable gift some day.

With Mount of the Sun. You will be very rich, and your name will be known from one end of the land to the other.

With Mount of Saturn. No matter what may happen to you in life, things are always going to turn out for the best in the long run.

With Mount of Mars. You will win great honor for heroism, possibly in the service of your country.

With Mount of the.Moon. A reputation of honesty and reliability will serve you in good stead, and if you have a talent for business you probably will find yourself in a position of trust involving vast sums of money.

With Mount of Venus. Your house will always be thronged with friends and acquaintances, for your company will be loved and valued. This will be because of your naturally sunny nature, your sincerity and your true devotion to those who are close to you.

THE MOUNT OF VENUS. Normal development shows a passionate disposition and a number of ardent love affairs. There is also the danger that you will be of a flirtatious or fickle nature, drifting from one intense amour to another. However, this can be controlled and is nothing to worry about. In general this stands for an admiration and adoration of the opposite sex and shows that with a knowledge of the affairs of the heart a happy marriage can eventually be counted on, in which there will be much joy and gaiety. Music and dancing and song are indicated, and in general a gracious and pleasant life among friends and acquaintances. Whether the individual's warm and healthy interest in life and nature will ever express itself in the arts depends on other signs in the palm. However, he will always be known as one who "lives well" and who knows how to relish the best in life.

Lack of the Mount promises a rather austere, cold life in which love will not have much part and where even an intellectual appreciation of the beautiful in life will not bring the possessor a great deal of joy, for the blight of selfishness will warp his outlook.

Overdevelopment shows an unfortunate situation. Here is wantonness, a lack of self-discipline and a luxury-loving nature that will even stoop to licentiousness and riotous living. Talents and special aptitude may be completely wasted because of an unbridled desire for sensual pleasures. This is also the sign of the faithless lover, and the individual's promises will never carry much weight.

With Mount of Mars. This merely emphasizes the bad characteristics which are to be expected with an overdevelopment of Venus. Now there will be a restlessness to proceed from one orgy of pleasure to another. Little appeal can be made to reason in these circumstances.

With Mount of the Moon. If the lines of the palm are not favorable, the individual will never be able to be trusted in love, for he himself will probably seldom know where his heart really inclines. If they are favorable, this is a sign of an elopement or some very fanciful episode involving a Prince Charming or a Cinderella (as the case may be) with everything coming out happily in the end.

THE MOUNT OF MARS. Normal development in a man shows a great way with the ladies. It is the sign of the dashing type who sweeps them off their feet, consequently one can expect a number of very romantic episodes. The same sign in women indicates high spirit and pride, which will attract the bold and vigorous type of man. In either case love will be deep and glowing and will have a dash and style to it that is usually only found in the movies or in novels. It may be coupled with adventure of some sort—the honeymoon may be to some distant land or clime where hidden danger lurks but where the reward is great. From this type of person you can expect a complete frankness and a sincere charm which will win many friends and followers. Daring and courage will take him into many strange and exciting places, and all through his life he will know action and even danger; but where a weaker type might cringe with fear, he will thrive on the stimulation such a life will bring.

Lack of this Mount indicates cowardice and is a sign that the individual will never be able to stand up for his own rights and will always give in rather than face a quarrel.

Overdevelopment is not a good sign. Here the bravery will soon become bragging and insolence. A tendency toward cruelty may lead to some outrageous behavior.

With Mount of the Moon. If the lines of the palm are favorable, this indicates a career having to do with ships and sailing. By extension this can also be considered to include aviation. Hence the possessor may be either a pilot in the air or on the sea. If the lines are unfavorable, this means very foolhardy ventures will be undertaken which will come to no good.

THE MOUNT OF THE MOON. Normal development means travel of some sort, probably to regions which have not yet been completely explored, such as the jungles of the Amazon, the valleys of Tibet, or the wilds of Siberia. A love of the strange and mysterious will cause this, and all through life there will be a fascination for the exceptional, the rare and the unexplained. There is also a sign of laziness when the need arises to think through a problem clearly, hence the individual will have to be specially on guard lest his taste for the strange and unknown lead him heedlessly into a position of great danger. People will always come to him for consolation and sympathy, for he has a naturally kind nature, although he may cling to acquaintances who are really unworthy of him merely because he has a sentimental regard for them and what they once represented in former days.

Lack of this Mount shows an unimaginative nature which can hope for very little more than a plodding, dull existence, usually in a single locality throughout life.

Overdevelopment is a warning against acute melancholy. The individual will be disturbed continually by the most frightening dreams which he will be able to find little explanation for. In his waking hours he will be sad and dispirited, worrying about terrible things in the future which will never occur. He will have to remember that half of the slights and unkindnesses which he imagines he has been made the victim of are really non-existent, and that an oversensitiveness on his part is leading him to suppose things which do not exist. Unless he guards against this too active imagination, it will hold him back in his career and thwart his chances for success and advancement by alienating him from people who are in a position to help him.

THE SEVEN SPECIAL SIGNS

The seven special signs (Fig. 5) may occur any place on the palm, but when they appear on the Mounts, they have particular meaning.

1.—THE DOT

On Mercury—You are about to suffer some sort of loss in your business affairs.

On the Sun—Something is going to occur which will damage your reputation in the eyes of the world.

On Saturn—Be on guard against evil which may affect the entire course of your life.

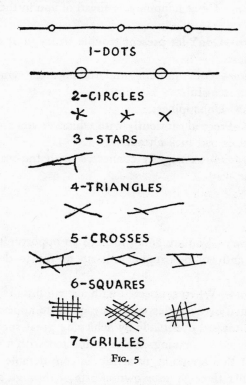

FIG. 5

On Jupiter—You are going to lose some money.

On Venus—Someone you love dearly is going to lose something valuable.

On Mars—You are going to find yourself in a difficult situation.

On the Moon—Beware of worry and mental strain.

2.—The Circle

On Mercury—An unpleasant experience connected in some way with a lake, a river, or the sea.

On the Sun—Great happiness is ahead of you in the very near future.

On Saturn—Don't let present trouble worry you; everything is for the best.

On Jupiter—Your present undertakings are going to be completely successful.

On Venus—Unhappiness.

On Mars—Proceed cautiously with whatever you are planning to do; there is bad luck ahead.

On the Moon—A tragedy connected with the water or the sky in some way.

3.—The Star

On Mercury—You are going to have an opportunity to cheat somebody and not be caught. It is up to you to decide what to do.

On the Sun—When connected with a small line: If you refuse to be downed by obstacles which are going to appear, you will reap a rich reward eventually by achieving great success in the line you are now pursuing. When connected with a number of small lines: You are going to acquire a considerable amount of money, either through your own efforts or through a legacy of some sort. When by itself and not linked to any lines: Watch your step; a mistake may spoil your hopes of complete success.

On Saturn—A grave warning; you may be led into doing something which will involve some sort of punishment.

On Jupiter—Your hopes are going to be completely realized, especially in matters of the heart.

On Venus—Trouble arising directly from a love affair. Watch out; Cupid isn't always kind.

On Mars—Intense jealousy may lead you to commit some very rash deed which you will be sorry for the rest of your life.

On the Moon—If other indications of the hand are unfavorable, this indicates grave temptation.

4.—THE TRIANGLE

On Mercury—Keep your eye on political affairs; you will find something which you can turn to your immediate advantage.

On the Sun—Some field of higher learning is going to assist you to reap a great reward.

On Saturn—Trust your hunches or any suggestions that may come to you in dreams, for something very favorable is about to come your way.

On Jupiter—You are going to need great tact to accomplish your purpose in the near future.

On Venus—Don't try to take advantage of the person who loves you; it will come to no good.

On Mars—Something you do in connection with the nation's armed forces is going to win you great praise, possibly advancement.

On the Moon—Follow your daydreams intelligently and you will be very successful.

5.—THE CROSS

On Mercury—A robbery; beware.

On the Sun—Connected with a small line: You may count on something very helpful in realizing your present goal. By itself: Your present objective is not going to be achieved immediately. If it is wealth you are after, you may never realize complete happiness with it.

On Saturn—You will never have any children.

On Jupiter—Married life was intended for you and will bring you your greatest joy and satisfaction.

On Venus—A divorce or a broken engagement.

On Mars—You are going to get into a fight because of your own bad temper. It will be you who should apologize.

On the Moon—You are too easily influenced by foolish superstitions.

6.—THE SQUARE

On Mercury—You are going to face bankruptcy but will be saved from it unexpectedly at the last moment.

On the Sun—Somebody is going to try to take advantage of you, possibly cheating you in a business transaction, but you probably will detect the deceiver and outwit him completely.

On Saturn—You will be miraculously saved from disaster.

On Jupiter—Rely on your common sense and don't listen to the advice of even those who wish you the best in the world, for it is your own basic instincts that are going to lead you to achieve your goal.

On Venus—You are going to lose your freedom temporarily.

On Mars—Your temper is going to be provoked, but you must keep your head and not fly off the handle.

On the Moon—Don't let your dreams carry you away; keep your feet on the ground and try to look at things as they are, not as you would like them to be. In that way you are going to get what you are after.

7.—THE GRILLE

On Mercury—You are going to be invited to join in some very dishonest business; if you do you will regret it.

On the Sun—You are going to overestimate yourself as the

result of some achievement, and if you don't watch your step even your friends are going to grow sick of your vanity and desert you.

On Saturn—A streak of bad luck.

On Jupiter—Don't let success go to your head; you are going to be greatly tempted to become self-satisfied and conceited.

On Venus—You are going to be justly accused of being too inquisitive.

On Mars—A warning. Be wary of your next step.

On the Moon—A bad spell of the blues and discontent.

THE LINES ON THE MOUNTS

Short lines occasionally are found on the Mounts, and they have a special meaning. As a rule they run vertically (that is, parallel with the four fingers—see Fig. 6 A).

Occasionally short lines are found on the Mounts which run crosswise (that is, from left to right—see Fig. 6 B). These are special cases and are known as crosslines. All lines referred to below are vertical unless noted as crosslines.

On Mercury. *One line* is a sign that you are going to come into possession of some money quite by surprise.

Several lines—An appeal is going to be made to you for financial assistance, for you have a reputation for generosity.

Several lines and the presence of a well developed Mount of the Moon—If you have ever had any desire to become a physician or a surgeon, you should follow this inclination, for you have many natural qualifications for this profession. In a woman's hand this signifies that she will become the wife of an engineer.

A quantity of little short lines—You must check your tendency to be talkative or your friends and acquaintances are going to find you rather a bore.

One crossline—You are going to suffer a setback through no fault of your own.

ON THE SUN. *One line* means you will be rich and greatly admired.

Three lines—You have genuine talent which is never going to be fully appreciated.

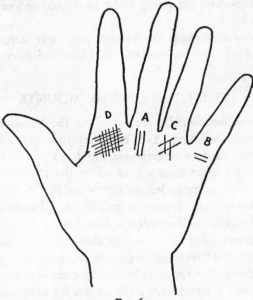

FIG. 6

Several lines, crossing one another (See Fig. 6 C)—Whatever desires you have to write, compose, or paint will never bear fruit for you are too analytical and think too much about your inspirations.

ON SATURN. *One line* signifies happiness and good fortune beyond your wildest dreams.

Several lines—Things are not going to go well for you.

One crossline—Your progress is going to be slow but steady and you may reach a very prominent position eventually.

ON JUPITER. *One line* indicates that what you had thought was unlikely to succeed is going to be very successful.

Several lines—You should keep on trying even though there will never be any great success as a result of your effort.

Several lines crossing one another—You are going to gain the reputation of one who lives a very unrestrained sort of life. This is not very favorable.

A network of very fine lines (See Fig. 6 D)—Many minor disappointments.

One crossline—An investment which you are counting on is going to turn out badly.

ON VENUS. *One line* signifies that your love is going to be returned with faithfulness and devotion.

Several lines—You are going to be disappointed in a friend who will not properly appreciate a kindness you have done.

Several lines crossing one another—You should not marry in haste, no matter how great the impulse, for you have a very deep and passionate nature which is not always as wise as it is loving.

ON MARS. *One line* indicates an action of great bravery which will earn you the reputation of a hero.

Several lines—This is not favorable. You will love so intensely that you will more often be cruel than kind. You may spoil your chances of happiness by a display of terrible rage.

One crossline—Beware a hooded figure coming in the night.

ON THE MOON. *One line* signifies that there is hanging over you some strange and menacing power. Look out for groups of eleven and seventeen.

Several lines—You are going to be troubled with many little problems; love is not going to turn out happily.

One crossline—You will achieve success through great mental effort, possibly at the cost of your peace of mind.

Several crosslines—A bird will bring you great sorrow.

THE PRINCIPAL LINES OF THE HAND

The principal lines of the hand are represented in Fig. 7. They are classified in three groups: the Major Triad, the Minor Triad, and the Lesser or Auxiliary Lines.

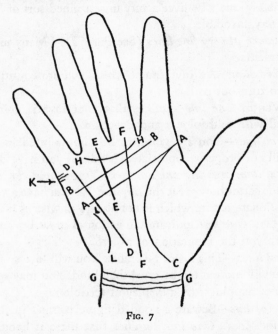

FIG. 7

The Primary (Major) Triad consists of the Line of the Head (A-A), the Line of the Heart (B-B), and the Line of Life (A-C).

The Minor Triad consists of the Line of Health (D-D), the Line of Apollo (E-E), and the Line of Fate (F-F).

The Auxiliaries are the Bracelet, sometimes called the Rascette, which are the lines about the wrist (G-G), the Girdle of

Venus (H-H), the Lines of Marriage (indicated at K), and the Line of Luna (L-L).

These lines may not always be single and solid. In fact, they generally are characterized by certain special markings. The main types of these markings are indicated in Fig. 8.

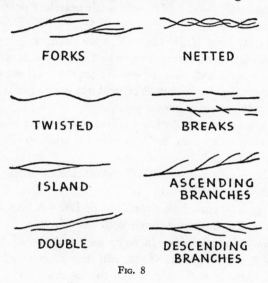

FORKS NETTED

TWISTED BREAKS

ISLAND ASCENDING BRANCHES

DOUBLE DESCENDING BRANCHES

Fig. 8

The Line of the Head

This line is a gauge of one's intelligence. When it is well defined, straight, and runs well across the palm it is an indication that the individual will always display good judgment in decisions. He will make an excellent executive, for he has a natural ability to estimate the difficulties of a problem and think things through to a satisfactory solution.

A very long line, running clear to the edge of the palm, means that he will be successful in business affairs but he may not always be an ideal companion because he will be rather calculating and exacting. For this reason he may not make an ideal mate, for he will be too demanding. He will set standards that are rather unreasonable for the ordinary mortal. Affection, sympathy and warm-heartedness will not be marked traits in his make-up.

Long, with Mounts of Mars, Jupiter and Saturn well developed—You will pursue your goal with ceaseless determination and vigor.

Long, with long Heart Line—You are going to get your way not by blustering or threats but by tact and diplomacy. You will be the one who will always pour oil on troubled waters.

Long but dimly outlined—You will not keep your word when your friends are counting on you.

Very short but well outlined—You will never accomplish all you have set out to do, for you will not stick to the job until it is finished.

Very short and dim—You will never have the energy to carry out your plans.

Running downward near the Line of Life—A love affair ending unhappily—largely through your own fault.

Downward and ending in large and widespread forks (See Fig. 8)—A sign of genius. If you will only persist and believe in yourself, there is nothing that you cannot do.

Downward and ending in a small fork—You will use deceit and cunning to gain something you desire very greatly.

Downward and continuing to the Mount of the Moon, with Girdle of Venus well developed—You are going to take great risks, either in connection with love or some business enterprise.

Downward with short Heart Line—Your stubbornness and headstrong disposition will bring you bad luck until you learn self-control.

Ascending toward the Heart Line—A trying experience.

Ascending in the second half toward Mercury—You will not

be gifted with originality, but you will achieve success by imitating others.

Netted (See Fig. 8)—A slight tendency toward nervousness.

Twisted and ascending toward the Mount of Mercury (See Fig. 8)—Temporary despair.

Twisted with Breaks (See Fig. 8)—You may be subject to forgetfulness.

Twisted with several Islands (See Fig. 8)—Financial difficulties with great temptation to dishonesty.

Double line (See Fig. 8)—You will receive money from a relative.

With Breaks under the Mount of Saturn—A number of serious problems to solve.

With Breaks under the Mount of the Sun—A quarrel with a loved one which will never be mended.

Breaks near the point of union with the Life Line—Unhappiness which will last only for a short time.

Breaks under the Mount of Mercury—A quarrel with a loved one over money matters.

Many Breaks throughout the line—An increasing melancholy.

Descending Branches (See Fig. 8) *with a downward sloping line*—An idealistic nature will prevent you from ever achieving great wealth. You will prefer to let the morrow take care of itself without trying to lay plans for your future.

Branches descending and touching the Life Line—The warning of unhappiness to come.

A Branch ascending (See Fig. 8) *to the Mount of Jupiter*—Great wealth as the result of a brilliant scientific discovery or outstanding success in business. Several Branches ascending to Jupiter mean increasingly greater wealth. But if Jupiter bears the sign of a Cross, this is an evil omen.

Branch ascending to the Sun—You will acquire reknown in painting, sculpture, music or literature.

Branch ascending to Mercury—Success in motion pictures or on the stage; also success in business.

Branch ascending and joining with Heart Line—Marriage ended suddenly.

Branches ascending to Heart Line but not touching—Your life will be profoundly changed by persons around you.

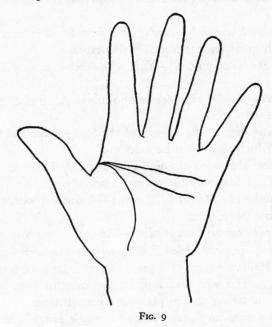

Fig. 9

Joined with Heart and Life Lines at point of origin (See Fig. 9)—You may meet with sudden tragedy.

Joined to the Heart Line midway across the palm—Serious problems lie ahead.

Joined with Life Line for a considerable distance before separating—Shyness. You may become overly assertive and domineering because you wish to cover up your natural timidity.

Or you may be the typical retiring type and seldom assert yourself. In either case you must work to overcome this problem, for it will handicap you in many ways.

Not joined with Life Line (See Fig. 10 A-A)—A life filled with activity and daring.

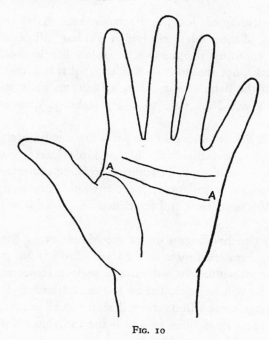

Fig. 10

Separated by some distance from Life Line at point of origin —Beware of overconfidence. You may be riding for a bad fall.

Joined to Life Line by Netted Lines—You are going to make the most money doing something you do not like to do.

White dots on the line—You are going to make a surprising discovery.

Black dots—An unpleasant situation.

Cross on the line—A fall.

Star at the end of the line—An unexpected ending.

A circle on the line—Impending trouble.

THE LINE OF THE HEART

When well defined, long, and straight this shows true and devoted love of the noblest sort which will last "till death do us part." For enduring happiness throughout life it should not contain breaks, nor should it be too long, for if it extends from one edge of the palm to the other, it indicates an intensity of passion that will lead only to bitter jealousy, quarrels, and heartbreaks.

When this line is lacking in the palm there will never be any great love in the individual's life and his interests will be focused largely in himself. In addition to being rather cold and selfish, he probably will never trust anybody very completely, and as a result his friends and acquaintances probably will never trust him.

Normally this line begins under the Mount of Jupiter.

Beginning between Jupiter and Saturn—Love is not going to come to the individual; he will have to seek it. However, when he finds it he will be rewarded by a true and lasting devotion. In his marriage there will be comradeship as well as love. There will be an ideal family life, in which the individual will make a very kind and loving parent.

Beginning under Saturn—There will be a great passion in your life which will not last nor will it ever be duplicated.

Beginning under Saturn, extending clear to edge of palm—An overpowering love, to which you will sacrifice everything, will lead you into a situation which will require great boldness and daring if you are to escape safely.

Long and dipping upward close to the Girdle of Venus—An

acute attack of jealousy. If there are many breaks in the line this jealousy will destroy a great love.

Long and dipping downward momentarily then resuming its course—Duplicity, offering good grounds for jealousy and anger.

Long and dim—Faithless love, ending in great quarrels, with tears shed.

Running downward toward Head Line—An increasing tendency toward sullenness and a selfish, unfriendly disposition.

Downward while Life and Head Lines are joined for some distance—Too much self-consciousness is going to hinder your efforts to love and be loved. You will appear to be cold and calculating even though your feelings will be deep and sincere, and you will have a hard time convincing the object of your affections that you really are serious.

Netted line—You will never be able to make up your mind whom you love best and so your affections will constantly be changing.

Netted and dimly outlined—Violent passions which will never last; a danger of flirting or philandering; an unsettled marriage.

Netted and beginning under Saturn—Spinsterhood or bachelorhood, as the case may be. The failure to marry will not be because you are not loved but because you will scorn the love which is offered you, believing it unworthy of you.

Double line—A long-suffering, deep love will lead you to many personal sacrifices even at the cost of your pride and in the end will bring you nothing but great sorrow.

One to four Breaks—Signs of broken engagements, one break meaning one broken engagement, two breaks meaning two engagements, etc.

More than four Breaks—An inconstant love, fickleness, lies and duplicity possibly ending in divorce.

Break under Saturn—The engagement will be broken off largely because friends of the other party will interfere in what first started out as a trifling lovers' quarrel.

Break under the Sun—The breaking off of a very foolish engagement in which the partners are obviously mismatched and would never be happily married. This is a very fortunate sign.

Joined with the Head Line at any point—A grave warning; sudden unhappiness looms ahead.

Branch descending and touching Head Line—A love affair which will be terminated shortly before the wedding day.

Branches descending but not touching the Head Line—Many love affairs which will all exert a tremendous power to change the life of the individual. This may involve changes in place of residence, in occupation, in financial status.

Branch descending to Mount of the Moon—A quarrel.

Branch descending and cutting Fate Line—The individual will be left to live a life of solitude.

Ascending branches—True friends and many happy times together.

Branch ascending to Saturn—Love which will not be returned, may even be spurned.

Branch ascending to the Sun—A marriage troubled by interference of in-laws.

Branch ascending to Mercury—Marriage or engagement troubled by constant quarrels over money—usually one partner reproaching the other for extravagance.

Fork at beginning under Jupiter—Wealth and fame.

Fork under Jupiter with one prong sloping toward Head Line—Somebody whom you trust is going to take advantage of you.

Forked at beginning between Jupiter and Saturn—In seeking to get what you want you are going to make some very serious blunders.

Forked at the end, with one prong going into Mount of Mercury—A sign of a divorce.

Unforked or unbroken at the edge of the palm under Mercury —There will be no children in the marriage.

White dots on the line—An ardent lover who is never spurned.

·*Black dots*—Your wishes are going to be thwarted by someone prominent in public affairs.

Cross on the line—Mounting debts, bankruptcy.

Island in the line—Infidelity.

Circle on the line—A serious and unsuspected situation will arise.

THE LINE OF LIFE

To estimate how long you will live, spread the fingers and place the point of a pencil between the index and middle fingers. Now trace a vertical line (indicated by dotted line in Fig. 11) down the palm until you come to the Life Line (at point A in Fig. 11). This point on the Life Line represents about the twentieth year. Now follow the curve of the Life Line down around the Mount of Venus to where it touches the first wrist line (at point B in Fig. 11).

If the Life Line does not extend all the way, you trace the path it would take if it ended at point B (as is shown by dotted curved line in Fig. 11). Point B represents 100 years.

Now all you have to do is locate the middle point (C in Fig. 11) of the curve A-B. Then you divide each of the halves into four equal parts. This will give you eight divisions between A and B, each standing for a decade. Thus with A standing for the twentieth year, D stands for the thirtieth year, E the fortieth year, and so on. The point where the Line of Life actually ends on this scale gives the approximate length of the subject's life.

In Fig. 11, the Life Line ends halfway between C and G, which means the individual will live to be about 65.

If the Line of Life is lacking, it is the sign of an indefinite span of life.

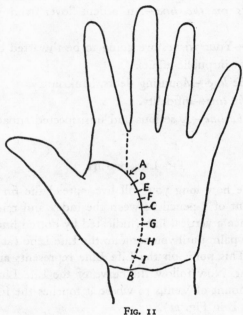

FIG. 11

If the Life Line is well marked throughout its length—It is an indication of a well-balanced life which will never undergo any violent changes of fortune, such as poverty and misery one year and unexpected riches the next, or periods of excellent health followed suddenly by intervals of illness.

If the line is thick in some places and thin in others—This shows a series of unexpected turns in fortune, together with alternating moods of melancholy and of happiness.

Pale in certain sections—This is a sign of rather difficult years, but one cannot always determine the time of life when these will occur on the basis of the time scale given.

Netted—A frailty which may never be completely overcome. The individual should guard against exposure to the elements and overwork.

Joined with the Head Line by a series of netted lines—Your fortune will often be endangered through rash acts undertaken without due consideration of their consequences.

Separated at the beginning from the Head Line—You will use up much energy in reckless actions which will not bring enough reward to merit the effort.

Double line—Bad luck and other unfavorable signs which are shown elsewhere in the hand will not be so serious when the Life Line is double in certain sections.

Breaks—These represent unfortunate and unexpected conditions.

Ascending branches—Good fortune coming from the efforts of the individual.

Branches ascending through the Heart and Head Lines—Wealth and honor will be yours as a reward for brilliant work.

Descending branches—You will be a failure for lack of application and perseverance.

Fork at the beginning of the line—If other signs are favorable, this means many people will come seeking your advice on personal matters; you may be able to capitalize upon this in some business or professional way—as a lawyer, doctor or investment broker. If other signs are unfavorable, you will waste much time in foolish activities that will get you nowhere.

Fork in middle of line—You are going on a number of long journeys that may take you out of the confines of your native land.

Fork at the end—You may be dependent on the charity of others in your old age.

Fork at the end with one prong touching Fate Line—This shows a life which will be lacking in excitement; the individual will get "stuck in a rut" and will probably never get out except by great effort.

Fringe at the end of line—A peaceful old age is in prospect in pleasant surroundings but with no great wealth.

White dots on the line—A condition involving one of the five senses.

Black dots—Worries over family relationships and finances.

Star—Despondency.

Triangle—After an illness there will be a long convalescence.

Island—You are going to have unexpected visits from friends you have not seen for years.

THE LINE OF HEALTH

This is also known as the Line of the Liver, or the Hepatica.

If the line is long, well defined and straight—It indicates a long life, with a capacity for business or the stage. It also indicates that the possessor will prosper in his chosen line of work and will seldom if ever be ill for any great length of time.

Short and dim—Unless care is taken, you are going to have trouble with your teeth.

If the line is missing—It is a very favorable sign if there is no health line in the palm, for that means that the individual is never going to be bothered about his health. He will be free to do whatever he likes, for illness will never hamper him in carrying out his plans.

Beginning at the Bracelet, not joined with Life Line—A sign of a busy life requiring frequent trips away from home, though never for very great lengths of time. If it also lies close to the edge of the hand, ocean travel is indicated.

Ending in Mount of the Sun—A sign of a fabulously wealthy

business enterprise which will be built up largely through the individual's own efforts.

Ending in Mount of Mercury—Friendship with famous or near-famous persons, resulting from the line of work the individual is in.

Ending between Mounts of Moon and Mars—The individual has a gift for prophecy which may be a great asset to him some day.

Netted—Loss of hair must be guarded against.

Double—When the line is double in certain sections it is a sign that whatever diseases are indicated in the palm will not be as serious as they might otherwise have been.

Breaks—Illnesses.

Ascending branches—You are going to change the line of work in which you are accustomed to earn your living.

Joined with Life Line at start—Spells of giddiness.

Linked to Life Line by netted lines—Muscular ailments, possibly gout.

Joining the Heart Line—A weakness which must be guarded against.

Forked—A tendency toward despondency.

Circle on the line—Minor misfortunes while hunting or driving.

Star—There will never be more than one child if the subject marries.

Triangle—An illness from which the patient will recover quickly.

Island—The vocal organs affected by improper use.

The Line of the Sun (Apollo)

The presence of the Line of Apollo, or the Line of the Sun as it is sometimes called, always indicates an aptitude for the arts.

If it is not to be found in the hand, it may be assumed either that artistic interests and pursuits will have little appeal for the individual or that the individual will have little talent in that direction.

Though the line always starts in or near the Mount of the Sun, it may not always end in the same place.

Ending in the center of the palm—It indicates that artistic success will only come after a good deal of struggle and disappointment.

Ending at the Life Line—Artistic pursuits probably will become the main activity of life, being treated seriously and not as a hobby. There will be a reasonable amount of success, both financially and artistically, and the individual will be recognized by the public as a man of talent if not of genius.

Ending near or on the Heart Line—Recognition and success will not come until very late in life after many discouraging and apparent failures.

Ending in Mount of the Moon—Success, when it comes, will not be entirely due to the individual's efforts alone. There will have been help of some sort from friends or loved ones. Possibly the wife or sweetheart will have been the great source of inspiration, without which the artist never could have achieved his goal.

If the Sun Line is clear and well defined—A robust, healthy physical condition will give plenty of energy for the exacting tasks of the artist and will result in sound accomplishment.

If thin and pale—The impulse toward artistic things will never be fully expressed, since there will be lacking the driving energy that is needed for true artistic creation. The individual may become a fairly gifted amateur or one who "plays" at art, or he may even become a critic.

Long and extending into a very hollow palm—This is a bad sign, suggesting the "evil genius" type. The individual's creative powers will be employed in unethical ways, or he may become the dissolute artist, with little respect for moral standards or conventions.

With well developed Mounts of Jupiter and Mercury—This indicates a good commercial success as well as an artistic one. The individual will be well paid for his art works, whether they be paintings, statues, songs or plays and novels.

Beginning just below the Mount of the Sun—This indicates a delay of some sort. Possibly the career as an artist will not begin until well along in middle life—after children or family cares have ceased to require so much attention. Or it may signify a delay in the full realization of the individual's talents —he may work for many years without producing anything very worth while.

Crossed by a marriage line—This indicates an art career handicapped by the responsibilities of a family.

Twisted—This indicates a talent wasted in the wrong field of activity—for example, a failure as a writer who would have been a much better painter or composer, or a bad sculptor who should have been writing poetry instead.

Accompanied by several shorter lines on Mount of the Sun— This shows a scattering of energies, an attempt to succeed in several lines of art instead of a concentration upon one field of activity.

Breaks—Two or three breaks indicate a certain amount of failure. If the line is badly broken throughout its length, it means success will never be very great.

Branch connecting with Mount of Mercury—Too great an interest in the money to be made from art will dull the inspiration of the individual and result in bad imitations of the work of other people.

Branch connecting with the Head Line—Ability in writing of poetry, novels or plays.

Ascending branch leading to Saturn—Much of the artist's life will be spent in poverty, with the demand for the necessities of life always hampering true inspiration.

Fork at beginning on Mount of the Sun—Creative ability along several lines which may help the individual to achieve success in more than one field of art.

Fork at end of line—Recognition and great wealth from a successful career.

Island on the line—Some misfortune which will directly affect the artist's work.

Star on line of Mount of Saturn—Great public acclaim, with the individual's name and picture appearing frequently in magazines and newspapers.

Circle on the line—Much of the wealth realized from art work wasted in gambling and other excesses.

THE LINE OF FATE

A clear, well defined Fate Line starting at the base of the palm and extending well up near the base of the fingers indicates a steady and gratifying progress toward success in life, with no major setbacks or failures of fortune. If the line is entirely absent, a very dull existence is foreshadowed, with no great satisfactions or achievements.

If too long, the line may mean misfortune. Thus if it starts on the wrist so as to cross one or two of the lines of the Bracelet (See Fig. 12 A), there is grief and sorrow in prospect. This will come through the individual's efforts to better his condition and will result from his striving too hard to win his objectives. If the line should extend through the Mount of Saturn to the middle finger above, this, too, shows that there will be sorrow brought on largely through the unintentional efforts of the individual himself.

If the line starts from the Life Line (See Fig. 13), it is a very favorable sign, showing that the individual's ambitions are going to be realized in the course of things to come. However, this will depend to some extent on whether the Fate Line itself is

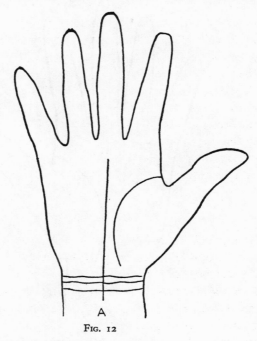

A

FIG. 12

clear and well defined and contains none of the unfavorable omens in the following list. If it does contain some of these, the chance of realizing complete success will be lessened to some extent.

If the line starts in the Mount of the Moon—Your life is not going to be entirely under your own control. Other people are going to have a certain amount of influence in the way things shape up. If success is indicated elsewhere in the palm, this means that the success will come because of the help of an outsider. If failure is shown elsewhere, then it will not be deserved, for you will be the victim of some evil person's actions.

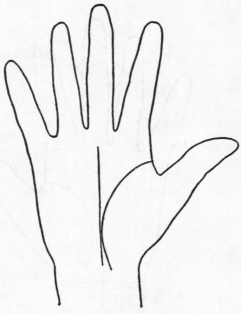

Fig. 13

If the line starts in the middle of the palm—Do not expect any great change—for better or worse—during youth or early middle age. After that there may be a struggle of some sort. Its outcome will be indicated elsewhere in the palm.

If it ends in Mount of the Sun—Riches are to appear without any effort on the part of the individual.

If it ends in Mount of Mercury—Business will exert the greatest influence over the life of the individual.

Netted—A netted Fate Line means complications. Netted

near the Head Line means complications having to do with business and indicates legal difficulties—lawsuits, etc. Netted near the Heart Line means complications in matters of love—not only "another man" or "another woman" but also divided loyalty between parents and one's spouse, etc.

Twisted—Great sadness, possibly even misery. If twisted only in one section, a limited period of mourning is indicated.

Dim and hard to see—Many projects on which you are counting will seem to be coming out satisfactorily· and then at the last minute will disappoint you badly.

Growing very dim at the end—A failure to keep up-to-date in views about life will lead to increasing failure to make good and probably will cause unhappiness because of an inability to see facts as they are.

Break—A decided change in fortune, probably a new occupation or life in entirely new surroundings.

Cut through by several short lines—Tragedies and unhappiness, though not permanent.

Ascending branches—Several different occupations or professions during life.

Branch ascending to Head Line—A hobby or a sideline of work having to do with intellectual activities. If there is a star on this branch, success will come unexpectedly through. this hobby.

Branch leading to Mount of Mars—A great deal of hard work to achieve whatever goal is sought—possibly some setbacks and grief.

Branch ascending to Mount of Jupiter—Assistance from persons of great influence or renown in public life.

Descending branches—Loss of wealth through bad investments; loss of jobs.

Branch leading to Mount of the Moon—Great peril through the individual's own foolishness.

Black dot—Financial difficulties, many unexpected bills amounting to large sums of money.

Cross—Eventual happiness through love which will triumph in spite of the greatest obstacles.

Fork at end of line—A favorable omen reinforcing any good-luck signs in the palm and making success more certain. If bad luck is indicated elsewhere, this will help reduce it.

Fork at beginning of line—Circumstances in childhood which were not pleasant will have considerable influence in later life, sometimes for the worse, other times for the better.

Island—A public scandal or disgrace of some sort which will bring loss of some friends.

Triangle—A divorce or an ill-fated love affair.

A circle low on the line—News of a near friend or loved one.

The Bracelet

The lines about the wrist are said to indicate among other things a certain length of life. An estimate based upon them should be checked with the Life Line, and from the Bracelet and the Life Line an approximate life span should be determined.

The first line of the Bracelet at the base of the palm (See Fig. 14 A-A) represents about thirty-three years of life.

The second (B-B) stands for twenty-five to twenty-eight years, so that with two lines one can count on an age of from fifty-eight to sixty-one.

The third line (C-C) stands for about twenty-two years, so that with three lines in the Bracelet an age between eighty and possibly eighty-five is indicated.

If the lines are well outlined—A happy and eventful life in general is indicated. Whatever troubles and sorrows come will be only part of the daily lot of all mankind, and since "Time can heal all wounds," in the long run the future will hold much that is worth while and that will give contentment and satisfaction.

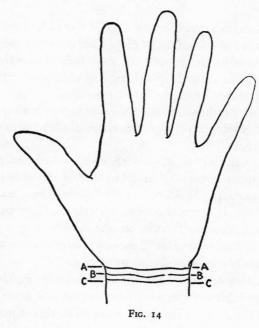

FIG. 14

If the lines are dim—Energy and time are going to be wasted in the pursuit of unrewarding goals. A reckless attitude toward money is also indicated, and the individual may find that, regardless of any fortune he may have amassed earlier in life, in his old age he will be poor and may have to depend on charity for his food and shelter.

If the lines ascend under the Mount of Venus—It is probable that the individual will lack imaginative powers and hence will never be very successful in any of the arts, in finance or the sciences.

If the lines ascend under the Mount of the Moon—You may never acquire great wealth, but this will not make you unhappy, for you will have found many other things in life to bring you contentment.

Netted—A netted first line is a sign of unending hard work, with little time for relaxation or play. This does not mean that success may not be the reward for such toil. However, if the second line is also netted, it is a sign of drudgery with little prospect of reward for all the effort expended.

Breaks—These indicate difficulties—setbacks in business, such as the loss of employment; a greater share of life's burdens than most people bear.

Branches ascending to Mount of Venus—Association with persons in higher stations of life than that of the individual.

Branches ascending to Mount of the Moon—Long travels by water or by air. If there is a cross on one of these branches, something unforeseen will occur on one of these journeys.

Branch touching the Fate Line—A disappointment while traveling, possibly by train, auto or airplane.

Branch cutting Mount of the Moon and ending in Mount of Mars—A long journey from which the traveler will never return. If the Fate Line shows a change in occupation, this journey may take the individual out of his native land forever.

Cross on first line—Wastefulness and extravagance after achieving position and a certain amount of wealth.

Triangle on second line—In some violent catastrophe of nature—a tornado, a storm at sea, or volcanic eruption.

THE GIRDLE OF VENUS

Since all other signs in the palm must always be taken into consideration in regard to the Girdle of Venus, the meaning of this line must be presented in two ways.

WHEN OTHER SIGNS ARE FAVORABLE. Under these circumstances the Girdle of Venus may prove to be an asset. If it is well outlined and without breaks the individual will achieve a reputation for wit and cleverness. His will never be a dull and stodgy life, for his imagination and resourcefulness will always come to the rescue no matter how uninteresting his circumstances may be. In other words he will usually be found in jolly company of people who like good things to eat and drink, who like to play and dance, who live at a fast pace for the thrills that are to be got out of life.

The danger in such a line is that the individual will be too clever for his own good. Gifted in many ways and stimulated by the efforts of his brilliant companions, he may waste his energies by trying to do too many things at one time. His greatest problem will be controlling his abundance of high spirits and learning to concentrate on only one or two lines of endeavor.

Breaks in the line—Many passionate love affairs which will never last more than a few months at a time.

Cutting the Heart Line—Love wrecked by too many other interests.

One end touching Mount of Jupiter—The finest type of wit. The individual will often be quoted by friends and acquaintances, and if he chooses to write, his work will rank with the best of the great humorous writers of the day.

One end touching Mount of Mercury—A spectacular business career, probably involving the founding of some tremendously successful enterprise.

WHEN OTHER SIGNS ARE UNFAVORABLE. In a bad hand the Girdle of Venus is a most unfortunate omen. If it is well outlined and without breaks it indicates a life wasted away in wanton pleasures and excesses of every kind. The cleverness and wit of the individual will be used only for the worst possible purposes, and he will spend most of his time carousing and in debauchery. His passionate nature will lead him down the "primrose path" and his willpower will be too weak to avert his final ruin. What talents he has will be dissipated and lost through drinking and overindulgence of every kind.

Breaks in the line—Reckless living will lead to a breakdown which, with an overdeveloped Mount of the Moon, may lead to despondency.

Cutting the Heart Line—Debauchery destroying a fine and beautiful love; financial ruin and the depths of misery.

One end touching Mount of Jupiter—Lying, stealing and cheating until all honor and reputation are lost.

One end touching Mount of Mercury—Embezzlement or forgery in a desperate attempt to regain money lost through gambling, wine, women, and song.

MARRIAGE LINES

The number of Marriage Lines has nothing to do with the number of marriages the individual is going to have.

A number of short lines with at least one of them cut by a small vertical line indicates that there will be several serious love affairs during the individual's life, and the heart may even stray after marriage in some of these.

Lines which slant downward indicate early separation in marriage.

One long line amid short ones—There will be one great love in the individual's life which will never be forgotten, even though the individual will probably marry someone else.

Lines slanting upward—Marriage upset by a child.

Breaks—Marriage will terminate in divorce or permanent separation.

Double line—Violent quarrels and reconciliations during marriage.

More than one double line—Violent quarrels during marriage leading to temporary separation.

Marriage Line touched by a line rising from Head Line—The marriage will be opposed by members of the other party's family.

Marriage Line touched by line rising from Heart Line—Marriage will be opposed by members of the individual's own family.

Line extending to the Mount of the Sun—A certain amount of wealth as a result of marriage.

Branches descending toward the Heart Line but not touching—Financial circumstances will make it impossible for the couple to have as large a family as they wish.

Branches descending toward Head Line but not touching—The other partner in the marriage will be found in some sort of profession or business.

Branch ascending to a grille on Mount of the Sun—Troubles connected with the marriage because of illness of one of the partners.

Fork on the inside end of the line (See Fig. 15-A)—The individual will break the engagement shortly before the wedding day because he has fallen in love with someone else.

Fork on the opposite (outside) end of line—The partner in the engagement will break it off shortly before the wedding day because he (or she) has fallen in love with someone else.

One or more lines touching a grille between Mounts of the Sun and Mercury—The individual should avoid marriage, for great disaster would be involved in it.

Triangle—Serious trouble in marriage lasting for about a year.

Netted lines—Many difficulties connected with marriage. Before the wedding there will be opposition to it. Afterward there will be trouble. There will be financial burdens to assume which have not been anticipated.

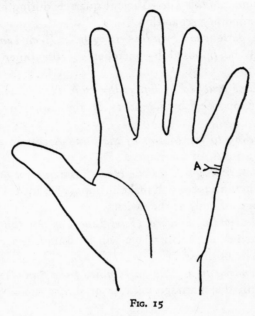

FIG. 15

Island—Serious quarrels with the in-laws which are going to put a strain on the affections of the two partners in the marriage.

Star—Loss of something valuable while traveling.

Circle on one of the lines—May mean an accident.

THE LINE OF THE MOON (LUNA)

Long and straight—The individual should never trust his imagination, for it will attempt to lead him into situations which are fraught with great difficulty if not danger. He will do best to trust the advice of others at all times, for he lacks a practical frame of mind and can easily deceive himself into believing that an idea is sound when it is in reality most visionary and rash.

Short and straight—The individual will be best suited to some occupation which will require a good deal of traveling.

Short and twisted—A lack of reverence for sacred things will lead to a serious accusation against the individual.

Long and twisted—The individual will be troubled by strange dreams which cannot be explained.

Forked at the upper end—A great deal of traveling by train.

Forked at the bottom—Much traveling on sea or in the air.

Double line—Reinforces the forecast that would be made if the line were single.

Ascending branch—A loss of money in old age.

Island in the line—Beware of advice from strangers.

GOOD OMENS ON THE FINGERS

Cross on index finger—Great happiness through a sudden elevation in life to a position of honor and esteem.

Cross on little finger—Unexpected honors bestowed in one's chosen line of work.

Grille on index finger—An opportunity for advancement coming unexpectedly when things appear to look blackest. The sign of the "silver lining" in the dark cloud.

Grille on ring finger—A journey leading to great wealth.

Square on middle finger—A large sum of money coming through a distant friend or relative.

Square on ring finger—Brilliant career with much public acclaim and an old age heaped with honors.

Square on little finger—Happiness and success after much endless toil and discouraging setbacks.

Triangle on middle finger—Domestic happiness, with children achieving great fame and material success.

Circle on index finger—An idealistic love in which the affection is returned.

Circle on little finger—Ambitions gratified as a result of some kind act by one whom the individual knows only slightly.

Circle on ring finger—Fame in a career, bringing with it wealth and honors from foreign governments.

Black dot on middle finger—Great responsibility, with some sorrow, but in the main a favorable omen.

Star on little finger—A second marriage in which there will be wealth and much happiness.

Star on index finger—Sure success.

EVIL OMENS ON THE FINGERS

Cross on middle finger—Malicious gossip.

Cross on ring finger—Loss of a loved one's devotion.

Grille on middle finger—Beware of large, open spaces, for here lurks a threat to safety.

Grille on little finger—May indicate an accident.

Square on the index finger—Bitter jealousy that may wreck more than one career.

Triangle on index finger—Trouble in connection with a spider or some sort of reptile.

Triangle on ring finger—Love for a person who is already married.

Triangle on little finger—Need for caution while among strangers.

Circle on the thumb—Possible failure in business.

Cross on the thumb—A failure followed by separation from loved ones for a long period of time.

Black dot on index finger—A short stay in a small room.

Black dots on little finger—An upsetting experience.

White dot on thumb—A disagreeable journey by air.

Star on middle finger—A domestic animal, possibly a house pet, will cause anxiety.

Star on little finger—Unfriendly interference.

Star on the thumb—Discord in the family.

II

What Your Birthday Signifies

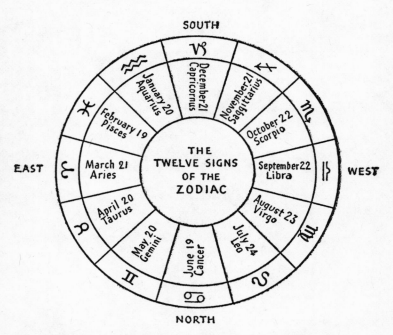

To FIND OUT what your birthday signifies, you must first locate it in the following list of the Signs of the Zodiac. Here you will find the general predictions for your type. Then turn to the

List of the Decans (Page 76), where you will find more specialized information, including the names of your ruling planets. Finally, consult the List of the Planets (Page 111) and you will learn how these powerful influences will affect your life.

THE SIGNS OF THE ZODIAC

The Zodiac is the pathway in the sky through which the sun and the planets appear to move. In ancient times sages and seers divided this pathway into twelve sections, or signs, and gave each a name. In the course of the year the sun moves through each one of these signs in turn. Your ruling sign is the one in which the sun happened to be when you were born. (All dates given are inclusive.)

CAPRICORN THE SEA-GOAT ♑

DECEMBER 22 TO JANUARY 19   SIGN OF CAPRICORN

If you are born under this sign, probably the best advice that can be given you is to try to cultivate a sense of humor, for there is a danger that all through life you will take things much too seriously and will not have all the fun which you deserve. If any great success comes to you, it will be entirely as a result of your own patient efforts. It will take time and the early part of your life may at times seem sadly lacking in the things you aspire to. But you should never be discouraged, for your greatest gift lies in your capacity for taking pains and in your fundamental common sense. Here also is something you will have to guard against, for your ability to plod along may also blind you to opportunities which require a certain amount of imagination and daring.

You will probably achieve best results in business which requires a steady, level head and industrious effort. Thus banking or office work such as is connected with governmental bureaus will hold the greatest opportunity for you. You will also shine in fields where scholarship is of importance. You might become a teacher or a research worker, but you must never expect to make a brilliant showing in the eyes of the world in general. Your gifts will be appreciated by the few rather than by the crowd.

In matters of love you will tend to be cautious and hesitant and, since you will not be one to decide on the spur of the moment, you probably will not marry early. However, when you do marry, it will be for keeps and you will make a devoted husband or wife and a very wise and loving parent. There will be one trait you will have to control if your marriage is to be a happy one. That is your tendency to brood over trivial things. You must always say what is on your mind, though you must do it tactfully. You will never be completely happy unless you are married, for your nature demands love and affection, and you will never realize a true expression of your finest talents until you are happy in marriage. In other words, it is the key to your future success in all lines of work.

You should get plenty of fresh air, and avoid worry as much as possible. Be very careful in your use of alcohol and tobacco.

JANUARY 20 TO FEBRUARY 19   SIGN OF AQUARIUS

One of the great problems that confront those who are born under this sign is the necessity of overcoming a certain shyness in human relationships. You have so many good qualities that it would be indeed tragic if they were not recognized and given full opportunity for expression. And a modest, retiring nature needs to be brought out not only for its own good but for the benefit of all those who come in contact with it. This is especially true in your case, for you will have ideas which, if given proper outlet, may lead to progress in many fields of activity.

AQUARIUS THE WATER-BEARER ≋

Yours is an original mind, and you should always rely on your hunches, no matter how out of the ordinary they may seem to be, for they may work to your great advantage.

Your originality of thought will probably result in the discovery of a new way of doing things in business or science; in the arts it will stamp you as a very independent type. No one will ever accuse you of imitation.

Though you do not make friends quickly, you will never lack for them, for you have a natural way with people, and in the long run you will always attract a host of admirers. You will have to curb a tendency to be impatient or contemptuous of persons who are not as quick to understand problems as you are, and you will also have to fight a sensitive nature which will permit you to imagine insults that have never occurred.

Your chances of success may be lessened by a disposition that is a bit too easygoing. Take care that friends and acquaintances do not impose on you and take up too much of your time, which you will always be so ready to give. There is also the possibility that you may be cheated or deceived by unscrupulous persons who will take advantage of your sincere direct nature.

Many businesses and professions will hold opportunities for you, but you must take care not to get into a line of work which puts you in a rut, for your independent nature will never tolerate monotony and such an occupation will only make you miserable.

You probably will do a great deal of traveling, though this should be a pastime with you. In your every-day work you should remain located in one place for considerable periods of time, otherwise you may be tempted to become a rolling stone.

In love you will tend to conceal your affections, and it is possible you may marry without ever knowing a very romantic period of courtship. This should be a warning to you to make an effort to be more demonstrative with your loved one, lest he or she misunderstand and suspect you of indifference.

FEBRUARY 20 TO MARCH 20   SIGN OF PISCES

Yours will never be a dull, stodgy existence. Your whole life will be filled with restless activity, and there is the danger that you may never accomplish very much because of this. Yours is a naturally loving and generous temperament, and one of your greatest weaknesses is the ease with which people can take advantage of you by appealing to your warm and sympathetic spirit. In fact it is possible that you will always be more concerned about the welfare of others than about your own or that of your immediate family.

Persons of your type can easily become the rolling stones of life, the ne'er-do-wells, the jacks-of-all-trades. Pleasant, companionable and always ready to lend a helping hand, they never seem to be able to center their attention on some one particular goal. These cases, of course, are the extremes, but they should serve as a warning to you. You should remember that charity begins at home, and that not every person who appears to be honest is really so.

PISCES the fishes ♓

In money matters in particular you will have to curb your generosity, and it would probably be best for you to obtain the advice of someone of sound business judgment before you make any investments or take financial risks of any sort.

Whatever your faults, however, you will never lack for true friends, who will overlook every shortcoming out of genuine affection for you. For this reason you will not be able to rely on their judgment too often, since they will be willing to indulge you in your failings.

Lest this present too one-sided a picture of what lies before you, it should be added that with self-discipline you can rise to great heights, especially in literary activities or occupations in which you are called on to deal with numbers of individuals, such as nursing, law, medicine, etc. You are especially fitted for any calling which renders a service to humanity or which requires a sympathetic knowledge of the ways of the human heart (as in literature). And self-discipline ought not to be too hard for you, either, for you have courage and determination, and these qualities are going to bring you honor and prestige.

You will probably marry early and you will undoubtedly have several love affairs—some, it may be, even after you have spoken your marriage vows. However, this is not so much a sign that you have an untrustworthy nature as it is an indication that you will always try to surround yourself with an atmosphere of affection and love.

ARIES THE RAM ♈

MARCH 21 TO APRIL 20   SIGN OF ARIES

Persons born under this sign are not meant to work under anybody else. To be completely happy you should be as independent in action as possible, for you have the marks of the leader or the trail blazer. Success, when it comes to you, will arouse the admiration of all those about you, for it will represent no ordinary achievement. On the other hand you will have to learn a great deal about self-control if you are to achieve everything you set out to accomplish. Your boundless energy and enthusiasm, for which you will always be so much admired, will have to be held in check or it will lead you to undertake too many things at one time. You will always be tempted to rush eagerly into some new line of activity before you have made really satisfactory progress in the work you are already doing. Probably the hardest thing you will ever have to learn is to take advice without becoming angry and resentful. Courageous and impetuous, you will always be the first to champion a new cause, oftentimes without giving it sufficient careful consideration. For that reason you may expect to make many blunders and mistakes. You can avoid some of these if you will always remember to "look before you leap."

This last piece of advice is especially noteworthy in matters of love. Never, under any circumstances, should you consider an elopement. With some other types an elopement might turn out all right, but in your case it will nine times out of ten be ill-advised, since you are always going to be one who acts in haste and repents at leisure. Every time you fall in love—and it will be often—you are going to think it is the great, enduring passion of your life. You will be ready to sacrifice everything for it—and like as not in six weeks' time you will not only be bored, but will be looking for some new romantic adventure. For this reason you should not marry until after a fairly long engagement. If after a year you find that your devotion is still as intense as ever, you may be sure that you have found the right person. In that event your marriage will be not only happy but exciting and one that will never grow stale.

You will probably do a great deal of traveling during your life and will meet many kinds of people. You will be popular and will make friends easily. However, if you want to keep them and avoid a lot of sorrow for yourself, you will have to learn to control your temper and your tendency to "boss" people. Even friendship will not last if you allow your instincts in this direction to get out of hand.

As has been indicated, politics, business or the arts will be suited to your temperament—anything in which you have a chance to shine by yourself. Do not attempt to enter in business partnerships of any sort, for co-operation is one of the things that will not come easy for you. You will have to guard against working too hard, and must learn to relax and take things easy.

TAURUS THE BULL ♉

APRIL 21 TO MAY 20   SIGN OF TAURUS

Your life is going to result in constructive achievement which will win the admiration and praise of your fellows. There is very little to prevent you from being a success in your chosen line of work, for you are never going to let obstacles defeat you, and you are always going to find a way out of every difficulty. You will achieve happiness and contentment through determined and persistent effort, and you will have a reputation for wisdom and stability which will win you promotions and continual advancement. When your community wants to get something accomplished, you will be one of the first on whom it will call.

You will be happiest when you are doing some sort of creative work, such as building houses and bridges or developing a business, or—if you are a woman—in making a home and raising a family. Your interest in efficiency may also express itself in the arts, where you will be noted as a fine craftsman or a very conscientious performer.

You will make close friendships easily and you will enjoy many of them. Even strangers will recognize in you the traits of sympathy and understanding and will often turn to you for advice or help. One thing you must learn to do is to be more expressive of your feelings, otherwise even your friends and loved ones may wrongly accuse you at times of coldness or indifference.

Obstinacy will probably be your worst fault, and this will show itself in a number of unusual ways. One way will be your refusal to accept the changes in your daily life which will surely come as science and invention make new contributions to progress. You will always want to insist that the old way of doing things is better, and you will have to keep this viewpoint under control if you want to remain up-to-date. You will have to be on guard, too, about becoming prejudiced without taking the trouble to study all the facts in a given case. This might even harm your chances of success in some instances, so it is worth keeping in mind.

In general you will enjoy very good health, but you will have to watch out not to overeat or drink to excess, for you will always be fond of good food and will usually find yourself financially able to gratify your tastes. You should always take plenty of exercise and get out in the open as much as possible.

May 21 to June 21   Sign of Gemini

You are going to find that a number of differing lines of work appeal to you and you are going to want to undertake almost all of them at the same time, for you will easily become bored with just a single job. Your greatest problem will be learning to concentrate your energies and to control your enthusiasm, which will always be driving you ahead and leading you to rush headlong into a new venture without first weighing all the facts carefully.

Failure for you will never come because of a lack of talent or ability; if you do not make a success of your life it will be because you can't decide on what you want to specialize in, and since this is an age of specialists, you would be wise in starting right now to make up your mind which career you will be happiest in and then to stick to your decision.

Anything which calls for an alert mind will be suited to your tastes, and it would be better for you to pick some sort of pro-

GEMINI THE TWINS II

fessional work than a business career, for the latter often involves a lot of humdrum detail for which you are likely to have little patience. You will be happy in anything connected with science or the arts, and you are likely to shine in a position that calls for oratorical skill.

In matters of love you will be very changeable and sensitive. There is a danger that you will be accused of being fickle, and you may be tempted to blame your own whimsical changes of heart on the imagined slights and neglects of the other party. Thus if you wish to have a happy marriage, you will have to concentrate on making it happy, just as you will have to concentrate on everything else in life that you want to make a success of. Guard against being too easily irritated by trifles. Although you will get over your quick bursts of temper in a very short time, another person whom you have offended and who has a less changeable temperament may not forget so easily.

The rash word spoken in haste will too often be your undoing, both in matters of love and in friendships. You must learn to understand how your many-sided disposition works, or you will never realize why it is that people will so often misunderstand you and take offense at things you do.

One of the best outlets for your restlessness will be in taking up hobbies. If you feel you simply must have a change, take up a new hobby. In the long run this will be more sensible than constantly shifting from one job to another on the slightest pretext.

You will make money easily and lose it just as quickly, so you will be wise to find some friend whose opinions you can trust and to allow yourself to be guided by him or her in major decisions in your life. This will not be hard to do, for you are going to have many friends who will be genuinely concerned with your welfare.

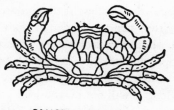

CANCER THE CRAB ♋

JUNE 22 TO JULY 21   SIGN OF CANCER

All your life you are going to worry entirely too much about what other people think of you. You are going to waste precious time looking for hidden meanings in casual remarks. It is something you ought to strive against with all your might, for in the first place it is never going to be possible for you to please everybody, and second, you are going to have far more friends than enemies.

You should learn to keep your emotions in control as much

as possible for your own peace of mind. Strangely enough, though you will often be plagued with self-doubt and shyness, others will place great confidence in you and will come to you for help in making their decisions. You will be much more sure of yourself when advising someone else about the proper course of action to take than when you are trying to make a decision for yourself. If you can only learn to look at your own problems as calmly and wisely as you do the problems of others, you may go far in the world, for in the main you will know what is the right thing to do. Remember to have faith in yourself, and half your battles will have been won at the start.

As has been indicated, you will have many friends and in matters of love you will give and will receive deep and loyal affection. When you feel fits of moodiness coming on, you should seek the company of those who are dear to you, for in them you will find a source of strength, and their companionship will help dispel the baseless fears and anxieties which will sweep over you from time to time. In your business or professional life you should pick a career which brings you into contact with people and activity. Although your instincts may suggest a hermit's life and an occupation that permits a certain amount of solitude, this will not be good for you, since what you need most in life is to develop your social side and to learn to come out of your shell. With the proper surroundings you may learn to overcome many of your retiring traits and take full advantage of the very capable and admirable nature which is yours.

Any career which calls for judgment and understanding sympathy for the trials and tribulations of mankind will be suited to you, for you will always be able to put yourself in the other fellow's shoes and see his point of view. Travel will be good for you, but you should plan to marry and settle down eventually in a home that will be your refuge and castle. You should never marry except for love, for without it all the riches in the world will not make you contented. Your health will be good if you do not worry too much.

LEO THE LION ♌

JULY 22 TO AUGUST 22   SIGN OF LEO

Under this sign are born persons to whom the world looks naturally for leadership and guidance. One of your greatest assets is your ability to inspire confidence in strangers who come in contact with you, and if you learn how to use this trait wisely, it should lead you to a position of prominence and affluence. You are likely to rise rapidly in a time of great national emergency when courage and enthusiasm in the face of overwhelming obstacles will be especially sought after.

The only factor which may imperil your chances of success will be your inability to realize that all people are not guided by the same high-minded motives as you are. Since you will be the first to give credit where credit is due, you will not always recognize flattery for what it is, for you will assume that praise is given to you as you give it to others: in recognition of genuine merit. Thus it may happen that you will place trust in a person who is only trying to lead you on to his own advantage. In this way you may be misguided and receive unsound advice. To put it briefly, you must be on your guard against the yes-man, who will agree with you even when you are in the wrong simply because he is anxious to obtain favors from you.

One other trait which, if allowed to go unchecked, may spoil some of your friendships is a tendency to domineer. It is to be expected that you will dominate and hold positions of authority, but you must cultivate tact in your daily life, remembering that people are more easily led than they are driven. By using diplomacy you will always be able to have your way, which will usually be the wisest course of action.

In business, industry, politics or trade you will inevitably rise to an executive position, with wealth and honors heaped upon you.

You will never be guilty of having trivial love affairs or shallow friendships. You will be assured of a happy and successful marriage if you always remember to consider the feelings of those close to you. Shun any sort of domestic quarrel, for when angered you may say things that you will live to regret deeply. With your children you must guard against being too strict.

AUGUST 23 TO SEPTEMBER 22   SIGN OF VIRGO

Whatever else your life may bring it is very probable that you will spend your old age in contentment and peace, surrounded by material comforts of every description, for no one will ever be able to accuse you of having wasted your life. Through careful and diligent work you are going to build up a modest fortune, and though you may never create a sensation in the world because of the brilliance of your accomplishments, still you will never have regrets about what you have done. Nor should this be taken to mean that you have no chance of achieving fame and fortune; there is nothing to prevent you from becoming famous. However, if you do, it will be entirely as a result of your own painstaking and ceaseless efforts. Great fame will never come to you by accident, as it often does to others. You will earn it the hard way.

Your temperament is such that you will achieve your greatest success in some occupation which requires patient and faithful attention to details. Any sort of office work of a clerical nature; accounting, laboratory research in physics or chemistry, statistical estimates—in general these are the types of work in which you probably will find the greatest satisfaction. And as every

VIRGO THE VIRGIN ♍

one knows, it is the plodding laboratory scientist who often unearths one of the great discoveries of the age and so climbs to fame. Thus it cannot be said that your life will be monotonous or devoid of any great interest.

You must learn to cultivate tact in your dealings with others, for too often you are going to be inclined to be overly critical. In many instances your judgment will be the correct one, but unless you are more considerate of the feelings of those about you, the way in which you state your opinions will offend people and hinder you in accomplishing what you have set out to do. A sense of humor will help you to understand the failings of people and will often carry you much further than the plain logic of your arguments. You must learn to forgive shortcomings when you see them and strive for a more tolerant and easygoing attitude about life in general.

It would be wise for you to marry early in life before you become too set in your ways. Though you may never be a very romantic lover, you will make a very fine helpmate, and your marriage should be happy and successful because it will be based on a solid foundation of worth. If you are a man you will be a good provider; if you are a woman you will make an excellent housewife. For complete happiness in marriage you should not insist on having your own way all the time.

LIBRA THE BALANCE ⚖

SEPTEMBER 23 TO OCTOBER 22   SIGN OF LIBRA

You are blessed with one of those rare gifts which should smooth out the path leading to success in whatever field of endeavor you should become interested in. You are always going to be able to get along with people easily. No matter what chance may bring in your life, you will have no difficulty in meeting strangers and making the proper impression on them. Not only will this faculty help you in making many friendships and keeping them, but it will also improve your chances for advancement in business or the professions and will eliminate many obstacles which might confront a different type of person. For this reason you should make a very good executive or manager who has many persons working under him.

Whenever you want something, never listen to the advice of friends (regardless of how well meaning they may be) who may tell you that you should use force to obtain your ends. You will succeed much better by persuasion and reason. Many persons who cannot be budged in their opinions when browbeaten will listen to your arguments and wind up by agreeing to do as you wish. Thus you are well fitted for certain types of business, the legal profession, salesmanship, or education. Just remember to be yourself and follow your own instincts when confronted with a problem involving dealings with persons who may be opposed to you. If you don't try to scheme or bluster you will win every time, even though at the outset it looks as if you could not possibly succeed.

In matters of love, however, you will always have to remember that the emotions and not the reason are the source of people's actions. Many times it will seem to you that you have every logical argument for doing something and will be unable to understand why your partner makes objection. In marriage you will have to remember that your partner demands all of your affections and will resent bitterly a tendency which you will have to show deep interest in others of the opposite sex. You may be accused of fickleness, and you in your part will resent this, attempting to argue that you can have more than one love interest in life without being faithless. If you insist upon this attitude you may bring sorrow to yourself.

OCTOBER 23 TO NOVEMBER 23   SIGN OF SCORPIO

There will be nothing tame or dull about your life. You were born to fight hard, to love deeply, to hate bitterly and to live at top speed. Though your life will seldom lack excitement it will not always be a happy one, and unless you guard against the overdevelopment of certain traits, it may end unhappily.

First of all you will have to become master of your temper. If you do not, you will quarrel frequently not only with your associates in daily affairs but with those you love. You are capable of violent hates which, if allowed to run unchecked, will sour your views on life and rob you of happiness and peace of mind. You may spoil your chances of success by flying off the handle or through sheer stubbornness and refusal to listen to reason. You must not give way to suspicions or jealousy, and the desire for vengeance may lead you to rash acts which will recoil to your disadvantage.

SCORPIO THE SCORPION ♏

If you will only learn to control this temperament, you will be able to direct the force of your personality into many useful channels which will lead you to ultimate success. No one will ever be able to accuse you of lying down on the job, and though early in life you will face many obstacles and may find the going very difficult, you have the strength to fight your way through and to win. If you will only listen to all sides of a question before you act, you will not fail to make the right choice, for you have a shrewd eye and will be able to see where your advantage lies every time. In this way you will achieve power and fortune, and it is very likely that in the later years of life you will find contentment and security.

You will succeed in many lines of activity, preferably ones where there is opposition and the need for a forceful, driving energy.

In love you will be ardent and will have no difficulty in attracting members of the opposite sex. If you are a man, don't let your cave-man nature run away with you. If you are a woman, you must learn to temper your ardor with reason, for love does not always end happily, and if it dies, you must remember that there are always other fish in the sea. In either case, jealousy is the greatest pitfall in the path of those born under the sign of Scorpio.

SAGITTARIUS the archer ♐

NOVEMBER 24 TO DECEMBER 21   SIGN OF SAGITTARIUS

You have a better than average chance of achieving success and possibly fame in life. It will be wiser for you to select some career where you are not compelled to work with too many other persons. You will find most congenial the job which allows you a certain amount of liberty to do as you think best and where you will not have a boss standing over you every minute of the day. You will always be resentful about receiving directions on how you should do your work, and so to avoid friction you should try to find something which will put you on your own much of the time.

Though there will seldom be quarrels or disputes to mar the even course of your life, you will occasionally flare up when you feel that you have been crossed, and so you must guard against these brief flashes of temper, which will never last very long but which may alienate some individual who is important to your success. On the other hand there will be times when you should show more determination to gain your point and should not give in readily merely to avoid an unpleasant exchange of words. This is especially true in regard to sudden inspirations which you are going to have every now and then. Do not let people argue you out of these ideas or hunches which come to you without explanation, "out of the blue" as it were. In almost every instance you will meet with remarkable good luck if you follow your instincts.

In matters of love you will have to learn one very hard lesson if you wish to marry and have a happy home life. That lesson is that you are never going to find anybody who quite lives up to your ideal of the opposite sex. No one will ever find perfection in this life, but we can all find happiness if we just learn to overlook the faults in our loved ones and friends and take satisfaction in their good qualities. You are very liable to make blunders in your choice of a partner. You will be so eager to find your ideal that you may be temporarily blinded to the real person before you. Then when you do finally see the actual personality, your disillusionment will be keen and you will make no attempt to hide your feelings. This, of course, will probably wreck your romance. You have two very important things to remember: there are no angels among mortal men, and always use tact when you are tempted to say what is on your mind without any sidestepping or evasion.

THE LIST OF THE DECANS

DECEMBER 22 TO DECEMBER 30.*

If your birthday falls early in this nine-day period, the planet Jupiter has the greatest sway over you, with Saturn exerting a secondary influence. If you were born late in the period, the

*All dates are inclusive.

planets' positions are reversed and Saturn dominates, with Jupiter secondary.

You will always have to guard against a tendency to "cross your bridges before you come to them." It is all right to be careful and avoid risks, but there is a kind of cautiousness which is quite as foolish and sometimes as costly as wanton reckless-ness. Your danger will be that you will spend so much time try-ing to make a wise decision that in the end you will lose the opportunity to make it. Remember, opportunity only knocks once. In business matters you will always show good discrimi-nation, and it is not likely that your enemies will find it easy to get the better of you or defeat you. Keep that in mind and have the courage now and then to take what may seem to be a rather risky chance. You will find you were wise to do so.

In love and marriage you will have to show tact and thought-fulness to be completely happy, for you will have a tendency to be selfish in your love. This applies not only to your relation with your wife or husband but also with your children. Always try to see their point of view, or someday you may be accused of being a parent who "doesn't understand." This would be tragic for you, for you will pride yourself on being a model father or mother, as the case may be.

You will have trouble connected with journeys, and you prob-ably will know alternating spells of good and bad fortune.

Persons born late in April or August will make the best friends or marriage partners. Saturday is the best day for action. Lucky colors are purples and blues of all kinds. Numbers which will be associated with good fortune are 8 and 5. Lucky gems are the turquoise, amethyst and sapphire.

DECEMBER 31 TO JANUARY 10

The planets which exert an influence are Saturn, Mars and Venus, and they dominate in the order named.

You will always be noted for industriousness and good judgment, but you will have to remember that "all work and no play make Jack a dull boy." Not only will you have to learn to have a little fun now and then, but you must constantly be on guard against moodiness and depressing thoughts. Don't let the blues get hold of you, for if you will concentrate on real things, not imaginary problems, you are likely to go far in the world. You can attain what you set out to achieve, for you are a tireless worker and your enemies will never be able to get the better of you.

In addition to the usual forms of business, fields where you are most likely to succeed include forestry, lumbering or large-scale farming or ranching. There is also a possibility that you will make a name for yourself in some branch of the military service or in surgery.

Women born in this period will be wonderful home-makers, and their greatest happiness will come from domestic life. Men born at this time will have to guard against unreasonable jealousy and a tendency to lord it over their sweethearts and wives. The later the marriage, the more successful it will be for both sexes.

You will have to guard against overeating, which may bring disastrous results, for you have a rather delicate constitution.

Persons with whom you will find the greatest harmony, either in love or in marriage, are those born between the middle of April and the middle of May, the middle of August and the middle of September, and the last half of December. Your favorable days are Saturday and Friday, in that order. Your lucky colors are blue and the deep reds. Your lucky gems are the garnet and sapphire. Numbers associated with good fortune are 8 and 9.

JANUARY 11 TO JANUARY 19

Your planets are Saturn, Mercury, and the Sun, and they exert influence in the order named.

You have the chances of becoming very successful in some sort of government work or in trades connected with mining and manufacture, but you must first overcome your desire to hold back fearfully, afraid to step out on your own. Lack of self-confidence will be your greatest liability, for there is no doubt that you will possess all the other qualities necessary to success. Never turn down an opportunity which involves great responsibility, for you will find yourself happiest when you are busiest.

In matters of love you must learn to say what you feel, for in many cases the other party may not even realize the depth of your devotion. This will be because you are too self-contained and undemonstrative. Therefore, you should try to break down your instinctive reserve.

You should marry a person born under the sign of Taurus, Virgo, or Sagittarius. Your most favorable day is Wednesday. Your lucky colors are deep blues and grays; your lucky gems, the onyx and garnet. Numbers which you will usually find associated with good fortune are 8 and 4. Water, when connected in any way with the number 3, should serve as a warning of danger to come.

JANUARY 20 TO JANUARY 31

Your ruling planets are Saturn and Venus, and they exert their influence in the order named.

You will probably spend most of your life championing one cause or another, for you will find the greatest joy in trying to be of service to others. This means that you may have an old age heaped with honors in recognition of your tireless devotion to some institution or profession. Since your talents lie either in the arts or sciences, it is likely that you may rise to a position of great trust in a laboratory, educational institution or hospital of some sort.

Although you may expect success in your chosen career, you are not likely to amass any great fortune in your lifetime, for the material things of life will never interest you as much as will the chance to do the thing you really like to do. You will be careless of money matters, and your natural idealism will prevent you from taking advantage of whatever position you may find yourself in.

Men born in this period will be good providers, however, and will need only the guiding hand of a more practical-minded wife. A woman born in this period will be very popular, but she will have to make a conscious effort to cultivate the feminine wiles, for her naturally direct nature may not always stand her in good stead when she is trying to attract the man of her choice.

Your most important day will be Saturday. You should beware of activities undertaken early in the week, since they may prove to be so much wasted effort. You should marry a person born in January or under the sign either of Virgo or Libra. Your lucky colors are blues and greens. Your lucky gems are garnets and opals, and the number associated with good fortune is 7.

FEBRUARY 1 TO FEBRUARY 10

Your planets are Saturn and Mercury and they exert about equal influence over your life and destiny.

Your greatest asset will be an ability to get along with people, and you can count on having many strong and loyal friendships. Tact and energy will bring you to a well deserved success, probably in some line of work which involves coming into contact with large numbers of persons. You will be happiest when you are doing something to help "the other fellow"; consequently a professional career as doctor, minister or social-service worker is probably the type in which you will enjoy the greatest success. In trades you will be best suited for work connected with machinery—electrical equipment or radio. One word of caution: your interest in your work may cause you to neglect your health, consequently you should be careful to take time out for fun and relaxation now and then.

Though you will be a devoted husband or wife, you will have to make an effort to express your feelings, for too often you will take love for granted, failing to realize that, like a garden, it blossoms best when given constant attention. Husbands born in this period may often become too absorbed in their business, and their wives will have to remember this failing and realize that it reflects in no way upon the depth of their husbands' love for them.

One trait of mind you will have to guard against constantly is skepticism which may make you appear to be cold and calculating to outsiders who do not understand you completely.

You should marry some one born under Gemini or Libra or in the later half of January. Your most favorable day is Saturday. Your lucky colors are dark blues and greens; your lucky gems are agates and amethysts, and your most favorable number is 9.

February 11 to February 19

Your planets are Saturn, the Moon and Venus, ruling in the order named.

You must never become discouraged if your plans go awry because of the actions of persons about you. If you are able to have complete control of things, there will never be any failure, for you will have marked ability to plan a line of action and then carry it out. Because of this, and since the blunderings of others with whom you may be associated will always have a very discouraging effect on you, it would be best for you to choose some career in which you can work independently much of the time. In the arts this would be painting, sculpture or literature—in the professions, medicine, inventing, lecturing or independent research. In business a small independent enterprise will be the one in which you will be happiest.

In matters of love you should learn to speak what is closest to your heart, for a certain shyness will handicap you in your relations with the opposite sex.

You will find your closest friends and your ideal mate in those born under the sign of Gemini, Libra or Aquarius. Friday is your most favorable day, and your lucky colors are blues, ranging up through the greens. Your lucky gems are amethysts and crystals. The number which will be associated with good fortune is 6, and occasionally 9.

You must guard against fits of moodiness which will plague you when you feel that your ambitions have been thwarted. It will probably be your fate not to achieve success immediately, but you must not allow worries over the future to occupy your thoughts, for in the long run things are bound to come out better than they seem to be at first.

February 20 to March 1

Jupiter is your ruling planet, and if you were born in the first half of this period, Saturn also exerts a powerful influence.

Indecision will probably be your greatest handicap, so you must always remember that your chances of success lie in acquiring self-confidence and assurance. Once you have overcome this obstacle, you will go far in your chosen field, for you will have many friends who will be glad to give you a helping hand as soon as they are sure that you will justify the trouble they take in your behalf.

You should do very well in the arts or the learned professions

—teaching or the law. In the exact sciences you may not fare so well, nor in routine business life.

In love you may be bitterly disappointed unless you first learn that idealism often makes impossible demands. You should never marry a person born under the sign of Libra, for only unhappiness can result. And you must be prepared to forgive and to forget, realizing that you, yourself, are not perfect and cannot, therefore, expect perfection of others. Unless you teach yourself to be less critical, it is possible that you will never marry at all.

You will have to be strict with yourself in matters of diet and drink, for you will tend to excesses which may undermine your health.

Choose your mate and your friends from those born under the sign of Cancer or in the last half of September or October and you will be assured of happiness.

Your best day is Tuesday; your lucky colors are purple and all shades of red, and your lucky gems are the amethyst and the pearl. The number with which you will most often find good fortune associated is 4. Of lesser importance is 2.

MARCH 2 TO MARCH 10

Your ruling planet is Jupiter, with the Moon exerting a secondary but important influence.

You are headed for very good fortune, provided you do nothing to harm your chances of success. Fame may be yours, and wealth, but you must always trust your own judgment rather than the advice of even your closest friends. Do not let yourself get tied up too intimately in the personal affairs of your acquaintances, for here lie pitfalls and hazards which may prove handicaps or may even defeat your aims in life.

You should do well in the professions or in finance, or if your tastes lie elsewhere you might try business connected with the arts—not the arts themselves, it should be emphasized. You would also make a good craftsman—one whose work calls for skill and dexterity, but you should avoid any activity that settles down into a humdrum existence with a great deal of daily routine.

In matters of love you will always be gentle and understanding, which points to a quiet and happy domestic life with few storms and troubles. If you are a woman, it might be wise to continue with a career—*if* your husband approves, for it will give you an outlet for many talents which would be lost in the routine of housework. However, if he should not approve, do not think that you will be losing anything of any great importance by giving up a career. You will always be happiest in your home.

You should marry a person born under Cancer or Scorpio, or in the last half of February. Here, too, you will find many of your closest friends. Your most favorable day is Thursday. Your lucky colors are mauve, the greens and indigo; your lucky gems are bloodstones and sapphires, and the number most frequently connected with good fortune is 3.

MARCH 11 TO MARCH 20

Your planets are Jupiter and Mars, and their influence is exerted in that order.

Your greatest problem will be in establishing some sort of order in your life, for there are going to be many interests which will be pulling at you from all directions, and you will have to guard against wasting your energies by having too many irons in the fire at once. You will find it doubly difficult to hew to the line, for you are going to be popular and have hosts of friends who will always be asking you to join them in some party or celebration. You will try to find many excuses for neglecting your work and will tell yourself that you are never going to get ahead unless you get out and meet people, etc. But this argument does not apply to your case, for you will naturally attract people who will be able to help you. Your main danger will be that you cannot settle down to a good job after you have landed it, so be on your guard.

It is probable that you will do a considerable amount of traveling and it is more than likely that you will find your marriage partner on one of these journeys. In matters of love you would be wise to go slow and not rush things, for not all people are possessed of such a warm and affectionate disposition as yours is. You will have a happy marriage, but it will not be without its quarrels and troubles. It will be essential for you to make a special effort to understand your partner's point of view in these disputes.

You should marry a person born under the sign of Cancer, Scorpio or Pisces. Your favorable day is Monday; your lucky colors are rich purples and vivid reds, and your lucky gems are the bloodstone, beryl, and opal. You may expect good fortune most often with the number 3.

MARCH 21 TO MARCH 29

Your ruling planet is Mars, with Jupiter exerting a secondary influence.

Yours is a brilliant future if you can only guard yourself against the unfavorable aspects of your character. You will by nature assume a leading role in every activity in which you participate, for your executive ability, enterprise and imagination will seldom find an equal among your fellows. You will forge rapidly ahead in whatever line of work you choose to concentrate upon, and here is where the word of warning is necessary. Your greatest failing will be to let yourself become sidetracked from your main purpose. You must never let your energetic nature get out of control, for your impulsiveness will often lead you to become impatient when things do not move along as rapidly as you think they should.

Possessing marked executive ability, you will shine in any position where you have charge of a number of people. Industry and the business world are your special fields, and you will probably make a considerable name for yourself in blazing a trail in some new and unexplored enterprise. Where you are most likely to fail is in routine work which is so often vitally important to get a new business venture on a solid footing. You must learn to see a thing through to the finish before embarking on a new venture, otherwise your life will be filled with brilliant beginnings and very mediocre endings. Learn to keep your feet on the ground and to keep plugging along even when you are tempted to quit the job for something which seems less monotonous.

In matters of love you will probably sweep the other sex off its feet, but in marriage you will have to remember that life is not all romance and that in domestic affairs an attention to the practical side of life is essential for true happiness. You should marry a person born in the last half of March or under the sign of Cancer or Sagittarius.

Friday will be your best day; your lucky colors are the reds and yellows, and your lucky gems are bloodstones and aquamarines. The number most often associated with good fortune will be 2.

MARCH 30 TO APRIL 10

Your planets are Mars and the Sun, in that order of influence.

You will never lack for courage and energy when confronted with obstacles and you will usually win your point if you can only learn to keep your temper and to conceal your impatience with persons who are less quick than you are. You will find yourself best suited to occupations in which you are called upon to direct other workers, which means that in business, politics or military affairs you are sure to make a mark in the world. You will need to be more cautious in decisions than most people, for you will always want to rush ahead without first weighing all the facts in the case. This may lead to rash and misguided acts unless you are careful, and might bring about a most disastrous defeat. For it is your destiny never to do anything by halves. If you succeed, it will be a brilliant triumph; a defeat would be equally spectacular. Therefore be more than usually prudent in financial transactions.

With members of the other sex you will have to guard against being too dominating, and since you will never take love lightly, you will be in danger of ruining your happiness through unfounded jealousy or possessiveness.

You should marry persons born under the sign of Aries, Leo or Sagittarius. Your lucky colors are tan and orange; your gems are the diamond and topaz. Your best day will be Tuesday, and the number most often associated with good fortune will be 8.

April 11 to April 20

Your planets are Mars, Venus and Jupiter, and their influence is exerted in that order.

Your future is particularly golden. Pleasure, success and true happiness will be yours if only you follow your instincts and do not let your enthusiasm cloud your judgment and permit you to waste your talents in fruitless and inconsequential activities. You will have many friends and opportunities will constantly open up before you as if by magic. Your biggest problem will be in learning to make the wisest choice. Like others born under this sign you must learn to accept routine and to finish what you have started before embarking on some new venture. You possess talents which can carry you far in business or the arts and sciences. Some sort of career is definitely indicated for you, but you should be careful not to tell too many of your good ideas to anyone who will listen, or you will find that someone else with less imagination but more enterprise has appropriated your own ideas and capitalized on them to your disadvantage.

You will be intense and idealistic about your love and will have to check a tendency to try to rule your partner's life completely, failing to realize that both courtship and marriage are give-and-take propositions. However, you have the capacity for achieving great happiness as a devoted mate and loving parent.

You would best marry a person born in the first half of April or under the sign of Leo or Sagittarius. Your best day is Monday. Your lucky colors are the yellows, light greens and blues; your lucky gems are sapphires and diamonds, and your most favorable number is 1.

APRIL 21 TO APRIL 29

Your planets, in the order in which they exert their influence, are Venus, Mercury, and Mars.

You are always going to be known for your good common sense and ability along practical lines. For this reason you may expect to succeed in any business line which requires sound judgment and reliability. Life is going to be relatively smooth and easy for you, for you will not pick quarrels or try to dictate to the other fellow how he should live. This does not mean that you are going to be imposed upon, for you will always stand up for your rights, and you will usually find they are respected because people are going to recognize instinctively that you cannot be trifled with. Your greatest fault will be obstinacy when you feel that your point of view has been ignored. You will have to learn to be tactful when you do become aroused, for your anger, which you will seldom feel, will blind you by its intensity when it does finally become stirred.

You must always remember not to neglect the romance in your marriage, for its greatest appeal for you probably will be in the comforts that domestic life provides rather than in the adoration of your partner. As a parent you will be inclined to be overindulgent and may spoil your children with too much attention. Otherwise you will be an ideal father or mother and your home will undoubtedly be the center of your life.

You will be a success in any sort of business or profession that requires methodical effort and "brain work."

You should marry persons born in the last half of April or August or under the sign of Capricorn. Your best day will be Friday; your lucky colors are yellow and orange, and your lucky gems are diamonds and moonstones. The number most frequently associated with good fortune will be 5.

April 30 to May 10

Your planets are Venus, the Moon, and Mercury, exerting their influence in that order.

To achieve success in life you have only to be sure that you become engaged in a line of work that you enjoy. You possess all the attributes of industry, perseverance and intelligence to make you go far in your chosen career. But never undertake something which does not appeal to you, even though you think that it may lead you to fame and fortune. You will never be able to drive yourself by sheer will power to success; you will have to get there through the joy of doing the job. If you have instincts for the stage or screen, they are worth following, for you will have the persistence to undergo untold hardships—in fact, they will not seem like hardships to you, but more like part of the game. You also would be good in any business which brings you in contact with the public.

Your marriage should be a happy one, though you must remember not to let the romance go out of it. Don't take it too much for granted. There is only one rock on which your matrimonial ship may founder, and that is jealousy. There is only one way for you to deal with that problem, and that is to be completely frank about your feelings.

You should marry a person born under the sign of Taurus or Capricorn or in the first half of September. Your best day will be Tuesday. Your lucky colors are pale greens and blues. Your lucky gems are the emerald and turquoise. The number which will be most often associated with good luck is 6. Your most auspicious day in matters of love will be Wednesday, and you may also find the number 4 favorable in this connection.

MAY 11 TO MAY 20

Your planets are Venus and Saturn, and they exert their influence on your life in that order.

There will be only one thing which will stand in the way of your eventual success and that will be a tendency toward moodiness. You will have to remember that one of the surest ways to fail is to worry constantly over whether you are going to succeed. You must learn to ignore the doubts and fears that will continually creep into your mind, for you have the best chance for success if you will only follow your instincts and persevere. Determination is your greatest asset and you can make almost anything of your life if you really want to. You should succeed in business having to do with construction or manufacture or in any of the creative arts, such as painting, sculpture or writing. Also you should make a name for yourself in anything which requires judgment in matters of taste—architecture or commercial designing.

You will have a happy marriage but you will have to watch out for jealousy. In friendships you will be intensely loyal, and you must never allow your moody spells to affect your relationships with others. Learn to laugh at what you will often imagine to be slights and neglect, for you will have a tendency toward self-pity, usually without the slightest justification.

You should never avoid responsibilities, for people are going to have confidence in you and ask your co-operation and advice, and you are going to find your greatest happiness in overcoming obstacles and proving your ability through hard and determined work.

You should marry a person born under the sign of Taurus, Virgo or Capricorn. Your best day will be Tuesday; your lucky colors are blue, gray and brown, and your lucky gems are the opal and emerald. The number most often associated with good fortune will be 6.

MAY 21 TO MAY 30

Your planets, in the order in which they exert their influence, are Mercury, Venus and Jupiter.

Your greatest danger in life will be that you may become the rolling stone that gathers no moss. This will come about because you will find at least half a dozen careers open to you. You will have the necessary talent for all of them and also the desire to undertake any one of them. Making up your mind which one to concentrate on will be such a difficult job that you may never come to a final decision, but will spend your entire life drifting from one thing to another. Thus if failure comes to you, it will not be because you lack ability, but because you have too much and have never been able to make up your mind what to do with it.

You are going to have to learn to concentrate and discipline yourself if you ever want to be successful. If you can accomplish self-discipline, you will have a brilliant career. You should be successful in a variety of professions: medicine, the law, literature, journalism. The ministry or finance should also be suitable fields for your type.

In love you are going to be both ardent and changeable and you probably will fall in love many times before you marry. You must try not to do so after you marry, however.

You should marry a person born in the latter half of May, September or January. Your most favorable day will be Wednesday. Your lucky colors are blue, green and gray, and your lucky gems are the emerald and agate. The number most often associated with good fortune will be 6.

MAY 31 TO JUNE 10

Your planets, in the order in which they exert their influence, are Mercury and Mars.

Like all others who are born under the sign of Gemini, you are going to be the victim of an incurable restlessness. This is going to have its advantages and disadvantages. On the favorable side it will mean that you will never settle down in a rut. Your life will be filled with interesting events; you will always be on the side of progress and change. With your alert mind you will constantly be probing into unexplored fields of knowledge and you may achieve success by some startling discovery or the development of a new way of doing things. On the unfavorable side, however, lies the possibility that you may never be able to stick to anything long enough to see it bear fruit. You may be so busy switching from one line of work to another that you will never find time to complete all the marvelous projects which you have dreamed of accomplishing.

You will make friends easily and have many love affairs, but you will always have to be on your guard against a tendency to quarrel and bicker about unimportant details. This may lose you many of your dearest friends in the long run, and it may even have tragic consequence in regard to your marriage. You must try to moderate your feelings and to learn not to fly off the handle too easily.

Business which is connected with travel should be suited to your temperament. You might also make a very fine teacher, since you will always be interested in the new generations that are coming up in life.

You should marry a person born under the sign of Libro or Aquarius. Your most favorable day will be Wednesday, and you need not be afraid of undertaking actions on Friday. Your lucky colors are green, yellow and pale blue; your lucky gems are the pearl and topaz. The number most often associated with good fortune for you will be 5.

June 11 to June 21

Your planets, in the order in which they exert their influence, are Mercury, the Sun, and Saturn.

If you can only bring yourself to settle down in one line of work and stick to it, you should achieve great success in journalism, education or the law; or in finance, banking or the brokerage business. Your ready wit will give you a great talent for public speaking, and this, combined with a great talent for making friends easily and naturally, should fit you for any sort of political career or executive office in connection with a large organization of individuals, such as a fraternal order or a professional or trade association.

Do not allow yourself to worry too much about the future. You will never be at a loss for a job. Your greatest problem in this connection will always be to make up your mind which of a number of positions you are going to take.

If you wish to be happy in your marriage you will have to learn to concentrate on that, too, and not let outside interests in business absorb all your attention and devotion. If a woman, you are liable to be the kind who spends all her time running clubs and charities and neglects her home and family. If a man, you are liable to bury yourself in business and forget that you have a wife who would like to spend an evening in your company once in a while.

You should marry persons born under the sign of Libra or Aquarius. Your most favorable day will be Wednesday. Your lucky colors are the golden tans and the grayish blues. Your lucky gems are the pearl or moonstone and the beryl. The number most often associated with good fortune will be 8, and sometimes 5.

JUNE 22 TO JULY 1

Your planets are the Moon and Venus, of equal importance.

Your life is going to be filled with contradictions. On the one hand you are going to be restless and uncertain about your plans. You are going to be very interested in something one moment and completely indifferent to it the next. Yet on the other hand you are going to be able to stick to something, once you have convinced yourself that it is what you want to do, in the face of tremendous obstacles and discouragements. Your biggest problem will be making that first decision. You will make things easier if you don't fret about them too much.

In business or the professions you are likely to make a success at anything having to do with aviation, railroading or shipping. You might start out in some capacity which requires you to travel, later settling down to an executive position where the experience you have thus gained will come in handy. It would be wise for you to satisfy your craving for new sights and strange places early in life, so that in later years you can locate in one spot and have a home.

You will probably have a number of love affairs before you finally make up your mind, and this is wisest, for you will need to find a partner who is understanding and sympathetic and you should not choose blindly in the first fine rapture of new love. You should plan to have children, for they will bring you much happiness not only while they are growing up but after they have gone out in the world on their own. And you will make an ideal parent.

You should marry a person born in the last half of June, October or February. Your lucky colors are light yellows, blues and greens, and your lucky gems are the pearl, moonstone or crystal. Your most favorable day will be Monday, and the number most often associated with good fortune will be 2.

JULY 2 TO JULY 10

Your planets are the Moon, Mars and Mercury, exerting their influence in that order.

Life for you is going to be filled with many interesting events and people. You are going to travel considerably and make many unusual friendships, some of which will bring you very good fortune. There is the prospect that you will achieve wealth and hold considerable influence over the lives of many people. The only obstacle to your success is over-timidity about yourself and an exaggerated idea of wrongs that you imagine have been done to you. Always be on guard against self-pity in any form.

Any business or profession connected with publishing or with travel will be suited to you, and you also may find fame in the entertainment world or in education. Try to choose an occupation in which your mental powers will be called upon, for you are meant to work with the brain rather than with brawn.

You may not make friends easily, since on first acquaintance your manner may seem rather abrupt and severe. This will come from your attempts to conceal a natural shyness which you feel and you should try to cultivate a more gracious manner with strangers. However, once the ice has been broken, people will become devoted to you and will stand by you through thick and thin. This is equally true in matters of love, and when you do find the one whom you wish to marry, be careful that the first impression you make does not tend to frighten him or her away.

You should marry a person born under Scorpio or Pisces. Your most favorable day will be Monday; your lucky colors are violet and green, and your lucky gems are the ruby, agate and beryl. The number most often associated with good fortune will be 2, sometimes 5.

JULY 11 TO JULY 21

Your planets are the Moon and Jupiter, exerting their influence in that order.

Things are not always going to be rosy for you. You will have periods of very good fortune alternating with intervals when it seems that the whole world is against you. During these later times you will be inclined to accuse yourself unfairly of being the cause of your misfortunes. In many cases this will not be true, for much bad luck and good luck, too, is going to come your way quite by chance. If you will have the courage to stick things out and keep a stiff upper lip, good luck is going to outweigh the dark side of life in the long run. One thing you must always bear in mind: never retreat. Take the risk every time, for common sense and a good brain will carry you through many dangers where persons with less ability would fail.

The scientific professions and trade will be best suited to your tastes and will afford you the greatest amount of satisfaction.

Never let anything come between you and your friends for you will have need of them in time of trouble, and if you have played square with them, you will always be able to count on their aid and support. Your marriage will be the source of great comfort and happiness to you, although you may not marry until rather late in life. If you have no children of your own, you should adopt some, for your parental instincts should be cultivated.

Marry a person born under the sign of Cancer, Scorpio, or Pisces. Monday or Wednesday will be your most favorable days. Your lucky colors are silver gray and violet, and your lucky gems are the ruby, the opal and jade. The number most often associated with good fortune is 3.

JULY 22 TO AUGUST 1

Your planets, in the order in which they exert their influence, are the Sun and Saturn.

You should make a success of your life and rise to a position of considerable prominence, but you will have to be on guard against one thing. There will be many persons who will attempt to impose upon your generous nature and try to induce you to join them in enterprises or activities which cannot possibly benefit you and which may possibly harm you. Thus whenever you are called on for help or assistance, be sure to take time to study the situation carefully. Your immediate reaction will be to act without delay, but in the long run you will find it wiser to learn a little caution.

In the matter of a career you have a wide field to choose from. Any sort of executive work should be especially suited to your talents. You should be an ideal manager of a plant or store. Since people will always like to work with you (provided you learn to control your "bossy" instincts so that you can give orders without giving offense at the same time), any job where you come into contact with the public should be to your taste.

You are going to be surrounded by friends who are devoted to your interests. Your marriage should be exceptionally happy if you can remember not to try to "rule the roost" all the time.

If you fail to realize that marriage is a matter of sharing, a partnership where neither one dominates completely, you will be in danger of much unhappiness and possibly a separation.

You should marry a person born under the sign of Aries or Sagittarius or in the last half of July. Your best day will be Sunday. Your lucky colors are green, orange or gold; your lucky gems are the ruby and the topaz, and the number most often associated with good fortune will be 1.

AUGUST 2 TO AUGUST 12

Your planets, in the order in which they exert their influence, are the Sun and Jupiter.

You were born under the most favorable auspices, and you not only are likely to rise to great heights but in the course of a lifetime you are going to surround yourself with loyal and loving friends who will do many favors for you. This does not mean that your success is not going to be the result of honest effort. You will rise rapidly through your own merits in any position which calls for the ability to plan out a line of action and to supervise and direct the working out of the plan.

Marriage will bring you great happiness, it also may bring you unexpected fortune or fame. You will be given your own way in the home, but you should remember not to insist upon it on every occasion. You will always have what is known as "a way" with children, not only your own but all youngsters. Nor will you ever be one to condemn the younger generation and criticize it. This great gift of understanding not only will make you a wise and loving parent but will suit you for any position in which you have charge of persons younger than you—a dean or adviser in a university, for example.

You should marry a person born under the sign of Aries, Leo or Sagittarius. Your best day will be Sunday. Your lucky colors are purple and gold, and your lucky gems are the sardonyx and

the sapphire. The number most frequently associated \
fortune will be 2.

AUGUST 13 TO AUGUST 22

Your planets are the Sun and Mars, and they exert their influence in that order.

There is only one thing which may stand in the way of your eventual success. Being keenly enthusiastic over what you are doing, you may forget that to other people this enthusiasm may appear to be boasting or egotism. Unless controlled this trait may alienate persons who might otherwise have become your friends and have given you some valuable assistance. Also you will have to learn to be a good loser and to conceal your disappointment when you meet with failure or a rebuff. If you will only bear in mind that in the end you are bound to succeed if your talents have a chance to be seen, you will be able to take the momentary defeats in your stride without giving them a second thought. You will have to curb your desire for praise occasionally or you may be taken advantage of by flatterers who are out to benefit themselves at your expense.

Business and industry of all kinds are open to you. You should also find fame in politics, military affairs, the law or the theater. As you can see, the future holds many possibilities; it is up to you to learn self-control so that you may realize them.

Your marriage should bring you great happiness. There will be only one obstacle in the way of its success and that will be your tendency to be suspicious when you have no grounds for jealousy.

Remember to take a vacation now and then, and not go at top speed all the time. Even the most rugged constitution can crack under constant strain.

You should marry a person born under the sign of Aries, Leo or Sagittarius. Your best day will be Thursday. Your lucky colors are apricot, scarlet, and vermilion. Your lucky gems are the sardonyx and crystal. The number most frequently associated with good fortune will be 9.

AUGUST 23 TO SEPTEMBER 1

Your planets are Mercury and the Sun, and they exert their influences in equal degree.

In a world which is always looking for honest, painstaking workmen, you will never find yourself idle. You are going to prosper and make money, though you may never amass a tremendous fortune. If you achieve any great success it will not bring great riches with it, rather it will be fame and honors in recognition of your talents. It is possible that you will invent some new device or process which will earn great wealth for someone else. Fortunately you will not be discontented if this happens, for with you the satisfaction derived from your work will be adequate compensation. Besides you will have a fair share of the wealth, enough to satisfy most of your dreams.

Other occupations in which you may succeed include editorial work of some sort in which you are engaged in the preparation and publication of manuscripts, scientific pursuits, education, or anything which had to do with construction or manufacture.

You must cultivate your social side so that you do not allow yourself to become so absorbed in your work that you neglect your friends and loved ones. This is particularly true in regard to your marriage. You will have to learn to show your affections and not take love so much for granted. Above all you must learn not to be too critical when things go wrong in your domestic life. If you are a woman you face the danger of becoming a nagging wife unless you keep your critical tendencies in control. If a man, you must learn to keep quiet when the dinner is cold and to be tactful when you think your wife has been spending too much money.

You should marry a person born in the last half of April, August or December. Your best day will be Sunday, although Tuesday may also be especially important. Your lucky colors are blue and green; your lucky gems are the sardonyx and the agate, and the number most frequently associated with good fortune will be 5.

September 2 to September 11

Your planets are Mercury, Venus and Saturn, and they exert their influence in that order.

If you want to be happy, you should always keep busy, for you were not born to be an idler. Nor will it be difficult for you to find something to do, for your talent for logical thinking and keen insight will always be in demand. You will never have to worry about making decisions, for your instincts will steer you clear of any impractical or foolish schemes. The main thing you will have to guard against is being too suspicious of new ideas and projects that appear to involve a risk. You will work best under the direction of someone else, for by yourself you will too often fail to see the greater possibilities in a new venture.

Many types of business are suited to you and, strangely enough, you should to a certain extent be successful in the arts, especially architecture.

Do not let yourself become too practical in matters of friendship and love. Remember that though marriage may be a serious business, love has its lighter side. Try to enjoy your domestic life and do not be too finicky if things don't always go the way you would like to have them. Try not to exaggerate the faults of your loved ones and your friends, and never try to correct or improve them, for that is a temptation to which you may give way entirely too readily, and in the end it can only bring you unhappiness.

You should marry a person born under the sign of Taurus, Virgo or Capricorn. Your best day will be Wednesday. Your lucky colors are dark blue and slate; your lucky gems are sapphire and jasper, and the number most often associated with good fortune will be 4.

September 12 to September 22

Your planets, in the order in which they exert their influence, are Mercury and Saturn.

Life for you is going to get easier as you grow older, and many of the things which seem to be great obstacles and handicaps now will eventually prove to be quite harmless. You have a good chance of achieving fame through some activity you have engaged in. You will find success in occupations having to do with mathematics or science. You may also do well in literary work of some kind.

Don't try to analyze yourself and your friends too often, for this will only lead you to brooding and melancholy. You have a gift for studying problems and people and classifying them in your mind as one type or another, and you should try to turn this to some advantage in your business life but never in your personal life. Try to learn to take people as they come, enjoy their company and overlook their failings as much as possible. In matters of love you must realize that true devotion shows itself in deeds. Learn to display your affections, lest you be accused of being too cold.

You should marry a person born under the sign of Taurus, Virgo or Capricorn. Your best day will be Saturday. Your lucky colors are light blue and green; your lucky gems are the sapphire and jade. The number most frequently associated with good fortune will be 8.

SEPTEMBER 23 TO OCTOBER 1

Your planets, in the order in which they exert their influence, are Venus and the Moon.

All your life you will have to guard against oversensitivity. In your business life especially you must not take it too much to heart when you fail to receive what you consider to be justly deserved praise. Try to remember that people about you are busy and concerned with their own affairs and that often what you believe to be slights or criticisms of your actions are really not meant in that way at all. You will save yourself much worry and anxiety if you can learn to forget trivial little incidents which in reality have no relation to you whatsoever. If your superiors fail to commend you, it does not necessarily mean that they are dissatisfied with your work but rather that they have merely neglected to tell you that you are doing well or that they consider that such praise is unnecessary. If you are working at a job that you like, the chances are that you are performing your work competently and satisfactorily, for you have much natural ability and talent.

You should not attempt hard physical labor, but you will excel in the arts, in commerce or finance, or in the law, provided you have a position which brings you into contact with large groups of people. You need the stimulation that comes from working with others.

You should have a happy married life if you can recognize that matrimony implies certain obligations and responsibilities which cannot be avoided. Be extremely careful that you do not give cause for jealousy and suspicion, for it will be very easy for you to hurt the person you love deeply without being aware that you are doing so.

You should marry a person born in the last half of January, May or September. Your lucky colors are pale blues and yellows; your lucky gems are the sapphire and the opal. Your best day will be Friday, and the number most often associated with good fortune will be 6.

OCTOBER 2 TO OCTOBER 12

Your planets, in the order in which they exert their influence, are Venus and Saturn.

One thing always to bear in mind is the old saying that "every cloud has a silver lining." You are going to have spells of moodiness which you will have to learn to control so that they do not interfere with your work. You will be inclined to exaggerate remarks that others have made and which you believe to be directed at you in an unfavorable way. Nine times out of ten this will not be the case. If you can only remember that it is a basic trait of your nature that makes you suffer periods of unhappiness and the blues, you will be able to become philosophical about these dark clouds and the sooner you do, the less effect they will have over you. Remember that the world seldom lives up to man's ideals and the important thing is to hold fast to the ideals through thick and thin, for it is only in this way that men ever progress at all. You have a very fine and sensitive nature and it will have much to contribute to the lives of those about you if you will keep busy and never lose sight of your goals.

You will prosper in business which is connected in some way with the arts or, strange as it may seem, in the heavier types of industry—in mechanical engineering, construction work, mining and the like. In any of these spheres you should rise rapidly to a position where you are in charge of many persons.

Though your marriage may not always be happy, you should not remain single, for domestic life and the comforts of a home will mean much to you and will be a never-ending source of strength.

You may marry a person born under almost any s[...]
Sagittarius and possibly Cancer. Your best days will [...]
and Monday. Your lucky colors are green and pink; your lucky
gems are the opal and the carnelian, and the number most frequently associated with good fortune will be 6.

OCTOBER 13 TO OCTOBER 22

Your planets, in the order in which they exert their influence,
are Venus, Mercury, and Jupiter.

You will probably engage in a number of different kinds of
work during your life before you find the one which is most
congenial to you. In part this will be due to an inability to make
up your mind to stick at what you have started; it also will
result from an instinct to better yourself and to seize the best
opportunity that presents itself. Do not make a change without
considerable thought. If you always let reason guide you and
not a momentary dislike or feeling of restlessness, you will be
right in shifting to a new type of work. Don't let your wide
interests and your ability to adapt yourself to new circumstances
lead you to become a rolling stone.

A number of love affairs are indicated in your life. There
can be no harm in this if you are completely sincere in your
emotions, and it will help you to find your type of partner.
Do not marry in haste. You will have a very happy domestic
life.

You should marry a person born under the signs of Libra,
Aquarius or Gemini, although you need not be bound by these
signs in your choice. You will be least likely to find happiness
with one born under the sign of Capricorn. Your best day will
be Wednesday. Your lucky colors are pale blue and violet; your
lucky gems are the opal and the tourmaline, and the number
most frequently associated with good fortune will be 5.

OCTOBER 23 TO NOVEMBER 2

Your planets, in the order in which they exert their influence, are Mars and Venus.

Learn to take criticism as easily as you are able to give it, for you will find that at times the well-meant suggestions of your friends and associates will be of great benefit to you if only you will follow them. For complete success you will have to train yourself to consider the other fellow's point of view, even though you are convinced that he is in the wrong. If you acquire this faculty—and you were not born with it—you will be able to use it to your advantage, for it will help you to see yourself as others see you and open your eyes to weaknesses in yourself which you had not been aware of and which might be used to bring about your defeat. This is particularly important if you are going to enter business life, in which you should have a marked success.

You should also make a name for yourself in medicine or anything having to do with industrial chemistry. Transportation and architecture or bridge designing and construction are other fields that are open to you.

In matters of love do not let the warmth of your passion blind you to the true character of the other person. You might marry someone who shares none of your interests and tastes if you acted in haste. You are probably due for some heartbreaks, for you will never be one to take love lightly, and when it dies for the other person, your whole world will for a time seem to die with it. Choose wisely when you wed and you should have a marriage that will be completely successful, based on deep and lasting feeling.

You should marry a person born in the last half of July, October or February. Your best day will be Thursday. Your lucky colors are the reds and purple; your lucky gems are the opal

and beryl. The number most often associated with success will
be 9.

NOVEMBER 3 TO NOVEMBER 14

Your planets, in the order in which they exert their influence,
are Mars and the Sun.

If you will guard against the unfavorable traits of character
that are found in persons born under the sign of Scorpio, you
should rise in life to a position of power and control. Your
superiors will delegate to you many hard and difficult undertakings. This is not a sign that they are trying to make you the
goat but rather that they would not intrust such work to a
weaker individual and that they have confidence in your ability
to make good. To be a good executive, you will have to cultivate
tact and patience with those who do not possess the same
ability that you do. It is important to remember this, for an
executive must know how to handle subordinates, and if you
should show yourself to be hard to get along with, your chances
of promotion might be hindered.

To have a happy marriage you should learn to forgive and to
forget. Do not let your affections become too possessive—this
applies especially *before* marriage. Avoid any tendency you may
have to domineer in your domestic life.

You should marry a person born under the sign of Cancer,
Scorpio or Pisces. Your best day will be Tuesday. Your lucky
colors are the reds and brown; your lucky gems are the topaz
and crystal, and the number most often associated with good
fortune will be 3.

NOVEMBER 15 TO NOVEMBER 23

Your planets, in the order in which they exert their influence,
are Mars and the Moon.

Your choice of career should be guided by what talents you

possess. If you have a special aptitude for one of the arts, you may wisely take this up as your life work. But unless you show marked gifts which are recognized by competent judges, you should not allow the mere desire to become a painter, writer, musician or sculptor to deceive you into believing that you might be successful as one. There is a danger that you may waste your time trying to develop a gift which you do not possess, and unless you have recognized ability it would be better to keep your interest in art as a hobby and find your real occupation in medicine, transportation, the physical sciences, electricity, politics or military affairs.

It is possible that you will marry more than once. You will have many love affairs and not all of them will be entirely happy ones. Jealousy or too much possessiveness on your part may spoil many of them, and you will have to learn to moderate your affection if you wish your married life to be a success. Too fierce a love is often as dangerous in its consequences as one that is not constant. Your temper may be the cause of a divorce.

You should marry a person born under the sign of Cancer, Scorpio or Pisces. Your best day will be Monday. Your lucky colors are rose and blue; your lucky stones are the topaz and pearl, and the number most often associated with good fortune will be 2.

NOVEMBER 24 TO NOVEMBER 30

Your planets, in the order in which they exert their influence, are Jupiter and Mercury.

Be sure you get plenty of fun out of life. Don't spend all your time with your nose to the grindstone, even though you do find a great deal of satisfaction in work. You will never achieve the maximum results by making a drudge of yourself. If you work by yourself, and you probably will be happiest when you are doing so, resist the temptation to bury yourself in your work. You need the stimulation of having your friends and acquaintances around occasionally.

There are many types of work that will be suited to you. In the professions there is law, the church and diplomacy. You should also do well in publishing, education, merchandising or banking. But in all these you must find time in which to relax and take things easy. Otherwise you may become irritable and less efficient in your work.

Remember that frankness is a virtue which can very easily be overdone. You should be especially careful about this in regard to your friends. It may seem to you perfectly harmless to tell them to their faces about their petty faults and weaknesses, but you are not going to keep your friends very long unless you become far more tactful. You will have several love affairs which will be broken up by this habit of yours. There is also the possibility that you may be divorced for the same reason. If you can only find someone who really sees that this directness and lack of tact on your part is not a deliberate attempt to be uncivil, you can marry and have a most happy home life.

You should marry a person born in the month of July, November or March. Your lucky day will be Monday. Your lucky colors are purple and yellow; your lucky gems are the topaz and marcasite, and the number most often associated with good fortune will be 3.

December 1 to December 11

Your planets, in the order in which they exert their influence, are Jupiter and the Moon.

There will be many dangers in your life and many obstacles. You will be tempted to take things easily and to avoid quarrels, but you must learn to fight for your own point of view. As for the dangers, you will probably escape from many of them by what at the time appears to be nothing less than miracles. In fact, it may safely be said that if you do not succeed in life as you had intended, only you will be to blame, for in many ways you will benefit by unexpected turns of very good luck.

Any career which will involve a certain amount of travel will yield satisfying rewards; you will likewise be very apt to make a name for yourself in a position which requires organizing ability. The arts are probably the one general field in which you are least likely to succeed. Don't let yourself worry too much over trifles or imagined insults and slights.

In your marriage you are going to resent any attempt by your partner to demand a great deal of attention. You are not the type who will take easily to the restraints and responsibilities of marriage, and you should bear this in mind when picking a partner, avoiding anyone who has a deeply affectionate nature or whose jealousy might be easily aroused. With the type who likes to be the pal or companion, however, you should have a very happy domestic life.

You should marry a person born under the sign of Leo, Sagittarius or Aries. Your best day will be Tuesday. Your lucky colors are green and purple; your lucky gems are the turquoise and the moonstone, and the number most frequently associated with good fortune will be 4.

December 12 to December 21

Your planets, in the order in which they exert their influence, are Jupiter, Saturn, and the Sun.

Always trust in your sudden moments of inspiration. You will make your mark in the world entirely on your own, with very little assistance from any outsider. It may be some brilliant scientific discovery, an invention or some new method of doing things, but the idea will come to you unexpectedly and you will work it out almost completely by yourself. For this reason it will be good for you to plan to do a certain amount of your work in seclusion, but you should not become a hermit. It will not prove best for you in the long run to isolate yourself from the world.

You will have only a few friends, but they will be ones who understand and love you deeply, and their loyalty will always be a great help and comfort to you. In love you may not find complete happiness. There may be a divorce and you may decide that domestic life is not worth the individual liberty you have to forego when you marry.

Science, education or research work offer the greatest opportunities to you, although you are also fitted for industry, politics or the financial world. In trade you should do reasonably well, although you ought to cultivate hobbies to satisfy intellectual interests which you will find developing as the years roll by.

You should marry a person born under the sign of Aries, Leo or Sagittarius. Your best day will be Sunday. Your lucky colors are golden brown, magenta or puce; your lucky gems are the turquoise, and the number most frequently associated with good fortune will be 8.

THE SEVEN PLANETS

JUPITER. This planet is said to be associated with success. Persons born under its influence will be aided in business affairs and will be favored in matters pertaining to money. An ability to acquire and manage property and wealth is implied.

Jupiter confers mounting ambitions and a broad and wise outlook upon life. If its influence is excessive it may lead to fast and high living, with the danger of extravagance and wastefulness, not only of material things but of spiritual powers and physical energy.

It bestows upon its subjects the gift of friendship and the admiration and esteem of their fellows. Jupiter's people are fond of material comforts and are made unhappy if they are completely denied the luxuries of life. They assume responsibility easily and have a gift for directing the lives of other people without arousing resentment. They are endowed with good minds and have a keen appetite for sensual pleasures—eating and drinking and easy living. They do not possess great powers of resistance when confronted by temptation. As a result they may sometimes yield to dishonorable activities while occupying positions of authority, and as a result may suffer grave reversals of fortune. When Jupiter people succeed they do so on a large scale, and their failures or defeats are equally impressive.

A knowledge of these influences should help them to conduct their lives so as to reap the benefits and avoid the pitfalls.

THE SUN. The Sun endows its subjects with a love of beauty and definite talents in the arts which can be developed so as to bring them great fame and fortune. They are generally lucky in games of chance or commercial enterprises that involve a certain amount of risk. As the Sun is the golden orb of day, it is as if its subjects had the gift of the golden touch. They make money easily but since they do not possess shrewdness in the handling of large sums, they are liable to lose their wealth as quickly as they obtained it. They can easily be victimized by unscrupulous persons and should always seek the counsel of others in decisions affecting financial affairs.

They are usually happy and warmhearted and draw to them friends as a magnet draws iron. They have to learn not to confide in strangers, whom they are unable to imagine as being less honorable and upright than they are.

They are destined for honors and prominence and like to receive attention and admiration. They have to guard against a tendency to "show off," a failing which sometimes proves to be their undoing, either alienating the friendship of influential people or leading them to unwise and reckless actions.

The force of their personalities will carry them far in life, but they should avoid the temptation to run other people's lives for them without first being asked. They are especially successful in any work which calls for untiring energy and great activity.

A knowledge of these influences should help them to conduct their lives so as to reap the benefits and avoid the pitfalls.

MARS. Persons born under the influence of Mars are primarily men and women of action. Mars does not produce a reflective, thoughtful type in which the intellect dominates. They are inclined to be either suspicious or contemptuous of learning or mental activity, and this is unfortunate since it often hinders them from recognizing a dangerous and cunning adversary.

They are brave to the point of foolish recklessness and can be lured into perilous activities by flatterers who wish to do them harm. They are not given to beating about the bush, but always speak their minds frankly and without reservation, totally unconcerned about whether they have made enemies by so doing.

They are absolutely trustworthy when they have given their word and they are likewise relentless when they are seeking revenge. It is difficult to reason with them, and their temper, which is violent and liable to lead them into the gravest difficulties, is easily aroused by opposition.

They have to guard against boastfulness and offensive manners. Devoted to their friends and loved ones, they are fierce in their hates. In love Mars produces a violent passion which is often excessive in every way and can easily repel persons of finer sensibilities, a fact which Mars people always have great difficulty in understanding.

A knowledge of these influences should help them to conduct their lives so as to reap its benefits and avoid its pitfalls.

SATURN. This planet casts an unpleasant influence. It fosters melancholy and depressed spirits. It begets doubts and suspicions, and torments the minds of its subjects with countless fears and worries. It helps to bring out many qualities which we do not admire in human nature—miserliness, trickery, deceit, cruelty. That is not to say that persons born under its influence are necessarily guilty of these things. It merely indicates that there is a force in their lives which often works for evil and for which they must be on the lookout continually. They should resist even the slightest temptation to give way to these influences.

When they are plagued with their black moods, the subjects of Saturn should never plan to undertake anything of any importance. Rather they should wait until the spell subsides, for if they attempt anything while it hovers over them, nothing but failure will result.

Saturn also has a better side. It gives strength of purpose and determination and thus is a decided asset when one is confronted with one of life's graver problems. It produces a certain skepticism of mind which gives its subjects a shrewd insight into many things which might fool other people who are not so gifted. If Saturn helps to create schemers and plotters it also assists those who wish to lay plans for the future of a constructive nature.

A knowledge of these influences should help the Saturn subject to reap the benefits of his planet and avoid its pitfalls.

MERCURY. This planet favors an alertness of mind and body and endows its subjects with quick wit and keen insight. It has a sort of chameleon nature in that, in addition to its own powers, it reinforces the influence of whatever planet it accompanies. Thus if there are a number of unfavorable traits in one's make-up, Mercury helps to bring them out. The same is true with one's strong points.

In a way Mercury is a youthful planet. It lends vitality and quickness and a ready aptitude for learning new things even late in life. Its subjects are able to enter a wide variety of activities because they have an adaptable and versatile nature.

Mercury people are excellent in arguments and are usually able to win their points by the sheer brilliance of their discourse, even when they are completely in the wrong. This trait can consequently be turned to evil uses and used in tricky and deceitful enterprises. At its best this attribute of Mercury people produces eloquent orators and adept politicians and diplomats.

The subjects of this planet are very clever in commerce and industry and have a talent for amassing wealth. They can often take a business which is on the verge of bankruptcy and by brilliant management turn it into a veritable gold mine. In combination with Saturn, the influence of this planet is bad and is liable to lead to gigantic swindles or illegal practices.

Mercury people have to learn to make up their minds for themselves and not to be influenced too easily by others.

A knowledge of these influences should help them to conduct their lives so as to reap the benefits and avoid the pitfalls.

THE MOON. The Moon has a remarkably stimulating effect upon the imagination and consequently endows its subjects with one of the primary requisites for a career in the fine arts. However, it also produces restlessness and dissatisfaction, probably because it stimulates daydreaming and wishful thinking. Those under its influence are liable to change their minds all too frequently, never being able to make a decision and stick to it. They often drift from one occupation to another, and they seldom remain settled in one spot for any great length of time.

Since the Moon is the planet which is closest to the earth, its influence is felt by its subjects very intensely, and its power over them is especially pronounced when it is in the full. Moon people should be particularly wary of making decisions during the time of the full moon, for their minds will not be free then to act unhampered.

The Moon has a favorable effect on its subjects in regard to travel. It also confers special aptitude for businesses having to do with liquids, the ocean or rivers. It is also said to favor aviators and all who travel by air.

Moon people are apt to be easily disturbed in their minds and should not subject themselves to severe mental strain for any very great length of time.

VENUS. Next to Jupiter this is one of the most favorable of all the planets. It endows its subjects with fine taste and discrimination which fits them for many occupations having to do with the production of the so-called luxury goods.

Venus people are also artistically inclined, though unlike the subjects of the Sun, they are not so much gifted as creators of art as they are blessed with a keen appreciation for the beautiful. This enriches their lives and can be the source of great happiness for them. They should cultivate one of the arts as a hobby or pastime if their everyday life is not connected with artistic things.

Venus people are excellent "mixers." Everywhere they go they are welcome and they make friends easily and keep them forever. They are seldom quarrelsome and are generally genial and sociable. This characteristic is, in its way, a form of weakness, since it is always hard for a Venus subject to put his foot down and insist on getting what he knows he should have.

The planet favors warm and abiding love and makes for a

pleasant domestic life and a home filled with cheer and good will. The subjects of Venus make very good parents, taking pride and satisfaction in their children. They are inclined to spoil them, however, by being too easygoing and indulgent.

In fact the most serious flaw in the true Venus character is the easygoing carelessness which lacks real force and drive.

A knowledge of these influences should help the Venus subject to reap the benefits of his planet and avoid the pitfalls.

III

What Your Numbers Tell

WHETHER we realize it or not we all go through life bearing with us a special set of numbers. Men who have made long and profound studies of such things tell us that these numbers play a very important part in our lives, casting powerful influences over our actions and also giving us clues about our future.

In fact, *all* numbers are said to possess a peculiar power over human affairs. This influence comes from the mystical vibrations which each number radiates, much as a radio station sends out unseen and unfelt vibrations into surrounding space. And since we are constantly coming into contact with numbers in our daily lives, it is natural that we should be directly affected by them for better or for worse.

However, the most important numbers to us are the special ones which are perpetually connected with us. They are the numbers of our name and our birth date, and it is considered extremely important that they should be in harmony with us and we with them, if we are to achieve success and happiness.

THE NUMBERS IN YOUR NAME

Each number between 1 and 9 is said to possess certain special meanings and to give off vibrations that exert a particular kind of influence over us.

Since every letter of the alphabet has been given a numerical value, it is possible to add together the letter values in your name so as to arrive at certain basic sums or numbers. On the basis of these you are then able to make predictions about your future and to guide yourself in decisions concerning such matters as love, business, etc.

The number values of the alphabet are as follows:

A — 1	F — 5	K — 3	P — 7	U — 5
B — 3	G — 8	L — 2	Q — 4	V — 3
C — 4	H — 9	M — 1	R — 6	W — 7
D — 4	I — 7	N — 5	S — 9	X — 1
E — 2	J — 6	O — 8	T — 2	Y — 8
				Z — 6

In analyzing your name there are three numbers to look for:

A—The Personality Number. This governs or modifies your relationships with those about you and has particular significance in matters of love and friendship.

B—The Vocational Number. This is associated with your occupation in life. If it is in harmony with the type of work you are doing, whether that be in commerce or one of the professions or in the home, then it will be a help to you in every undertaking. If it is not in harmony, however, it will act as a brake upon your efforts and tend to hinder you in your accomplishments.

C—The Destiny Number. This may also be referred to as your Monogram Number, since it is obtained from the initials of your name. It has an important influence upon the general good or bad fortune in your life and should be harmonious with your fundamental character or what is sometimes called your psychological type.

THE PERSONALITY NUMBER

To find your Personality Number you must use the name by which most of your friends and acquaintances call you. If your given name is Patricia but most of your friends call you Pat, then you will find your Personality Number in Pat, not in Patricia. For it is the influence which the name Pat has over you that affects you most frequently in your daily associations with those about you. Let us see how to find Pat's Personality Number.

Consulting the foregoing table of the alphabet we find that P is 7, A is 1 and T is 2. Add these three numbers together— 7 plus 1 plus 2 equals 10. This sum must be reduced to a single number, so we add together the two digits—1 plus 0—and the total is 1. Thus 1 is Pat's Personality Number.

In finding any one of the three numbers in your name, always add the letters together until you reach a single number between 1 and 9.

Let us take another example, the name Rita. The number values are as follows: R—6, I—7, T—2, A—1. The total is 16. Add the two digits together—1 plus 6 equals 7. Rita's Personality Number is 7.

Thus in Pat's case the number 1 has a special influence on her relationships with her friends, her family and with her boy friend. With Rita it is 7 which is constantly affecting the way she gets along with people in her social life.

By consulting the *Table of Personality Numbers* which follows both Pat and Rita can learn what sort of influence their names are having upon them. It may be that their Personality Numbers are not completely in harmony with their own individual personalities.

A glance at the table will show that Number 7 radiates vibrations of a subdued, thoughtful nature and is not favorable to jollity and high spirits. It may be that Rita is a sociable girl and is fond of parties and dancing and good times. In that case it would be wise for her to alter the spelling of her name slightly, or possibly to adopt an entirely new name which is more in harmony with her personal likes and dislikes. By substituting an E for the I in her name, she can adopt 2 as her Personality Number, which is much more favorable to one who likes fun and good company. It may help her in capturing more quickly the attentions of the young man on whom she has set her heart. At any rate 2 will not tend to drive away admirers as 7 inevitably will do.

Table of Personality Numbers

1—This is a very friendly number. It is conducive to enthusiasm and good spirits. For a person who is naturally sociable and warm-hearted it strengthens and enhances these qualities, while with shy and retiring natures it helps to overcome timidity and lends encouragement to friendly instincts. While it assists in creating admirers and loyal followers it likewise intensifies the hatred of enemies. The person dominated by this Personality Number is likely to be the center of a large circle of friends. In matters of love this number makes for powerful affections in which there is the danger of possessiveness and a tendency to dominate the partner unduly.

2—The influences of this number produce a very romantic disposition, with the affections very easily stirred. It is favorable to love affairs—many of them—in which the spiritual element is dominant. The number also enhances one's powers as a conversationalist and makes for general affability and friendliness. It helps in attracting friends, for it brings out the traits of tactfulness and kindness and suppresses tendencies toward bickering and sarcasm. It makes its subjects particularly sensitive to criticism and in general radiates a gentle, amiable spirit.

3—Three is a gay and happy number and promotes an atmosphere of good feeling and generosity. Persons under this influence are, therefore, always welcome company and eager to lend a helping hand or cheer up those who have the blues. If one's personality is not a very social one to begin with, the number 3 tends to lessen shyness and make it easier to strike up new acquaintances. It promotes a spirit of joyous comradeship which is very hard to resist. In matters of love it is conducive to a very deep, passionate nature and it does not favor light or passing affections.

4—The influence of this number is not very helpful in social affairs, for it is inclined to foster a "business before pleasure" attitude which is not entirely favorable to making friends and striking up new acquaintanceships. Persons under its influence are sometimes tempted to bury themselves in their work because they consider the pleasure of good company to be a waste of time. Hence for a person who is basically shy this number is not at all encouraging. In matters of love 4 produces caution and hesitation which would prove an asset (acting as a balance wheel) only in connection with a headstrong, fiery disposition.

5—This number bestows the gift of great personal charm, and it favors activity and gaiety, which are notable social attributes. Thus under the influence of 5 friends are made easily and hearts are won with little or no effort. But this is far from an ideal influence, for it also promotes a changeable, unstable nature, and persons who are completely dominated by 5 are usually notoriously fickle. Their warm-hearted affection, which seems so irresistible at first, cannot be counted on to last; they alternate constantly between enthusiasm and indifference, and are likely to leave a trail of broken hearts wherever they go.

6—This is the number of loyalty and devotion. It acts as a check on the person whose affections are likely to stray and it reinforces the home-loving, steadfast qualities of the domestic type. It promotes thoughtfulness in personal relationships and he who lives under its influence is apt to win many true friends because of his helpful, considerate manner. Though it does not ordinarily favor general merry-making, 6 does favor a quiet sociability. It is an ideal number for parenthood, since it brings faithfulness and unselfish love, and it sheds a very benign influence upon marriages in general.

7—This is not a sociable number. It is best suited to those of a serious, thoughtful disposition who actually prefer to live by themselves much of the time. Although it confers no ability for making new friends, it does favor a few deep and lasting friendships, and persons under its sway should cultivate these carefully, lest they live too completely the solitary, hermit life. The number 7 offers no assistance where tactfulness is required, consequently those who are affected by it often blunder and do things which are generally misunderstood by those about them.

8—Like number 7 this number does not confer any great amount of tact, but it does radiate a spirit of determination which, in matters of love and friendship, often goes far in overcoming bad first impressions and in ultimately winning the affections of the desired person. "Faint heart never won fair lady" seems to be the motto of those influenced by 8, for oftentimes they fall in love with someone above them in social position, marry against the advice of all their friends, and achieve great happiness with their chosen partners when all the odds seemed to be against them. However, with persons in whom they are not particularly interested, they are frequently abrupt and uncivil.

9—Persons who are influenced by this number are subject to very intense emotions. When in love their affection is fierce and deep, and they are never happy when paired with a person whose devotion is light or changeable. They make friends easily, being endowed by the number with considerable personal magnetism. Their greatest danger lies in the ardent and passionate nature which 9 favors. Unless kept in hand it can be a destructive force, overpowering the will and judgment of the individual.

THE VOCATIONAL NUMBER

This is the number which can either help or hinder you in your business career or whatever your daily work may be. To find it you use your full name, and in this case you do *not* use nicknames or contractions. First you find the number of your given name. Then you find the number of your middle name— or names—if you have any. Last you estimate the number of your surname. Then you add these numbers together and reduce them to a single figure. This is your Vocational Number. Let us take an example.

Our friend Jack White is a salesman in a clothing store, and although he is doing fairly well and is in no danger of being fired, he is still not satisfied with his work and feels that he would like to change to a different occupation. Jack knows that there is an opening in the general offices of a large manufacturing company, and he wonders if he should give up his steady salesman's job and try the office position. Somehow the idea appeals to him but he is not sure. His Vocational Number will give him a suggestion.

To find this number he must use his complete and formal name. That means that he must use John, not Jack. Following the method explained in the preceding section on *The Personality Number*, we find that John adds up to 1. John's middle name is Wilbur, which adds up to 3, and White gives the figure 9. Now we add together these three name numbers—1 plus 3

plus 9—and the result is 13. Combining the digits—1 and 3—
we get 4, which is Jack's Vocational Number.

Consulting the following Table of Vocational Numbers, we
find that this would be a wise move for Jack to make, since the
manufacturing company presents a type of work which is in
harmony with Jack's Vocational Number, and it is very probable that he will make much quicker progress in his new job
than he is now making at the clothing store.

On the other hand if Jack had not known about the opening
with the manufacturing company and had still been unsatisfied
with his progress as a salesman, he could have changed his
middle name to Arthur, which adds up to 2. When this is taken
with the 1 for John and the 9 for White, we get 12, which reduces to 3. This Vocational Number is in harmony with the
selling or merchandising that Jack is engaged in. It is quite
probable that the Vocational Number 4, which goes with JOHN
WILBUR WHITE, has been hampering Jack's progress as a
salesman, whereas the 3, which will go with JOHN ARTHUR
WHITE, will surround Jack's business activity with an entirely
different influence that will help him to advance more rapidly.

Table of Vocational Numbers

1—This is the number that is favorable to many types of
independent or original work. It offers special assistance to
those who are planning or designing. It favors the person who
tries to perfect a new method of doing things or develop a new
kind of machine. Teachers and lecturers, research men in the
mathematical sciences, and managers are all benefited by the
vibrations of this number. Anyone who is trying to do something which has never been done before will be aided in his
efforts by this influence.

2—This is a number that confers tact and diplomacy upon its

subjects. Those who are in charge of any sort of arbitration or mediation—judges, and the like—are all favored by 2. It also has a helpful effect upon those who deal with large numbers of figures, or persons whose work is connected with cataloguing or filing in any way. It has a positive influence for sound and wise judgments and it endows those whom it affects with patience and keen insight into all types of business or commercial enterprises.

3—This number is extremely helpful to all those who are in occupations which require a great deal of contact with the general public. The vibrations of 3 thus are favorable to performers on the theater or concert stage, to men and women who have things to sell, to the public-relations counsel, the publicity man, the advertising agent, or the radio performer or writer. They are very beneficial to those who feel the need for self-expression or who are unable to work at anything which is monotonous and does not call for enthusiasm and energy. To a more cautious, plodding type of personality this number may be harmful, acting as an irritant and distracting the individual in his daily tasks.

4—This is the number of industry and constructive work. It is favorable for the builder or the engineer, the city planner, the craftsman, the mechanic. It is suited to anyone who works in a large industrial plant or is connected with a factory that produces finished goods of any sort. Enterprises which require a combination of shrewd intelligence and dogged persistence are encouraged by 4. On the other hand the number is not favorable to the arts or any activity in which the use of vivid imagination is called for.

5—This number never casts a beneficial influence over any job that involves routine. Rather it is the number for the go-getter; the man who is brimming with new ideas; who likes to take a chance and do things on a big scale. It favors the adventurous kind of occupation, the one in which there is probably more thrill and risk than real security. Persons who like to feel sure of their jobs and who are never completely happy unless they know when the next paycheck is coming in should avoid this number, since it will exert a distracting influence over their lives and prevent them from realizing contentment and peace of mind in their work. On the other hand, those who cannot stand to be put in a rut will be greatly helped if their Vocational Number is 5.

6—This is an ideal number for a housewife.* It is the number that promotes honest and devoted service. It is helpful to all who are engaged in positions of trust or responsibility for the welfare and lives of others. Thus it is the ideal number for the nurse, the mission worker, the social-service official. It favors the healing arts and all who answer the call to public duty. It makes for reliability, and thus enhances a person's chances of promotion to positions where authority and confidence are needed.

7—The number 7 is favorable to all occupations in which the person works by himself a great deal. It gives hope and persistence to the struggling artist and confidence that he will eventually succeed. What is more it reinforces those personal gifts through which he will ultimately achieve success. It is not favorable to individuals who have to work in co-operation with other people. In the main it should be remembered that 7 is the number of the "lone wolf," the man who makes his way alone and unaided.

8—This is the number that favors executive work of all sorts. Management in business, industry or finance is strengthened by its influences, and it is especially valuable to those who are

---

*A married woman should use her own given name and middle name together with the surname of her husband when she is looking for her Vocational Number. Thus if Sue Jane Smith marries Bob Jones, her Vocational Number after her marriage will be found in Sue Jane Jones.

determined to win a position of wealth and power in the face of great odds. It gives determination and business insight. But though it holds the promise of great reward in the long run, it is not a number that leads to quick and easy success. The number 8 stands for hard work, many disappointments and the probability of success only after many years of struggle. To persons who become easily discouraged it may not yield many benefits and may only make them worry and fail where another individual with stronger will power would keep plugging along in spite of every discouragement and many reverses.

9—In business and commerce the number 9 makes for shrewdness and cleverness, though with certain overly enthusiastic personalities it also may lead to cunning. It is most helpful to those in the arts who are more interested in success than in genuine merit. It brings out versatility and brilliance though it sometimes produces a flashy rather than a lasting success. To persons with a practical turn of mind it is not extremely helpful, for while it endows those under its influence with imagination, it does not produce the patience that is so often necessary for the mastery of important details.

THE DESTINY NUMBER

The Destiny Number, which is sometimes known as the Monogram Number, is the one which has the most direct influence upon your happiness in life. To find real contentment and satisfaction in our daily lives is a very important goal with all of us. Do we have the courage and the faith to meet the trials and sorrows of life unafraid and with our chins up? It is a most important question.

Our Destiny Number can be of great help to us in adjusting ourselves to life about us, provided it is in harmony with our basic personalities. If you are a sober, studious type you cannot be completely happy if your Destiny Number, which affects you every moment of your life, is one that radiates gaiety and restless enthusiasm. Your fundamental nature is constantly clashing with this number whose vibrations surround your monogram, and you cannot achieve the peace of mind that you desire. Likewise a merry, sociable individual will always find a dark cloud slipping between him and the sun if his Destiny Number is of a quiet or passive nature.

Fun-loving Donald Robert Brown likes to be the life of the party, but there are days when uncontrollable fits of moodiness seem to take all the joy out of living. Then he no longer seems to be his true self; his friends even notice the change. What is the cause? There is a clash somewhere. Basically Don is a happy, light-hearted individual. But look at his Destiny Number.

To find the Destiny Number we add together the initials of our name. (Married women always use the initials of their maiden names.)

Don's initials are D.R.B., which give 4 plus 6 plus 3. Added together these make 13, and adding the two digits we get 4. By consulting the following *Table of Destiny Numbers* we find that Don's Monogram or Destiny Number is not in harmony with his personality. So let him change his middle name to Frederick. The monogram is now D.F.B.—4 plus 5 plus 3—which gives 12, which in turn reduces to 3. This is a much more harmonious number, and quite in keeping with the merry spirited person that Don really is.

Table of Destiny Numbers

1—This number is most suited to persons who are fond of adventure and who get a thrill out of bold and daring action. They are not bound down by convention either in thought or in action, for they honestly enjoy exploring the possibilities of the new and untried. As will be seen by consulting the number values of the alphabet, the word Pioneer adds up to 1. Such persons are always the first to lay aside the old way of doing things and to proclaim the advantages of progress and change. A person who is sensitive to what other people think about him will not be happy with 1 as his Destiny Number.

2—This number is most suited to the more conventional type of individual, though that does not necessarily mean one who is old-fashioned or one who refuses to keep up-to-date in his thinking. Rather he is the person who wants to study all possible sides of a question before coming to a decision. He is always open to suggestion and will never turn a deaf ear to any reasonable argument. The number 2 is for the helpful individual who likes to work with others and is capable of taking criticism as well as of giving it.

3—This is the number of the enthusiastic, whole-hearted person who likes to express his feelings and share them with others. Number 3 is most congenial for the individual who cannot be happy without many of the comforts and luxuries that would be called frivolous and useless by a more restrained, "common-sense" person. It is the number that favors the man or woman with a wide variety of interests, and is not suited to persons who are ready to sacrifice everything for the sake of their career, some special ambition or the realization of a cherished dream.

4—This is the number for the person who likes to keep busy and has little use for idleness or wasting time. It is the number of efficiency and usefulness, and it goes best with the matter-of-fact man (or woman) who really enjoys and takes pride in his work and in doing a job as well as he possibly can. Persons who have a practical turn of mind and always pay especial attention to details which more careless individuals would overlook will be happiest under the influence of the wholesome vibrations of 4. It is not a number for the flighty or restless temperament.

5—This number is for the individual who places greatest store in his personal freedom and liberty of action. The vibrations of 5 are in harmony with an energetic, variable temperament—the personality that demands constant change and is stifled when it is forced to conform to a fixed pattern or way of doing things. It is not suited to the person who places security and peace of mind above all other considerations, for with such an individual 5 can only produce unhappiness and anxiety, since its influence is disturbing and can never produce a soothing or calming effect.

6—This is the number of the solid citizen, the person who takes pride in being "civic-minded" and is always ready and eager to engage in any work that will serve to better the community at large. It is the number of co-operation and favors the man or woman who likes to be a part of a group undertaking, where responsibility is shared and all are working toward a common goal. It is especially suited to persons who are willing to undertake tasks for which there may be little recognition or reward and who "carry on" quietly while others are attracting all the attention and praise.

7—This is the number that is most suited to the person who strives constantly for perfection in all things. He is not easily satisfied and consequently is often impractical in that he will refuse to accept anything that is less than perfect. Whereas a less exacting individual might be willing to compromise with his ideal, the person to whom 7 is best suited will always do without rather than try to make the best of things as they are. This type of person is fond of solitude and quiet and spends a great deal of time in thought. The number 7 is not at all suited to an active, lively personality.

8—This is the number best suited to the person who combines idealism with practicality. It favors the man who sets a a goal for himself and then plugs away tirelessly until he has accomplished what he set out to do. He may have to alter his standards or accept a compromise now and then, but regardless of all else he will stick with his problem until it has been solved to his satisfaction. This is the number for the individual who is fired with ambitions of wealth and success and who is ready to sacrifice everything to achieve them.

9—This number is suited to the individual who is recognized as a leader among his fellows. The vibrations of 9 are particularly powerful and endow those influenced by the number with boundless energy and inspiration. They are happiest when they are planning on a broad scale and making decisions which will affect the welfare of many individuals. This number is not suited to persons who get "stage fright" in the presence of large crowds or who prefer the peace and quiet of domestic life to the ceaseless activity and excitement of public affairs. In their case 9 can only make them miserable.

THE NUMBER IN YOUR BIRTH DATE

The Spiritual Number

There is one more number which is associated with us throughout our lifetime and which, consequently, is of the greatest importance to us. This is the Spiritual Number, and it is contained in the birth date.

The Spiritual Number differs in one very marked respect from the three numbers that reside in the name. We can never change the Spiritual Number to suit ourselves as we can change our Personality, Vocational, or Destiny Numbers, since it is derived from the numbers of the day, month, and year when we were born.

However, there is no reason why we should want to change our Spiritual Number, for it does not have quite the same relation to us that our name numbers have. The Spiritual Number indicates the basic traits of personality with which we were endowed at birth—in other words, it gives us a clew to our worst faults and to our redeeming virtues. It does not offer us a forecast of our future so much as it presents a guide that we may follow, if we choose, in our daily conduct.

It might well be called the Conscience Number, since through it we can obtain knowledge about ourselves which, if wisely applied, should help us to achieve success and happiness and a reasonable measure of the good things which life has to bestow.

Mary Brown was born on the twelfth of April, 1910. April being the fourth month of the year, her birth date reads: 4—12—1910. Adding the digits together this reduces to 4—3—11, which further reduced leaves 4—3—2. These added together give 9, which is Mary's Spiritual Number.

Mary can now consult the Table of Spiritual Numbers and find out the underlying pattern on which her character is based. She will be able to discover the good points of her nature which will help her to succeed in life and she will also find a warning about those tendencies that she must guard against if she wishes to realize complete happiness.

In studying the following table it must always be remembered that the good and bad traits listed here are those which are conferred on us at birth. *In the course of our lifetime these traits may become greatly modified by experience or by the other numbers associated with our names.* Some of these basic traits may be emphasized and brought out, while others may become suppressed and seem to disappear completely. However that may be, these are the personality factors which we have to start with, and whether they are at present active or dormant we should benefit greatly by learning about them. For by conscious effort we can develop the good ones so as to make the most of the possibilities they offer, and at the same time we can learn to keep the bad ones under control. A word to the wise is sufficient.

Table of Spiritual Numbers

1—One of the great virtues indicated by this number is the ability to maintain an independence of mind. This person is blessed with a strong will which can resist undesired suggestions or temptations. He is able to think for himself and make decisions without being influenced by others. He can always be counted on to do what he thinks is right, regardless of the opinion of those about him. However, he must guard against an assertive pride which may tempt him to try to rule over others with an iron hand. He must learn to control his temper, especially when he has to take orders from others. Of course, some of these traits may be emphasized, modified or counteracted by other numbers in the name.

2—This is the number of the individual who possesses tolerance. His motto is "Live and Let Live" and he can be counted on to mind his own business and also to give credit to others when credit is due. He has a basic urge to be helpful and co-operative without trying to boss everybody. However, there is a flaw in this favorable picture. Though he is able to overlook great faults, he is inclined to be too critical in matters of unimportant detail. He must guard against impatience and becoming petty where it would be better to ignore minor shortcomings. These traits may be modified by other numbers in the name, but they are still present in the character.

3—This is the number of the generous, forgiving nature which is very sympathetic to the troubles of others and which shuns all that is petty and mean. An easygoing nature is indicated by 3, one that remains calm in the face of adversity and is not easily made the victim of worry. But there is the danger that the individual may be too easygoing and may become careless, indifferent and lacking in the necessary concentration and determination which insists that the path of duty be followed regardless how unpleasant it may seem. There is also the danger of overindulgence in purely sensual delights. These traits may be modified by other numbers in the name, but they are still present in the character.

4—This number indicates a fundamental urge to be orderly and business-like in the conduct of one's affairs. There is a praiseworthy sense of responsibility and a basic liking for work, provided it is suited to the individual's tastes. On the unfavorable side is a certain lack of imagination which may stand in the way of real progress and achievement. The individual must guard against an innate desire to remain secure in a dull rut— a drudge or a stick-in-the-mud. The fear of loss of position or rank may hold back a personality that otherwise might achieve great things. These traits may be modified or counteracted by other numbers in the name, but they are still present in the character.

5—This number indicates a determined approach to the problems of life, though the individual may be more apt to make good resolutions than to carry them through to a successful conclusion. A basic curiosity about life is indicated, which is a sign of a healthy and active mind. There is imagination and resourcefulness in the face of danger or obstacles. On the unfavorable side there is the tendency to be hasty and to act without sufficient forethought. Unreliability may be a besetting sin of the 5 personality. These traits may be modified or counteracted by other numbers in the name, but they are still present in the personality.

6—This number indicates courage which arises from inner convictions and an ability to see through the false and the sham and to hold to that which is good and true in spite of temptations. There is loyalty to deep-rooted ideals, and self-confidence which gives strength and purpose. On the unfavorable side there is the danger of obstinacy and an urge to argue too much over small points. The 6 personality should guard against worry and fears for the future. There is also a fundamental danger of indulging in self-pity and assuming the attitude of the martyr without cause. These traits may be modified or counteracted by other numbers in the name, but they are still present in the character.

7—This number indicates great breadth of vision and a comprehension of life's problems and trials. The mind is able to analyze characters and situations and judge them at their true worth. The individual will always strive to be completely honest with himself and will probably be his own severest critic. On the unfavorable side we find that this clear and judicial frame of mind may lack warmth and sympathy with the frailties of human nature. There is a danger that the individual may be accused of having a "holier than thou" attitude. These traits may be modified or counteracted by other numbers in the name, but they are still present in the personality.

8—This number indicates an ability to keep working toward a goal until it is reached. There is no compromise with imperfection, for only the best is demanded and accepted. The individual has the innate power to command the respect and attention of others about him. On the unfavorable side there is the danger that he may be snobbish and unfeeling in his attitude toward those whose talents are not equal to his. He should guard against sacrificing the feelings of others to attain his goal. Ruthless ambition could become one of his besetting sins. These traits may be modified or counteracted by other numbers in the name, but they are still present in the character.

9—This number indicates great warmth of emotion, with the

feelings ruling in many of the decisions of life. Basically there is a desire to love and be loved and a great appreciation for the feelings of others. The finer instincts of the nature are easily appealed to, but on the unfavorable side it should be noted that this may lead to sorrow or unwise moves, since the individual may easily become the dupe of ,unscrupulous persons. He should guard against letting his feelings get the better of the dictates of reason. These traits may be modified or counteracted by other numbers in the name, but they are still present in the personality.

A GLIMPSE INTO YOUR FUTURE

THE MYSTIC NUMBER

The ancient Egyptians and Chaldeans were among the first civilized peoples to delve into the mystery of numbers and the strange influence which they are said to have over the lives of human beings. From them there has been handed down a number of spells and formulas, the origins of which are shrouded in the mists of time.

From priests who conducted their weird and secret rites on the banks of the Nile hundreds of years before the pyramids were built has come a Table of Mystic Numbers which has been used for centuries as a key to unlock the hidden meaning of the future. This Table, modified and adapted to fit the requirements of present-day life, can be used in connection with the numbers of your birth date and your name to foretell events which are in store for you in the days to come.

To find your Mystic Number and the message which awaits you from out of the depths of the past you add together the numbers of your given names and surname plus your Monogram Number and the number of the year of your birth. Then you multiply by 2. An example will illustrate how this is done.

John Henry Brown was born in the year 1908. Consulting the alphabet table at the beginning of this chapter, he first finds the letter values of his name to be as follows:

J — 6	H — 9	B — 3
O — 8	E — 2	R — 6
H — 9	N — 5	O — 8
N — 5	R — 6	W — 7
28	Y — 8	N — 5
	30	29

These sums must be reduced, of course, to single numbers, so the digits are added together: 2 plus 8 gives 10, which further reduces to 1; 3 plus 0 equals 3, etc. Thus John's three name numbers are 1 — 3 — 2.

The Monogram Number (Destiny Number) is now obtained as has been explained previously, by adding together the initials of the name—in this case J. H. B. or 6 plus 9 plus 3, which reduces to the number 9.

Lastly the digits in the birth year are added together— 1 plus 9 plus 0 plus 8, which reduces to the number 9.

Now we can write out John's complete number series:

JOHN	HENRY	BROWN	J. H. B.	1908
1	3	2	9	9

These five numbers are added together in turn, but we do NOT reduce their sum to a single figure. The total of John's number series is 24.

The sum of the number series is now multiplied by 2, giving 48. *This is John's Mystic Number.* By consulting the following Table of Mystic Numbers, he will find the message of the past concerning his future.

The Table of Mystic Numbers ranges between the numbers 8 and 90. The reason for this has never been clearly explained, but some Cabalists and other students of the ancient priest lore contend that it is one of the riddles the Sphinx.

One last word of instruction for using the Mystic Numbers: if your number series should add up to a sum which is larger than 45, you do not have to multiply by 2, but can look in the Table directly for that number.

Table of the Mystic Numbers

8—If you refuse to allow anything to shake your confidence in yourself and maintain your will against all obstacles, you will realize your ambition. Be sure that no one suffers from an injustice because of your efforts to reach your goal, and trust the head rather than the heart.

9—There is nothing to prevent you from getting ahead except you yourself. Be sure not to fail for lack of will power—either to do the right thing or to refrain from doing the wrong. And keep your plans and your opinions to yourself, for the world is full of men who are ready to steal ideas as well as money.

10—Be sure that what you wish for lies within the realm of possibility for you. To hope blindly for something which it will be impossible for you to accomplish will lead you to sorrow and loss of fortune and position, for daydreams have ruined more than one promising career.

11—You will face several struggles in your life. Be sure that you are not in the wrong; do not let your passions sway you in trying to find out honestly all the facts. Once you know you are right, do not hesitate. If you win your battle, there will be great satisfaction for you. If you lose it, you will be honored for having fought a good fight.

12—Guard your actions carefully and in moments of crisis never allow yourself to hesitate. Train yourself in the small things of daily life to make immediate decisions, for some day your life or fortune may depend upon quick thinking. There is nothing which you cannot master if you set your mind to it. Remember that, when the clouds hang gray.

13—Before you realize the fulfillment of your wishes you must first acquire more knowledge.

14—You are going to be successful in some action. But be careful. Your happiness may be followed by sadness and trouble. Keep on the alert to avoid disaster and a reversal of fortune.

15—You will be confronted with a serious personal problem. Do not act in haste, but rather ask advice from someone you can trust and give the matter careful thought yourself. You may be sorely tempted more than once to speak your mind, but keep your thoughts to yourself and remember that actions speak louder than words.

16—Be sure that there is no dishonor connected with the goal you are striving for or that in your efforts to achieve it you are not going to be led into unworthy thoughts or actions. Then stick to your objective regardless of what may come, and one day you will realize not only happiness but also power and possibly fame.

17—There are obstacles looming ahead which will appear to be overwhelming. You are going to face problems which will appear to have no solution. However they are going to *seem* to you to be much worse than they really are. Remember that, take courage, act boldly and you will find that your troubles will vanish suddenly like fog on a bright spring morning.

18—You are going to be called upon to make a great sacrifice with little chance that it will be fully appreciated by those who are near to you. It may also happen in this connection that you will be wronged and will have your choice later of forgiving or of revenging yourself. It will be up to you to decide, but before you do, remember that hate often destroys the hater.

19—You are going to be greatly disappointed in some person

or some event. It will be hard for you to control your feelings or to refrain from reproaches and bitterness. If you will do so, however, there will be unexpected happiness for you.

20—Guard against distractions and influences which may lead to a wasting of your energies. You are going to face a test which will call for all the endurance and determination you possess. If you have not permitted yourself to become overtired and worn out spiritually as well as physically, you will come through with flying colors and your wishes will be realized.

21—You will have to keep a lookout against temptation which is going to come in an unexpected form, so that you will not recognize it for its true self at first. Your emotions will be violently aroused in some way. Be cautious, keep control of yourself. If you do not your very life may eventually be imperiled.

22—Unless you make a drastic change in your ways you are going to suffer a grave loss in fortune and in position because of vanity, unwise and reckless enterprises undertaken without proper thought, and downright carelessness and indifference to the consequences of your actions.

23—You are going to achieve success after you have undertaken further work in some sort of educational institution. The measure of your success will depend on how well you apply yourself to your study and how completely you are able to rule out certain distracting influences which are going to surround you.

24—This is a danger sign. You are headed for trouble of some sort and there are among your acquaintances some who are pretending to be your friends but who in reality are working against you in many ways which you do not suspect. Look out for flattering words and what appear to be extremely generous offers for your own good. They may be hiding the instrument of your downfall.

25—This is a very favorable sign. There is happiness ahead for you, and in some way it will be connected with love. Be sure that all is well in your home and that you do not express feelings that are not genuine and sincere. If you follow this advice, the happiness will be lasting. If you do not, it may fade quickly.

26—Look out lest you grow too smug and self-satisfied. You are in danger of slipping into a rut which will lead you nowhere. If this appears at first glance to be in no way connected with your life, think again carefully. Is there not some place where you feel that there is nothing to improve on, that you have done just about as well as anybody could? If there is, then this warning is intended for you before it is too late to bestir yourself and see if you cannot show further improvement.

27—Nothing but success is in store for you. You can have fame, wealth, happiness—it merely depends on how high you aim and how conscientious you are in your work. Of course, if you have no great ambitions, you will not realize great things.

28—There are some dark clouds hanging in your future. Trouble will come suddenly and without warning. You will need the guidance of a friend or loved one. Much is to be gained by prayer.

29—In order to carry your plans or your wishes through to success you are going to need the assistance of someone who holds a position of authority or power. Find this aid now before you proceed any further with the work in hand.

30—A person, of the opposite sex, whom you have not yet met is going to have a powerful influence in your struggle to achieve your goal. The person is somewhat older than you are and there is the possibility of friendship but not of love between you. You will not reach your goal until after you have found this stranger.

31—Do not underestimate the difficulties which lie between you and the realization of your dream. They can be overcome but not unless you work very hard and refuse to be disheartened by temporary setbacks. Don't expect help from others. It all depends on you.

32—You are never going to get anywhere in life until you give up certain plans which you now have in mind and which you believe will lead to wealth. There is nothing in them and you are wasting time and energy thinking about them and trying to put them in operation. If you insist in going ahead with them, you are going to lose money and a very fine opportunity.

33—Stick to your present line of work faithfully. You are going to have a lucky inspiration which will turn out to be of great benefit to you. It will be something that you may be inclined to laugh about at first, but eventually you will do something about it, and the most astonishing good luck will result for you.

34—Beware of some association you have in business or among your friends. There is trouble brewing, though it may not be the fault of your associate. You will face grave problems and your position in life will be menaced. You are going to have to be very careful of your personal affairs, especially in matters concerning money.

35—Trust in your own ideas and don't let others laugh at you and try to discourage you. You are going to do something that no one else has ever done before and it is going to bring you wealth and happiness. Do not confide your plans to too many persons. It would be better not to tell them to anybody.

36—This is a very lucky omen. You have nothing to worry over. Just keep on in the work which you are now undertaking and everything will turn out satisfactorily.

37—Be especially on guard against losing your temper. Don't let anything provoke your anger, for there is a danger that you may ruin a piece of good luck if you should become enraged. A number of lucky breaks will come your way and advance you rapidly toward success, provided you do nothing to spoil your chances. Anger is most likely to prove your undoing, although you should also avoid giving way in any manner to vanity or self-admiration. They, too, can lead you to disaster of an unexpected sort.

38—Unless you show more determination and strength of character, especially in the matter of putting things off from day to day instead of getting them done, you are going to suffer a great reversal of fortune. Be particularly suspicious of what seem to you to be good excuses for not getting things done immediately.

39—Everything at present is favorable to your success and happiness. Intelligence rather than force is going to help you surmount the obstacles in your path.

40—Ahead of you are arguments and quarrels. Some are connected with a court of law, and they involve both business and affairs of the heart. There is a danger of a breaking off either in marriage or in a romance. It will be largely up to you whether this break is permanent. You may not continue much longer in your present job.

41—You are going to be connected with some sort of secret work having to do with the government or with science. It will rest largely with you whether the work turns out successfully. You will have to choose your company carefully during the time and guard your speech against careless slips.

42—Ahead of you is travel. A number of journeys are indicated. One will be by land. Another will be by water. A third will be by neither, and it may end in sadness or in great joy. Taken as a group, these travels will prove to your advantage and you will be very happy among friends and relations.

43—You are going to receive help and encouragement from a person of considerable power and authority. This friendship will come unexpectedly and will grow to be one of the great influences in your life. Through it you may realize success, though it will be entirely up to you whether you win fame or not.

44—Marriage for you is going to be most fortunate. With it are going to come honors, probably in later life. You will also receive the attention of a beautiful and intelligent woman who will prove a very devoted and loyal friend. She will give you three pieces of advice. You should follow the second and third but not the first, though you must not let her know that you are disregarding her first suggestion.

45—Unhappiness is going to come to you because of the failure of an engagement to result in marriage. You may not necessarily be one of the parties involved. There is also going to be a great deal of difficulty and even danger for you because of the meddling and evil gossip of old women. Be especially wary of the interest of your elderly relations.

46—There is much sadness in store for you and a number of heartbreaks. You will lose a friendship which you believed to be loyal but which was based on flattery and duplicity. But if you are wise in choosing the ones to whom you confide your personal secrets, you will find a way out of your troubles. Help will come to you from a source where you had least expected it.

47—There is a danger that your feelings will prevent you from seeing the true state of circumstances around you and that you will meet disaster through a hasty and ill-considered action.

48—There will be one enduring love in your life which will bring you great joy and much courage to face the trials of fortune. You may not at first realize the value of this attachment, but time will test it to the utmost and will prove its worth.

49—Through the eyes of a little child you will see real happiness and a little kindness of yours will reward you a thousand-fold, making a number of your most earnest wishes come true.

50—There is unexpected success awaiting you after a period of struggle and disappointment. Cherish your friends and do not let anything separate you from them, for they are going to be very important in bringing about the realization of your dreams.

51—Jealousy and suspicion may ruin romance and marriage for you unless you are very careful of what you say and do. Great danger is in store for you in connection with love. You will be required to run a great risk, but you must have courage to carry on in the face of overwhelming obstacles. If you falter, tragedy may ensue.

52—Unless you heed the advice of those whom you trust, you are going to meet with a severe test. You are in danger of being misled by your heart. Think twice before making a decision which may alter the entire course of your life, especially in matters of love.

53—A strange man is going to be directly connected with the success of one of your enterprises. If you are a woman, this will be a love relationship. Act discreetly and you will enjoy a happy home life; act without due consideration, and you may bring great unhappiness upon yourself and on him. If you are a man, this stranger may become a close friend, provided you do not let the success he has brought to you go to your head and turn you away from your loyal acquaintances.

54—This is a sign that dishonor is in store. If you are unmarried, be particularly careful in choosing the person to whom you give your love. If married, be especially careful that you do not arouse the anger or jealousy of your partner.

55—A marriage, not necessarily your own, is going to bring you misery. You will receive attentions from a person of the opposite sex who is older than you are. Treat these with reserve, for all is not well in this direction.

56—Ahead of you is a happy domestic life with many children and lots of loyal friends. You may suffer momentary temptation at the hands of an old sweetheart of your youth. Do not yield to it, for it would only bring you unhappiness and lead you to a foolish step.

57—Beware of persons in positions that compete with yours. There will be one who poses as your friend but who will be seeking to do you harm. You have enemies who are anxious to bring about your downfall, but none of them is as dangerous as this pretended friend.

58—Your future is dark and not completely clear. There is a woman who will bring you no good. There is also jealousy and the danger of loss of reputation and honor. Prepare for great vexations and the failure of some cherished dream, possibly as a result of the woman's influence.

59—A person whom you have not yet met is going to have a great quarrel with you and become one of your bitterest enemies. Nothing will stop this person from trying to harm you. Avoid contact with firearms.

60—You are going to be called on to make a sacrifice for someone who is not particularly close to you. You will be able to refuse, but if you do, you may meet with unexpected misfortune from an entirely different direction. If you make the sacrifice, it will be a temporary setback to your plans, but in the long run it may prove the wisest course for without knowing it, you will have frustrated the plans of people who have evil intentions regarding your future happiness.

61—To attain what you desire you are going to have to take a great risk. There is something connected with your home life which will serve you in good stead, and if you act wisely, it will be the means of overcoming dangers and winning what you want.

62—There is trouble ahead of you in matters of business. A dangerous rivalry may test all your powers of resistance. You will need courage and above all wisdom if you are to come through these trials unscathed.

63—You are going to be involved in a legal action of some sort which will require your presence or the presence of your representatives in a court of law. As long as you show no sign of retreat or weakness, you have a good chance of coming out on top.

64—Be careful of your actions and those decisions which you will have to make in connection with persons around you. There is the danger that you will do something which you may regret for many years afterward. Be sure your motives are honest and that you do not act through selfishness or pride. Remember that things done cannot be undone easily.

65—There is grave temptation in store for you; also much sadness as a result of your failure to act decisively. All will be lost if you hesitate too long. At best you are going to have to endure in the face of great disappointment and defeat.

66—An unwise choice may lead you to the brink of disaster. You may lose your present position in life for a time. But if you will work diligently to make amends for your failure, you will ultimately reap a great reward and will know much happiness.

67—You are going to be the loser in a situation which will in some way be connected with the legal profession. There will be much anxiety and worry, and if your loved ones are to be spared, it will be necessary for you to assume a great burden. But in the end you will be a much greater personality.

68—There is danger hanging over you, which may involve a temporary upset of some sort. There is also a mystery which will have to be solved before you are delivered from your trials. Things will eventually come out all right if you use your head. You may even avoid this danger if you conduct yourself prudently.

69—You are not going to realize success immediately. There are going to be momentary triumphs followed by setbacks and disappointments. In all of these ups and downs you yourself will be largely responsible for the troubles which beset you. Try to avoid overconfidence and a carelessness about details when you are enjoying good fortune, for it will be at such a time that you will unwittingly pave the way for a subsequent spell of bad luck.

70—You are going to rise in the world, largely through the efforts of acquaintances of. the opposite sex. You must learn not to mix love with business. Remember that if your hands are full, you should not have your arms full at the same time.

71—Your success will be largely due to someone connected with politics or one of the learned professions. See that you do not abuse this association by becoming too demanding.

72—There are hardships in store for you, most of which you will not be able to avoid in any way. You may look to your friends for assistance and encouragement, but you will only triumph by drawing on the sources of strength which lie within you. Do not give way to self-pity or fear, and let the world see a smile on your lips at all times. In this way you can overcome defeat by laughing in its face.

73—Money is going to bring you sorrow. If you persist in sacrificing everything else in life in an attempt to amass a fortune, you will eventually wind up in the poorhouse. You will be far better off if you cultivate other aims, for in striving to achieve them you may come into peace and security.

74—Pay no heed to those who may try to persuade you to give up your present mode of life, telling you that fame and fortune await you in some different direction. You are going to reach happiness and contentment only by following the path which you are now taking.

75—Your own individual enterprises are never going to prosper very well. Time and again you are going to lay careful plans and then see them come to nothing. However, if you will take someone into your confidence and share your ideas, you may find success through your joint efforts. It may be that marriage will bring you the fortune which alone you will never be able to reach.

76—Success is not going to come to you without diligent effort. You may see others succeed without appearing to try very hard, but for you the rule will be conscientious work and much self-denial and discipline.

77—Through many hardships you are going to attain to wealth and happiness which will remain with you throughout the rest of your life. But in love you may never realize all your desires.

78—Beware of easy money, for what you earn without great effort on your part will be taken away from you in spite of everything that you can do to prevent it. You must learn to cultivate thrift, for otherwise you may waste what you now have.

79—You are going to receive money unexpectedly, possibly in connection with a will or a death. Then you will have to be on guard against false friends and advisers who will not have your interests at heart. Unless you are very careful you will fall into company which will bring you to your downfall.

80—You are going to attain the thing you most desire, but you will have to fight to preserve it, for there are enemies whom you do not now suspect who will be envious and will attempt to mar your happiness.

81—Success is going to come to you in some line of activity where you least expect it. It will not be in connection with what you are now aiming at. It may have something to do with persons who are considerably younger than you are, and you will know the devotion and loyalty of young friends.

82—There is happiness in store for you as the result of a very mysterious set of events. You will be wise never to let curiosity get the better of you and to try to inquire into the circumstances surrounding your unexpected good fortune.

83—Take heed of any decisions that you will be required to make in connection with the sea or the air. Disaster may lurk where you least expect it. If you are wise and prudent, you may avoid these dangers and come into good luck.

84—A profession is going to have a profound influence on your life, though you may never engage in it directly. You should keep your mind alert and broaden your knowledge of human affairs, for it will come in handy some day when you least expect that you will be called upon to act.

85—Something very favorable is going to happen to you as a result of a kindness which you once performed without fully realizing what you were doing. You will gain new friends and may even attain sudden and unexpected prominence.

86—You are going to come into some money, but it will bring you no good, for it has not been earned honestly. You will be wise to give away half of it to some charitable enterprise. This will break the spell that hangs over it and with the rest you may find happiness and contentment.

87—You will meet with a stranger who will give you an unexpected piece of advice. If you follow it, you will meet with an adventure in which your courage and wisdom will be tested. But if you act with discretion, good fortune will result.

88—There is a gift coming to you from a place far away. It will bring you happiness only if you are willing to share its benefits with others about you.

89—The way ahead of you is not clear. Proceed cautiously in all situations which require decision, and do not heed the advice of your friends too frequently.

90—You are going to find yourself unexpectedly allied with a large group of strangers in the pursuit of some common goal. If you are diligent and prove yourself trustworthy and reliable you may bring great distinction and honor to yourself.

HOW NUMBERS ANSWER QUESTIONS

Before leaving this chapter there is one more subject which should be considered. That is the method of answering questions by the Rule of the Pyramid. For this method we require a second alphabet table in which certain modifications have been made by students of numbers in accord with the ancient traditions of the Pyramid Rule.

A — 1	F — 8	K — 6	P — 5	U — 8
B — 5	G — 8	L — 5	Q — 6	V — 8
C — 6	H — 3	M — 7	R — 9	W — 3
D — 4	I — 7	N — 5	S — 9	X — 1
E — 2	J — 6	O — 8	T — 2	Y — 8
				Z — 6

When we wish to consult the Pyramid about some subject of interest to us, we first write down our question at the top of a sheet of paper, trying to keep our question limited to fewer than ten words. Let us take as an example the seven-word question: Am I going to win my bet? Beneath each letter we write the corresponding number value as given in the Pyramid alphabet table above. Thus:

A M   I   G O I N G   T O   W I N   M Y   B E T
1 7   7   8 8 7 5 8   2 8   3 7 5   7 8   5 2 2

Now we add the numbers of each word together, and if the sums are greater than 9, we add the digits together until we arrive at single numbers. Thus: 7 plus 1 equals 8; 7 remains 7; 8 plus 8 plus 7 plus 5 plus 8 equals 36, which is again reduced by adding 3 plus 6 to give 9, etc. Our seven words now may be represented by seven single numbers, as follows:

AM	I	GOING	TO	WIN	MY	BET
8	7	9	1	6	6	9

We are now ready to build the base of our Pyramid. Before the above line of figures we place the number of the words in the question, which is 7. This gives us a row of eight figures:

7 8 7 9 1 6 6 9

To erect our Pyramid on this base we place this row of figures at the bottom of the sheet of paper. Then we add together the first two numbers—7 and 8—and reduce that sum to a single figure (7 plus 8 equals 15 which gives 5 plus 1 or 6). This single figure we place above and between 7 and 8:

6
7 8 7 9 1 6 6 9

We now add the second and third figures in the row, which are 8 and 7, and reducing them to their single figure (6) we place that number above and between the second and third figures:

6 6
7 8 7 9 1 6 6 9

We now add the third and fourth figures together to produce a single number and place that above and between the third and fourth numbers, and so on until we have finished the second row of figures in the Pyramid:

6 6 7 1 7 3 6
7 8 7 9 1 6 6 9

We now add together the first and second numbers of the second row and place their sum above and between them, just as we did before, and continue the process until we have built up the third row of the Pyramid:

3 4 8 8 1 9
6 6 7 1 7 3 6
7 8 7 9 1 6 6 9

The building of rows is continued in the same fashion until we have completed the Pyramid and reached the summit, which is the figure 8. Thus:

```
        8
       1 7
      2 8 8
     1 1 7 1
    7 3 7 9 1
   3 4 8 8 1 9
  6 6 7 1 7 3 6
 7 8 7 9 1 6 6 9
```

The Pyramid has now given us 8 as the key to the answer of our question. All we have to do is consult the following Table of the Pyramid and under the number 8 will be the information we desire.

It should be noted that the answers in the Table are necessarily of a rather general nature. In some cases they may not appear upon first glance to offer any definite reply to the questioner, but if he will stop to consider all the circumstances which surround his query and ponder the words of the answer carefully, he will sooner or later discover the kernel of truth that applies to him. In the case of the sample question given above, the phrase "all signs point to failure" in the Table under 8 should be sufficient reply.

Critics of the Pyramid method have pointed out that the answer depends entirely on the words used in the question. This, of course, is true and is one of the reasons for the significance of the method. For it is the way in which the questioner unconsciously words his query that indicates his fundamental nature and gives the clew which the Pyramid is capable of interpreting. Thus the answers to all our questions inevitably lie within ourselves, and the Pyramid is but an instrument to help us read the secrets of our personalities.

The Table of the Pyramid

1—Rest assured that in good time success will be yours and your hopes will prosper, whether it be through your own doing or as the result of the most unexpected happenings.

2—There can be no success where hesitation has replaced determination. The opposite sex will have a powerful influence in retarding your enterprise and bringing a negative result.

3—You may expect gains, advancement or a broadening of activities if you will hold fast to your purpose and refuse to let yourself be swayed in doing what you desire to do.

4—Your expectations will far exceed your realizations, for disagreement and quarreling will undo your plans. This will happen because others wish to take advantage of you.

5—In a journey there is the prospect of much good coming to you. Your question may be answered after you have received an unexpected letter of considerable importance.

6—Expect assistance from someone of the opposite sex. What you desire is about to be fulfilled, and in the end you will not regret steps you have already taken.

7—You may anticipate positive results which will involve you in relations with large numbers of persons. If you refuse to be influenced by the advice of another, you will reap joy.

8—Ahead are many obstacles. You may sustain a reversal of fortune. All signs point to failure because of malice and ill will or incompetence on the part of others.

9—Ahead are many obstacles, but if you will keep a stout heart, all will be well. The greater your risks, the greater will be your ultimate rewards. Have courage.

IV

What's in the Cards

FOR CENTURIES playing cards have been used as a means of telling fortunes, and many methods of reading their meaning have been developed and passed down from generation to generation. There are presented here some of the more representative systems of the time-honored tradition of card divination.

GENERAL INSTRUCTIONS

Among practitioners of fortune telling by cards, or Cartomany as it is called, it is generally held that the cards should not be consulted too frequently. Some say that they should not be consulted more often than once a week; it is the opinion of others that they may be read more frequently, but under no circumstances should they be read more than once a day. And no sitting should last more than an hour or two at most.

It is not considered lucky to read the cards alone. Two persons are required for this. The one who wishes to have his fortune told is known as the *Questioner*. The one who assists him by reading the meaning of the cards is referred to in the following pages as the *Seer*.

In cutting the cards the Questioner should always use the left hand.

Before the reading begins the Questioner usually has to select a card which will represent him, and which is known as the Questioner's card. If the Questioner is dark-haired, with dark eyes and dark complexion, the King of Spades is usually chosen to represent a man and the Queen of Spades a woman. The King and Queen of Clubs represent, according to sex, the Questioner who has brown hair and brown eyes. Questioners with blue or gray eyes and light brown hair are represented by the King and Queen of Hearts, according to sex, while with blond Questioners, the Queen of Diamonds represents the women and the King of Diamonds the men.

THE TWO MAJOR SYSTEMS

There are two major systems for using the ordinary pack of bridge or playing cards in fortune telling. One system makes use of the entire deck of fifty-two cards. The other uses only thirty-two cards, the twos, threes, fours, fives and sixes being discarded. Since this later system is usually easier for beginners to master, it is presented first.

THE DECK OF 32 CARDS

After the lower cards, from twos through sixes, have been discarded from the regulation pack, the remaining thirty-two cards must be marked so as to indicate the top and bottom of each card. This may be done by putting a light pencil mark in one corner of each card. In this way the Seer will be able to determine at a glance whether the card has been laid down in normal or reversed position. This is most important, for the meaning of the card depends upon whether it appears reversed or not.

The Meaning of the 32 Cards

CLUBS

Ace—Good luck. Favorable news, possibly that the Questioner will receive money. A letter. *Reversed*—Good news but the happiness will be brief. The correspondence will not be pleasant.

King—A dark man, loyal friend, honest. *Reversed*—Worry or disappointment, good plans coming to naught.

Queen—A dark woman, a friend, full of devotion. *Reversed*—Unreliable, a coquette, jealous.

Jack—Dark young man, bright and amusing, bold and eager in wooing. *Reversed*—He is fickle, a flatterer.

Ten—Good fortune, ease and luxury. *Reversed*—A trifling failure, or travel possibly by air or water.

Nine—Unexpected windfall in the way of money. *Reversed*—A little gift, or some sort of difficulty.

Eight—Love from a worthy individual, bringing fortune and happiness. *Reversed*—Unworthy love, bringing trouble. Or papers bringing trouble.

Seven—Small money or business affair. *Reversed*—Difficulties over money. An unfavorable omen possibly involving legal matters.

HEARTS

Ace—Pleasant tidings, a love letter, the Questioner's home. *Reversed*—Change of place, a friend's visit.

King—Fair-haired man, loyal and friendly. *Reversed*—Disappointment connected with this person.

Queen—Light-haired woman, dependable and affectionate. *Reversed*—Unhappy love connected with her. She may be fickle.

JACK—Fun-loving young bachelor; possibly a child. *Reversed*—Young man linked with disappointment or unhappiness, possibly a soldier.

TEN—Very favorable. Good luck, happiness. A proposal. Helps to cancel bad cards. *Reversed*—Fleeting trouble, possibly a birth.

NINE—This represents the wish. Also slight troubles, but eventual success. *Reversed*—Fleeting troubles.

EIGHT—Love from a light-complexioned person. Marriage thoughts. *Reversed*—Love that is not returned.

SEVEN—Happy thoughts. *Reversed*—Boredom, ennui, possibly jealousy.

DIAMONDS

ACE—A letter. Marriage offer. *Reversed*—News that brings sorrow.

KING—Man with light hair (possibly gray), may be a soldier. *Reversed*—Deception or treacherousness, possibly connected with him.

QUEEN—Light-haired woman, rather common and vulgar, gossipy. *Reversed*—Difficulties caused by the malice of this woman.

JACK—A young man, an employee, someone in a subordinate position. *Reversed*—He causes trouble, cannot be trusted.

TEN—Journey or change of residence. *Reversed*—Bad luck as a result of the trip or change of residence.

NINE—Trouble coming, worries, annoyances. *Reversed*—Dispute in the family or between lovers.

EIGHT—A love affair. *Reversed*—Disappointment in love, affections spurned.

SEVEN—Teasing, unkind criticism, possibly a child. *Reversed*—A minor scandal or some small slander, based on a trifle.

SPADES

ACE—Satisfaction or pleasure connected with the emotions. *Reversed*—Sorrow or sad news.

KING—A dark man, possibly a widower; untrustworthy. *Reversed*—A dangerous foe. The wish to work evil.

QUEEN—A widow or an older woman. *Reversed*—A woman bent upon evil-doing.

JACK—A young man, possibly a student in law or medicine. An ill-bred young fellow. *Reversed*—A disloyal young man, deceitful and dangerous.

TEN—Misery and sorrow, loss of liberty. *Reversed*—The trouble will be of brief duration.

NINE—A bad omen. News of loss or failure. *Reversed*—Unhappiness for someone close to the Questioner.

EIGHT—Approaching disappointment. *Reversed*—A love affair or match broken up; dissolute living.

SEVEN—Anxieties; the making of a new resolution. *Reversed*—Silly scheming in love.

MEANING OF CARD GROUPS

4 ACES—Perils, loss of money or honor, separations. If one ace is reversed, these troubles are not so grave; if two are reversed, the danger is further lessened; if all are reversed, it is slight.

3 ACES—Brief anxieties, with good tidings to follow; if all are reversed they foretell a foolhardy action.

2 ACES—Some sort of partnership; the diamond and spade together indicate evil or misfortune to come. Other combinations are favorable. If one of the cards is reversed, the partnership will not be entirely successful. If both are reversed, it will fail.

4 KINGS—Advancement, wealth, honor. With each reversed card, the good fortune will be less but it will happen sooner.

3 KINGS—Something of great importance is to be started; the more cards that are reversed, the less successful it will be.

2 KINGS—A commercial alliance. One reversed means partial success. Both reversed mean failure.

4 QUEENS—A social affair. The more cards that are reversed, the more the fun will be spoiled by unexpected circumstances.

3 QUEENS—A gathering of friends. With each reversed card there is greater danger of scandal-mongering and trouble.

2 QUEENS—A talk between friends, with secrets given away. One reversed indicates rivals. Both reversed mean trouble for the one who learns the secret.

4 JACKS—A hilarious party. The more cards that are reversed, the wilder the hilarity, with possible trouble as an outcome.

3 JACKS—Trouble among friends, possibly from gossip. With each reversed card there is greater danger of a quarrel leading to blows.

2 JACKS—Loss of some sort, possibly theft. One reversed means the loss will not happen right away. Both reversed mean it will happen very soon.

4 TENS—Exceptionally good luck in store, especially regarding the Questioner's present undertakings. *Reversed*—The more cards that are reversed, the more hazards that must be overcome before success is reached.

3 TENS—Failure and trouble through legal proceedings. With each reversed card the trouble becomes less serious.

2 TENS—A lucky break coming without warning, it may involve a new kind of occupation. One reversed means it will take place very shortly. Both reversed mean some time will elapse before it occurs.

4 NINES—Unexpected occurrences. The more cards that are reversed, the sooner the surprise will come.

3 NINES—A most favorable sign. Increased prosperity, good health, enjoyment of life. Each reversed card represents an additional amount of brief worry and care before the good fortune occurs.

2 NINES—Some sort of success in commercial affairs. If one or both are reversed, this indicates small troubles and anxiety.

4 EIGHTS—New kind of occupation or a short trip. The more cards that are reversed, the sooner this will occur.

3 EIGHTS—The Questioner's thoughts regarding marriage and love. If any one is reversed, it means merely a flirtation.

2 EIGHTS—A short love affair. One reversed means a disappointment in connection with love. Both reversed mean a sadness resulting from the Questioner's previous actions.

4 SEVENS—Foes working in secret against the Questioner. The more cards that are reversed, the more likely their plotting will fail and they will be suitably punished.

3 SEVENS—Unhappiness, or the loss of friends. With each reversed card the unhappiness will be less severe.

2 SEVENS—Love that is reciprocated. One reversed means deception in love. Both reversed mean regrets over love.

MEANING OF SPECIAL COMBINATIONS WITH 32 CARDS

In addition to the above meanings of the individual cards and of groups of the same denomination there are also certain combinations of two or more cards which have special meanings when the pack of 32 cards is used. These are listed below according to the four suits for rapid identification. It should be understood that these meanings apply *only* when the cards listed appear *side by side*.

CLUBS

ACE—When surrounded by *diamonds* or with diamonds not more than one card away from it, the Ace of Clubs signifies money coming to the Questioner. With the *nine of dia-monds* it indicates legal business of some sort.

KING—With *ten of clubs,* an offer of marriage is to be expected.

QUEEN—With *seven of diamonds* this Queen indicates an uncertain outcome of events. With *Ace of Spades,* a tiresome journey.

JACK—With *Jack of Spades,* loss of money, unprofitable business ventures.

TEN—With an *ace* of any suit following this indicates a big amount of cash.

NINE—With *ten of hearts* this indicates the stage or screen, possibly a theater. With *nine of hearts* it foretells a will or legacy bringing good fortune to the Questioner. With *eight of hearts* it indicates a good time or celebration.

EIGHT—With *Ace of Diamonds,* money coming unexpectedly. With *ten of diamonds,* a trip in connection with a love affair. With *eight of diamonds,* true love.

SEVEN—With *Jack of Hearts,* a love affair in which one party is more interested in gaining social prestige or financial advantage than in true and unselfish devotion. With *ten of spades,* an omen of misfortune in the future.

HEARTS

ACE—When surrounded by *hearts* or with hearts not more than one card away from it, this indicates the beloved, or domestic bliss.

KING—With *nine of hearts,* a love affair with a happy future.

QUEEN—With *seven of diamonds,* joy coming unexpectedly. With *ten of spades,* a dangerous undertaking.

JACK—With *seven of clubs,* a love affair where one party is motivated by a selfish interest in gaining social prestige or financial advantage.

TEN—With *ten of diamonds,* a marriage ceremony. With *nine of clubs,* the stage or screen, possibly the theater.

NINE—With *nine of clubs,* a will or legacy bringing good fortune to the Questioner.

EIGHT—With *nine of diamonds,* travel to some distant place. With *eight of diamonds,* the beginning of new and important work. With *nine of clubs,* a good time or celebration.

SEVEN—With *Queen of Diamonds,* happiness overshadowed by jealousy.

DIAMONDS

ACE—When surrounded by *diamonds* this indicates the Questioner will prosper financially in his present occupation. With the *eight of clubs,* money coming unexpectedly. With the *seven* and *Jack of Diamonds,* a telegram or wireless message.

KING—With *eight of spades,* a sudden journey.

QUEEN—With *seven of spades,* success to be found in a small community, rather than in a large city.

JACK—With *Ace* and *seven of diamonds,* see Ace of Diamonds.

TEN—With *ten of hearts,* a marriage ceremony. With *eight of clubs,* a trip in connection with a love affair. With *seven of spades,* a lapse of time caused by a delay.

NINE—With *Ace of Clubs,* legal business of some sort. With *eight of hearts,* travel to some distant place.

EIGHT—With *eight of clubs,* true love. With *eight of hearts,* the beginning of new and important work.

SEVEN—With *Ace* and *Jack of Diamonds,* see Ace of Diamonds. With *eight of spades,* the need to ask for help.

With *Queen of Clubs,* an uncertain outcome of events. With *Queen of Hearts,* joy coming unexpectedly.

SPADES

Ace—With *Queen of Clubs*, a tiresome journey.

King—With *seven of clubs*, caution necessary in connection with investments.

Queen—With *Jack of Spades*, the Queen signifies a woman of most evil intentions.

Jack—See Queen of Spades.

Ten—With *Queen of Hearts*, an exciting venture.

Nine—With *Jack of Diamonds*, the advice of friends should not be accepted too readily.

Eight—With *King of Diamonds*, a sudden journey. With *seven of diamonds*, the need to ask for help.

Seven—With *ten of diamonds*, a lapse of time caused by a delay. With the *King, Queen* or *Jack of Spades*, this indicates a traitor posing as a loyal supporter.

MISCELLANEOUS

When a *heart* card of any sort follows a King or Queen of any one of the suits, that King or Queen represents someone who wants to be a close friend of or in love with the Questioner.

If a King, Queen or Jack has cards of the same number on either side (as *eight, Jack, eight,* or *Ace, King, Ace*), it is a sign of caution to the person for whom the King, Queen or Jack stands.

When the Ace, King, Queen and Jack of one color fall in that order, a wedding is indicated. If the *seven of clubs* is not more than two cards away from this sequence, the couple will have to face financial problems.

A number of *spades* in a row is a sign of misfortune.

A number of *hearts* in a row is a sign of more than one love match, also social gatherings and domestic joys.

A number of *clubs* in a row is a sign of success and happiness.

A number of *diamonds* in a row is a sign of money transactions, usually benefiting the Questioner.

AN OLD FAVORITE

Here is a very old and reliable method. The Questioner shuffles thoroughly the thirty-two-card pack, then cuts them with the left hand into two sections. From the upper section the Seer removes the bottom card and from the lower section he removes the top card. These two cards he puts aside, face down. They are known as the Surprise.

The Seer then places the lower section on top of the upper section. From this pack of thirty cards he deals off three piles of ten cards each, starting from the right and dealing to the left.

The pile on the left is known as the Past; the pile in the center is the Present, and the pile on the right is the Future.

The Seer now deals out the ten cards of the Past in a row from left to right, and proceeds to read them. He then does the same with the pile of the Present and the pile of the Future. Last he turns over the two cards of the Surprise. They represent a sudden turn of affairs which will have a direct bearing on the future success and happiness of the Questioner.

A MODEL

Here is a model deal to show how the cards may be read. The cards are shuffled and cut by the Questioner, a young woman represented by the Queen of Hearts. The Seer having dealt off the cards as directed, the pile of the Past is found to contain the following, reading in order from left to right:

Seven of clubs
King of hearts
Nine of clubs
Ten of clubs
Ace of hearts reversed
Eight of spades reversed
Jack of diamonds
Queen of spades reversed
Ten of spades reversed
Jack of clubs

First we consider the card groups. Two jacks refer to some loss which the Questioner has sustained. The two tens indicate a lucky turn of events which came unexpectedly. Looking for special combinations, we find the ten of clubs followed by the ace of hearts which refers to a large sum of money.

Now taking the cards in order we find the Questioner connected with some small affair having to do with business (seven of clubs) in which she was associated with a loyal and friendly light-haired man (king of hearts) and as a result of which she received an unexpected sum of money (nine of clubs). This apparently was the lucky turn of events indicated by the two tens and involved quite a large sum, as previously shown by the ten of clubs-ace of hearts combination, for she was enabled to enjoy ease and luxury (ten of clubs) and to change her place of residence (ace of hearts reversed). We also find the break-up of a romance (eight of spades reversed) in which the Questioner's interests were centered upon a young employee in some business firm (jack of diamonds). This may be the loss of which the pair of jacks speaks, and it was brought about by the interference of a woman who was bent on evil doing (queen of spades reversed). However the Questioner's heartache was not of very great duration (ten of spades reversed), for it is apparent that she soon transferred her affections and found a new interest in a dashing young man, who was both an amusing and witty companion and devoted swain (jack of clubs).

Now turning to the pile of the Present, we find the cards read from left to right in order as follows:

> Jack of spades
> Eight of hearts
> Nine of diamonds
> Nine of spades
> Queen of clubs reversed
> Queen of hearts reversed
> Eight of diamonds reversed
> Ace of clubs
> King of diamonds
> Nine of hearts

Looking for card groups, we find first three nines which is a very favorable sign and indicates increasing prosperity and good health. This is tempered a bit, however, by the presence of the two eights, one of them reversed, which speaks of a disappointment in love, a sign which must not be overlooked especially in view of the two queens, both of which are reversed, indicating a talk between friends with secrets being confided and trouble for the one who has learned the secret. The ace of clubs surrounded by diamonds as it is refers to money which is coming to the Questioner and the eight of hearts with the nine of diamonds indicates a journey to a distant place.

Now let us study the cards in sequence. We find the young man whom the Questioner is interested in at present. It may possibly be the amusing young fellow whom we found in her Past, and now we learn more about him, for he appears to be a student (jack of spades). It is clear that he is definitely interested in the Questioner, for we see that he is entertaining thoughts of marriage in connection with her (eight of hearts), but unfortunately nothing can be expected to come of this for we see that there is unhappiness ahead (nine of diamonds and nine of spades). We do not look far for the cause, either. It is a jealous coquette (queen of clubs reversed) who is going to steal his heart away. Any doubts we might have about this turn of events is removed by examining the next two cards. We find the Questioner's card (queen of hearts) which is in reversed position, meaning unhappiness in love, and as double proof, the eight of diamonds reversed is linked with it, indicating a disappointment in love. The disappointment is easily discerned. The jealous coquette is doubtlessly a close friend of the Questioner, for we find their cards side by side. Now the significance of the pair of queens previously noted becomes plain. Here are two girl friends having a supposedly friendly talk, with an exchange of confidences, and the Questioner learns to her sorrow that her trusted friend has proved disloyal and stolen the love of the Questioner's young man. Here is unhappiness in love, disappointment in and loss of a friend through love. The ominous warning contained in the nine of spades is indeed bearing fruit. The last three cards speak of other matters. We find a letter bearing good news (ace of clubs) and coming from an elderly, gray-haired man, probably an uncle or a grandfather (king of diamonds). It may be that this letter contains the money which we saw was coming to the Questioner, for it is through the letter that the Questioner obtains her wish (nine of hearts). This checks with the previous favorable indications found in the three nines, and it is possible that the wish may have something to do with travel to a distant place (which has already been noted). The money would provide the means for the realization of this desire and thus would allow the Questioner to enjoy a change of scene and a chance to forget the unhappiness of her friend's betrayal and her shattered romance.

The pile of the Future contains the following cards, from left to right:

> Seven of spades
> Queen of diamonds reversed
> Seven of diamonds
> King of spades reversed
> King of clubs reversed
> Ten of diamonds
> Seven of hearts
> Ace of spades
> Jack of hearts
> Eight of clubs

We first note two groups of cards with unfavorable meanings. The pair of kings, both reversed, speak of some sort of failure in a commercial enterprise or undertaking. The three sevens speak of great unhappiness. On the basis of the Past and Present it is possible to hazard a guess that these groupings signify that the Questioner's attempt to forget her unhappy love affair by concentrating on a business career is not going to be successful. But we must consult the individual cards first before we draw any final conclusions.

The seven of spades foretells anxiety and worry on the part of the Questioner, caused by the malice of a rather common and vulgar woman (queen of diamonds reversed). In addition we find unkind criticism (seven of diamonds) coming from a man who is an enemy of the Questioner (king of spades reversed) which will lead ultimately to the defeat of the Questioner's best plans (king of clubs reversed). When these predictions are considered in the light of the meaning of the pair of kings, they offer the picture of the Questioner, earnestly trying to make her way in business, being thwarted by a malicious woman, possibly someone who works with her, and by an employer who dislikes her and is constantly criticizing her. In the end her dreams of a career will be spoiled and she will be most unhappy. However beyond this gloomy period of trial and unhappiness we find a much different set of circumstances. A change of residence (ten of diamonds) will bring to a close the unpleasant chapter of the future and will usher in a period of happy thoughts (seven of hearts) and much emotional pleasure and satisfaction (ace of spades). And it is not hard to discern the cause for this sudden change for the better. It is a fun-loving young bachelor (jack of hearts) who is offering a worthy love that is destined to bring fortune and happiness (eight of clubs).

Last we consult the Surprise, where we find a proposal of marriage (ace of diamonds) linked with assurance of good luck and happiness (ten of hearts).

The Secret of the Sevens

The Questioner takes the pack of thirty-two cards and after shuffling them well cuts them into three sections. The Seer takes the section on the Questioner's right and places it on top of the section on the Questioner's left. The center section is now placed on top of these two.

Now the Seer proceeds to deal out the cards, right to left and face up, in four rows of seven cards each, with a fifth row of four cards.

Each row is considered as containing some message in regard to the future. The Seer first reads the meanings of the cards in the top row, proceeding from left to right, in order to find out the message or prediction contained in the row. He then consults the second row, and so on until he has covered all five rows.

Now the Seer locates the Questioner's card, the choice of which is explained in the *General Instructions* at the beginning of the chapter, and counts off seven from it in either direction. The two cards thus located (the seventh on the right and the seventh on the left of the Questioner's card) are read together

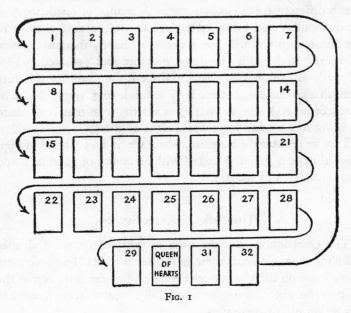

FIG. 1

as a special forecast relating to the Questioner himself. It should be explained at this point that in order to be able to count off seven in either direction, it is necessary to regard the five rows of cards as being in reality a continuous chain. Fig. 1 illustrates how this works. Card 7 at the end of the top row is considered to lie next to Card 8 at the beginning of the second row, and so on. Likewise the last card in the bottom row, Card 32, leads directly back to Card 1 at the beginning of the top row. Thus in counting off seven in either direction from the queen of hearts in the bottom row we arrive at Card 5 in the top row and Card 23 in the fourth row.

The Seer also locates the nine of hearts (wish card) and counts off seven in each direction to find the message concerning the Questioner's wish. Similarly he reads the message connected with the Questioner's home (ace of hearts), with the letter the Questioner is about to receive (ace of clubs), and with the Questioner's current love affair (eight of diamonds).

A MODEL

Here is a model reading of this interesting method.

The cards are shuffled and cut by the Questioner, who is a man represented by the king of diamonds. The Seer deals off the cards in the five rows as directed. Examining the first, or top, row for its message, he finds these cards in the following order from left to right:

> Ace of hearts
> King of diamonds
> Queen of hearts
> Ace of spades reversed
> Jack of diamonds reversed
> Seven of diamonds reversed
> Eight of spades reversed

Looking for groups we find a pair of aces, one reversed, which indicate some sort of partnership which will be only partly successful. In special combinations to be noted there is the queen of hearts which appears with the ace of hearts, the sign of the beloved. In this case reference is obviously made to the woman with whom the king of diamonds (Questioner) is in love. The seven of diamonds with the eight of spades foretells the necessity for asking for help. A study of the cards individually should make these points clearer.

First we find a love letter (ace of hearts) coming to the Questioner (king of diamonds) from a dependable and affectionate woman, with light complexion and fair hair (queen of hearts). It is evident that this woman's sentiments are returned, for we have already noted the special combination referring to the beloved. Consequently the king of diamonds and the queen of hearts must represent the partnership—one of affection rather than commerce, in this case—of which the pair of aces spoke, and we have been warned that this partnership will not be altogether successful. We do not have to look far to find this prediction borne out. Next to the Questioner's card we find the ace of spades reversed, which indicates unhappiness and discord. This is evidently because the letter was delivered by a young man who could not be trusted (jack of diamonds reversed) and who used his knowledge of the contents of the message to create a scandal (seven of diamonds reversed). The outcome of this unfortunate situation is the breaking off of the love affair (eight of spades).

In the second row we find the following cards, left to right:

>Seven of clubs reversed
>King of spades reversed
>Jack of spades reversed
>Ace of clubs reversed
>Ten of clubs reversed
>Seven of spades
>Nine of clubs

In this row we find a pair of sevens, one of them reversed, which indicates deception in love. As there are no special combinations here we can proceed at once to examine the cards individually.

There is at the outset a warning to the Questioner of money troubles (seven of clubs reversed) which are to come, and since

these are brought on by the scheming of an unscrupulous man
(king of spades reversed) it is probable that this enemy is a
rival of the Questioner's in love, having also instigated the afore-
mentioned deception. We find that this enemy is assisted in
his evil doing by a deceitful and dangerous young man (jack of
spades reversed) and as a result of their combined efforts a
most unpleasant correspondence is going to ensue (ace of clubs
reversed) which eventually will end in making it necessary for
the Questioner to make a journey (ten of clubs reversed) which
will be very unpleasant and filled with anxieties (seven of
spades). However in the end all will turn out for the best, for
the Questioner will, as a result of his journey, come into possession of an unexpected sum of money (nine of clubs).

The message of the third row is contained in the following
cards, reading from left to right:

> Queen of spades
> Queen of clubs reversed
> Seven of hearts reversed
> Nine of spades
> King of hearts
> Ten of hearts
> Nine of hearts

Looking for groups, we find a pair of queens, one of them
reversed, which tells us of a rivalry. The pair of nines speak
of success in commercial affairs.

It is evident that this message concerns the Questioner's business dealings. We see him associated in commerce with two
women, one an older type (queen of spades) and the other a
coquette (queen of clubs reversed). These women find themselves rivals for his interest, and though there is no evidence
that the Questioner entertains any special feelings toward either
of them, it is obvious that the coquette's interest in him is not

solely confined to business, for there is an indication of jealousy (seven of hearts reversed) at work. This situation is going to lead to trouble and the Questioner will suffer some sort of loss as a result (nine of spades). However, through the intercession of a loyal and trusted friend (king of hearts) matters will soon be straightened out and everything will turn out for the best (ten of hearts) and the Questioner will realize the success in his commercial affairs which the pair of nines suggested, for we see that his wish will be granted (nine of hearts).

The message of the fourth row is contained in these cards, reading from left to right:

> Eight of hearts
> Ten of diamonds
> Jack of clubs
> Nine of diamonds
> King of clubs reversed
> Eight of clubs
> Ace of diamonds

Studying the row for groups, we find a pair of eights, which indicate a short love affair. In the special combinations we discover the eight of clubs with the ace of diamonds, a welcome sign foretelling the receipt of an unexpected sum of money.

At the outset we find the Questioner entertaining thoughts of marriage (eight of hearts) which are interrupted when he is compelled to make a journey (ten of diamonds) in the company of a bright and amusing young man (jack of clubs). The journey, however, brings trouble and worry (nine of diamonds) and the Questioner sees his well-laid plans coming to naught (king of clubs reversed). But despite this misfortune his love is returned by a worthy individual (eight of clubs) and we find the brief courtship forecast in the pair of eights terminated by a proposal of marriage (ace of diamonds), which we may assume is accepted, since the eight of clubs indicates a love which will result in good fortune in happiness.

In the last row of four cards we find the following cards, reading from left to right:

> Jack of hearts
> Eight of diamonds reversed
> Ten of spades reversed
> Queen of diamonds

This message appears to be a warning to a friend of the Questioner, a happy-go-lucky young bachelor (jack of hearts), who is going to suffer a disappointment in a love affair (eight of diamonds reversed) and a certain amount of misery and unhappiness (ten of spades reversed) because of the idle chatter and tale-bearing of a gossipy woman (queen of diamonds). The unhappiness will fortunately not last very long, as is shown by the position of the ten of spades, which is reversed.

Finally we turn to the individual cards relating to the Questioner, his wish, his home, etc., and look for the special messages of the sevens in regard to them.

Counting off seven in each direction from the Questioner's card (king of diamonds) as previously described, we arrive at the eight of clubs and the king of spades reversed. This is a message informing the Questioner that in a love affair with a worthy individual (eight of clubs) he must beware the influence of a dangerous enemy who will seek to wreck his happiness (king of spades reversed).

Regarding the Questioner's wish, we count off seven from the nine of hearts and obtain the following message: The wish will be granted as a result of a letter (ace of diamonds) which will contain an unexpected sum of money (nine of clubs).

Regarding his home (ace of hearts), the count of sevens

brings the following warning: The Questioner's plans about his home are not going to materialize (king of clubs reversed) owing to difficulties concerning money (seven of clubs reversed).

Concerning the letter (ace of clubs) he is going to receive, the count of sevens reveals that it will contain unpleasant news.

Regarding his present love affair (eight of diamonds) the count of sevens predicts that there is going to be interference in the Questioner's romance by a young man who is a trouble maker (jack of diamonds reversed) and that the Questioner is going to have to make a journey (ten of diamonds) in order to patch things up.

The Fateful Eleven

The Questioner takes the pack of cards and shuffles it thoroughly. It is then cut into three piles. The Seer places the center pile on the one on the left, and these two together are placed upon the remaining pile, which was the one on the right.

The Seer now turns the pack face up and, picking off the three uppermost cards, chooses the one which ranks highest, regardless of suit. In case two of the three cards are alike (or all three are alike), choice of high card is made by considering clubs highest, then hearts, then diamonds and last spades. (It should be remembered that in this method the ace ranks above the king.)

Having chosen the highest of the three top cards, the Seer places it face up on the table and discards its two companions face down. Now the Seer picks off the next three cards of the pack and again selects the one of highest rank, placing it face up to the left of the previously chosen high card and discarding its two companions. This process continues, each selected high card always being laid down in the row to the left of the preceding one, until the entire pack has been exhausted. At the end two cards will remain instead of three. Of these last two the Seer chooses the one having the *lower* value and places it last in the row of selected cards. Its partner goes into the discard pile.

There are now eleven cards face up in the row on the table and twenty-one face down in the discard heap. These latter twenty-one are now carefully shuffled by the Questioner and handed to the Seer who proceeds to deal them out face up in two rows, one of eleven cards and the other of ten. The cards in these two rows are now read, each row carrying a message for the Questioner. Finally the original row of eleven selected cards is read for its message, certain portents being carefully noted. If the nine of hearts (wish card), the ten of hearts or ace of clubs happens to be in this row, it is an exceptionally favorable sign regarding the Questioner's future and helps to cancel the effects of any evil combinations. If the nine of spades is in this row, however, it is a warning to the Questioner to proceed with extreme caution in everything he does for the next two weeks or so.

In reading the cards the Seer must always remember to look first for groups and special combinations before proceeding to interpret the significance of the cards individually.

THE DOUBLE THIRTEEN

The Questioner shuffles the pack thoroughly and hands it to the Seer, who deals the cards out into two piles. With the left hand the Questioner now cuts the pile on his right, taking care not to look at the cut card. This the Seer removes, also taking care not to look at it, and places to one side face down as part of the Surprise. The Questioner then cuts the other pile in the same manner, and the Seer removes the cut card and places it face down with the first one as the second half of the Surprise.

The remaining thirty cards are now shuffled again by the Questioner and cut into two piles, from which the Seer removes the top and bottom card of each and discards them. The two piles are placed together again and reshuffled by the Questioner. The Seer then takes the pack and deals out two rows of thirteen cards each, face up. The message which each of these contains for the Questioner is now read, the Seer taking care first to note all groups and special combinations.

When this has been done the Questioner examines both rows and chooses a card to represent himself or herself, as the case may be. In this method any king may be selected to represent a man and any queen a woman.

Once the Questioner's card has been decided on, the twenty-six cards are gathered together and reshuffled by the Questioner. The Seer now takes the pack and deals out two rows of nine and one row of eight, right to left and face up. The Questioner's card is now located in one of these rows. The other two rows may then be ignored. The Seer studies the six cards nearest to the Questioner's card for any message which they may contain. These six will be the three to the right of the Questioner's card and the three to its left. If the Questioner's card is placed so near the end of the row that there are not three cards on either side, then there will be less than six cards to consider. In Fig. 2 this situation is illustrated. The Questioner's card (Q)

Fig. 2

is shown third from the left end of a row of nine. The shaded cards represent those which contain the special message. Three of these appear on the right of the Questioner's card, but there are only two to the left of it. Consequently only these two, plus the three on the right may be considered. In like manner, if the Questioner's card had appeared as the last card at the right end of the row, only the three cards marked A, B and C could have been considered for the special message.

After this reading has been completed, the Seer turns up the two cards in the Surprise and determines what unexpected event is going to affect the future success and happiness of the Questioner.

THE SINGLE THIRTEEN

The Questioner selects the card which is to represent him according to the directions given at the beginning of the chapter under the heading *General Instructions*. This card is laid face up in the center of the table. The remaining thirty-one cards are now shuffled by the Questioner and handed to the Seer, who deals off thirteen face down. This thirteenth card is placed face up on the table to the *right* of the Questioner's card. The Seer cuts the cards which remain in his hand and places the cut card face up on the table to the *left* of the Questioner's card.

The cards are now shuffled again by the Questioner and the Seer deals off eleven, placing the eleventh face up *above* the Questioner's card. The cards remaining in the Seer's hand are cut and the cut card is placed face up *beneath* the Questioner's card.

This process is continued until the layout shown in Fig. 3 is built up. The numbers indicate the order in which the cards are placed about the Questioner's card. Each time after the Seer has placed the cut card, the rest of the pack is reshuffled by the Questioner.

It should be noted that the Seer first deals off thirteen cards, placing the thirteenth in the layout. On the next deal he deals out only eleven cards, placing the eleventh card in the position bearing the number 3 in the diagram. The third time he deals off, he deals only nine cards, the ninth being placed in position No. 5 as indicated in Fig. 3. (The cut card after this deal goes in position number 6.) On the fourth deal only seven

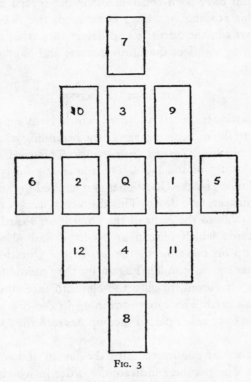

FIG. 3

are dealt off. On the fifth deal only five are dealt and on the sixth and last only three are dealt from the pack, the third going in position No. 11. The cards remaining in the Seer's hand are then cut for the last time, with the cut card going in position No. 12.

The layout is now complete and the reading may start. The Seer begins with the top card (position No. 7), considering

how it is related to the Questioner in connection with the card
beneath it (position No. 3). The cards in positions 10, 3 and 9
are considered as a group, since they adjoin one another. Likewise positions 10, 2 and 12 are studied together for related
meanings. The same naturally applies to positions 9, 1 and 11,
and 12, 4 and 11.

Though this is not one of the easiest methods, its adherents
claim great things for it, insisting that it can reveal much that
lies in the mysterious future.

THE FIFTEEN-SEVEN METHOD

This is an old peasant method, which is said to produce remarkably accurate forecasts of things to come. The Questioner
selects a card to represent him according to the directions given
at the beginning of the chapter under the heading *General
Instructions*. This card is placed face up on the table. He then
shuffles the remaining thirty-one cards and hands the pack
to the Seer.

Placing the pack face down on the table, the Seer proceeds
to turn over three cards at a time. If two are of the same suit
he takes the one with the highest value and places it face down
to the left of the Questioner's card. If they are all of the same
suit, he lays the three face down and in order next to the Questioner's card, starting on the left. If none of the cards are of
the same suit, he discards them. Three more cards are turned
up from the pack and the same process of selection and re-
jection is repeated. This continues until a row of fourteen
cards has been built up from the left of the Questioner's card.
If after the entire pack has been dealt out in this way there are
not fourteen cards next to the Questioner's, the discarded cards
must be reshuffled by the Questioner and the Seer must start
over again, dealing off three at a time.

When the fourteen cards have finally been chosen and placed in a row face down beside the Questioner's card, the row is bent around to form a circle, care being taken so as not to disturb the order in which the cards lie. Starting with the Questioner's card, the Seer now counts off seven around the circle. The counting may be done in either direction. The seventh card is removed from the circle and placed by itself face up. The card which was next to this one now becomes the starting point for a new count, and continuing around the circle in the same direction, the Seer counts off seven again, removing the seventh card and placing it face up to the left of its predecessor. The count continues by sevens, proceeding around the dwindling circle until all the cards have been counted off and placed in a row face up from right to left.

The message of this row is now read, the Seer paying special heed to groups and special combinations. When this has been done, the Seer picks up the two end cards of the row, places them together and notes their combined meaning. The two cards which now appear at the end of the shortened row are likewise picked up, placed together and "read." This is continued until only three cards remain in the row. These three are considered together for any special meaning they may have.

Next the fifteen cards are reshuffled and dealt out into three piles, each pile then being studied separately for its special added message.

Finally the fifteen cards are reshuffled and dealt out as follows: three piles of four cards each, which are known respectively as *The Questioner, The Questioner's Beloved* and *The Questioner's Home*. The three remaining cards are dealt out in a row and the middle one is laid aside as the *Surprise*. The two remaining cards are put together as *the wish*. The three big piles are then read in order for the messages which they contain. The message of the first obviously refers to the Questioner, of the second to his sweetheart, etc. The message regarding his Wish is read next, and last the Surprise.

THE STAR OF SEVENTEEN

The Questioner first chooses a card to represent him according to the directions given at the beginning of the chapter under the heading *General Instructions*. This card is placed in the center of the table face up and the remaining thirty-one cards are carefully shuffled by the Questioner.

The Seer takes the pack and deals off the first eleven cards, which are discarded. The Questioner reshuffles the remaining cards and cuts them into two piles. The Seer removes the top and bottom card of each pile and discards them. The cards which now remain are again shuffled by the Questioner and then handed to the Seer.

The Seer begins to deal them off, laying them around the Questioner's card in the order which is indicated by the numbers in Fig. 4. (The shaded cards in the diagram, marked 17, 18, 19 and 20, should be disregarded for the present.) Thus the first card dealt off is laid sideways to the right of the Questioner's card; the second sideways to the left of the Questioner's card; the third vertically above the Questioner's card, etc.

Once the seventeen-card star has been laid out, the Seer proceeds to read the cards in pairs, relating the message of each pair to the Questioner. The pairs are read in order as follows: 1 with 2, 3 with 4, 5 with 9, 6 with 10, 7 with 11, 8 with 12, 13 with 15, and 14 with 16. The nearer a pair is to the Questioner's card, the more immediate will be the results predicted in its message, though this is not a hard and fast rule. Nearness to the Questioner's card depends largely upon the order in which the cards are read. Thus the message of cards 1 and 2 has immediate significance, while that of cards 14 and 16 may refer to some event that will not take place until after a certain lapse of time.

It should be noted that from the observer's point of view

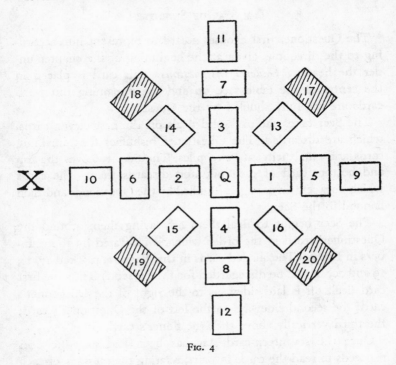

FIG. 4

(which is the Seer's) in Fig. 4, the cards numbered 1, 2, 7, 8, 9 and 10 are lying sideways, thus making it difficult to determine whether they are in reversed or normal position. To ascertain this it is necessary for the Seer to move around to the left side of the layout (at the point marked X in the diagram) in order properly to study these particular cards. After noting their values from this position, he can resume his seat and proceed with the reading.

A VARIATION

A variation of the Star of Seventeen is the Star of Twenty-One, which is preferred by some Seers, since it gives more evidence about the future of the Questioner. The Star of Twenty-One is laid out in precisely the same manner in which the Star of Seventeen is formed, with these exceptions:

Instead of dealing off and discarding eleven cards at the outset, the Seer deals off and discards only seven. The remaining cards are reshuffled by the Questioner and cut as before, with the top and bottom cards of the two piles being removed. After the final shuffle by the Questioner, the Seer lays them out in the same manner as previously indicated. The extra cards which remain after the sixteenth has been dealt are placed in the positions 17, 18, 19 and 20 as indicated by the four shaded cards in Fig. 4.

These last four cards are also read in pairs, 17 with 19 and 18 with 20.

The Lucky Star

Another favorite pattern based on the star employs only a total of fifteen cards. The Questioner's card is first selected according to the rules given at the beginning of the chapter under the heading *General Instructions*. This is placed face up in the center of the table and the Questioner shuffles the remaining thirty-one cards and then cuts them into three piles of approximately equal size.

The Seer now starts to build up the star. Taking the top card off the center pile, he places it face up and sideways above the Questioner's card. The top card of the right-hand pile is placed face up and sideways beneath the Questioner's card. The top card of the left-hand pile is next placed face up and sideways to the right of the Questioner's card. In Fig. 5 the positions

of the cards as they are drawn and laid out are indicated. The
Seer continues drawing cards off the three piles in the same
order: center pile, then right-hand, then left-hand. After the
fourteenth card has been placed as indicated, the rest of the
cards are discarded and the reading begins by pairs, as was

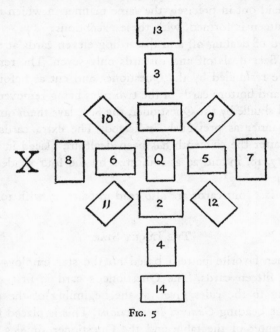

FIG. 5

explained under the *Star of Seventeen*. The order in which
the pairs are read is as follows: first 1 with 3, then 2 with 4,
5 with 7, 6 with 8, 9 with 11, 10 with 12, and last, 13 with 14.

As in the case of the *Star of Seventeen,* some of the cards
lie sideways. In order to determine whether they are in reversed
or normal position, the Seer must move around to the left side
of the layout (at the point marked X in Fig. 5) in order properly to study these cards, which are 1, 2, 5, 6, 13 and 14.

Special note must be taken of the message of the last two cards—13 and 14. In the *Lucky Star* method these last two cards are said to foretell something which is to occur in the very near future. In other respects the reading of the cards differs very slightly from that of the *Star of Seventeen*.

THE SIMPLE CROSS

First the Questioner selects a card to represent himself according to the directions given at the beginning of the chapter under the heading *General Instructions*. This is laid face up on the table and the remaining thirty-one cards are carefully shuffled and cut by the Questioner into two approximately equal piles. From each of these the Seer removes the top and bottom cards and discards them.

The Questioner reshuffles the remaining cards and deals out four packs of six cards each. Three cards remain in the Questioner's hand and these he discards. The four packs are now joined together again and shuffled by the Questioner and handed to the Seer.

The Seer deals off the first four cards and adds them to the discard pile. He now takes the remaining cards and turns them face up. The first one he places to the right of the Questioner's card; the second goes to the left of the Questioner's card; the third goes above the Questioner's card, and the fourth below it. The fifth is laid on top of the Questioner's card. The sixth card is placed on top of the first (at the right of the Questioner's card); the seventh on top of the second, etc., the process being continued until all the cards have been laid out. There is now a pile of four cards to the right, the left, above, and below the Questioner's card, as well as four cards on top of it. In Fig. 6 the order is indicated in which the cards are laid out in piles. Thus in the pile on the right are to be found cards 1, 6,

11 and 16, while piled on top of the Questioner's card are those numbered 5, 10, 15 and 20, etc.

The Seer now begins the reading. First he considers the message to be found in the pile of four cards to the left of the

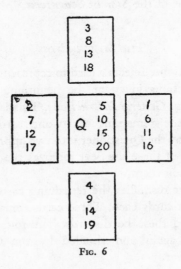

FIG. 6

Questioner's card, and then the message in the pile below the Questioner's card. These two refer to the Questioner's past. The pile to the right of the Questioner's card is considered next and then the one above it, these two referring to the Questioner's future. Last the Seer studies the four cards which lie on top of the Questioner's card. Their message relates to the Questioner's wish.

THE GYPSY CROSS

This method of card divination requires a second pack of fifty-two cards, in addition to the marked pack of thirty-two. From the pack of fifty-two an ace, two, three, four and five of any suit are removed and placed face down in a row on the table.

The Questioner now chooses from the marked pack of thirty-two cards one which will represent him. This is done according to the rules given at the beginning of the chapter under the heading *General Instructions*. This card is placed face up in the center of the table.

The remaining thirty-one cards are now shuffled carefully by the Questioner and cut with the left hand. The Seer now takes the pack and holding it face down lays the top card beneath the Questioner's card. The next card is placed to the right of the Questioner's card, the third goes above the Questioner's card, the fourth is placed to the left of it, and the fifth is placed on top of it.

The Seer then deals off seven cards and discards them. He then adds five more cards from the pack to the five which have already been laid down about the Questioner's card, following the same order as before—first below, then to the right, then above, then left and last on top of the Questioner's card.

Once more he deals off seven cards and discards them, and then he adds the next five cards to the ones already laid down, again in the same order as previously given. After this the two remaining cards in his hand are discarded.

There are now three cards in a pile above, below, on the right and on the left of the Questioner's card, and three on top of it. In Fig. 7 the order is indicated in which the cards are laid out in the five piles.

The Questioner now turns to the five cards from the full pack of fifty-two which were laid face down on the table at the beginning. Shuffling them so that he has no idea of their identity, he selects one and places it on the pile of cards below the Questioner's card, turning it face up as he does so. He then picks another of the four remaining cards and lays it on the pile at the right of the Questioner's card, turning it face up as he does so. This is repeated with the three remaining cards, they being placed in order upon the pile above the Questioner's card, upon the one to the left of it and lastly on top of it.

With these five cards—ace, two, three, four and five—lying face up, the Seer is now able to determine the order in which he

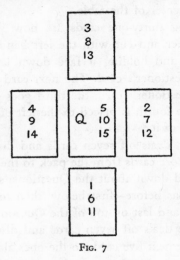

Fig. 7

will read the messages of the five piles. The pile on which the ace is lying is read first—the ace is not considered to be part of the message but merely an indicator of the order in which the reading shall proceed. Next the cards which lie under the two are read, then those under the three, etc.

Your Wish with 32 Cards

One thing that everyone wants to know is whether a wish will be granted, how soon this will happen and under what circumstances. There are a number of ways of answering these questions with the pack of thirty-two cards, and some of the more traditional methods are presented here, together with some of the less familiar ones.

The Questioner is warned that the cards should never be read more than once a week when seeking information about a wish.

An Easy Method. The Questioner shuffles the pack of cards and at the same time concentrates upon his wish, which, however, he does not reveal to anyone.

The Seer takes the shuffled pack and deals out nine cards right to left and face down. Then the Seer begins to turn over the cards one at a time, moving from left to right. As soon as he turns up an ace he lays this aside and continues on down the row of cards until he has turned them all face up. If he finds any more aces in the row, he also removes them and places them beside the first ace withdrawn.

He now gathers up the cards which remain in the row and replaces them in the pack, which is reshuffled by the Questioner. The Seer then repeats the process, dealing out nine more cards and hunting for aces. If all the aces have not now appeared, the Seer may repeat the process once more, dealing out a third row of nine cards after the Questioner has thoroughly reshuffled the pack. This must be the last deal, however, and if all the aces have not turned up by the time the third row has been searched, it is a sign that the Questioner will have to work very hard to obtain his wish.

The sooner the aces turn up in the three deals the quicker the wish will be granted. Thus if all four appear in the first row, it is the best possible sign that fulfillment will not be long delayed. This is not a usual circumstance, however, and the Questioner should not be disappointed if it requires three deals to complete the hunt. In such an event it merely indicates that the delay will be longer.

If, however, the ace of spades is the first ace to appear, the

Questioner is going to be confronted with great obstacles in achieving what he desires.

The Rule of Three. The Questioner begins by deciding which card is to represent him or her, according to the directions given at the beginning of the chapter under the heading *General Instructions.* This having been done, the Questioner shuffles the pack thoroughly, keeping the wish fixed in mind. Then the Questioner cuts the pack, and note is taken of the card which is revealed in the cut. If this card should happen to be the nine of spades, the omen is very unfavorable, and nothing more can be done, for this indicates failure to realize the wish.

In case the cut card is not the nine of spades, the pack is put together again and the Seer deals out the cards into three piles. Then he begins to look through each pile in turn to find the card which represents the Questioner. When that is located the other two piles may be discarded.

Now it is necessary to see if the cut card is in the same pile in which the Questioner's card appeared. If it is, this is a sign that the wish will be granted, and the number of cards which turn up between the cut card and the Questioner's card indicate the relative length of time it will take before the wish is granted. Should the nine of spades appear in the same pile with the Questioner's card and the cut card, it is a warning of great difficulty in obtaining the wish. If the nine of spades is not in the pile but more than six other spades are present, this is likewise a warning of trouble to come in connection with the wish.

If the cut card and the Questioner's card do not appear in the same pile, the outcome of the wish is very doubtful, and nothing can be predicted for certain. In this event the Seer should examine all three piles carefully until the wish card (nine of hearts) has been located. The cards which appear on either side of this—or if it is an end card in a pile, the two cards nearest to it—may provide some message for the Questioner regarding his wish.

The Message of the Aces. From the deck of thirty-two cards the Seer removes the four aces and places them face down on the table so that the Questioner does not know which ace is which.

The Questioner now shuffles the remaining twenty-eight cards thoroughly, silently concentrating on a wish. The Seer takes the pack and deals out the cards face down into four piles of seven cards each.

Then the Questioner chooses one of the four aces at random and turns it face up. This he places next to one of the four piles of cards. He then selects a second ace, turns it face up and puts it beside another of the four piles. In like manner he turns up the two other aces and lays them beside the two remaining piles. Thus each of the four piles of cards is now identified by one of the aces.

The Seer then hunts through each of the four piles in turn until he has found the nine of hearts (wish card). If the nine of hearts appears in the pile identified by the ace of spades, it means that the wish will not be granted. If it appears in the pile of the ace of clubs, the realization of the wish will depend entirely upon how much effort the Questioner puts forth. If he works very hard, he will win his desire very soon. If not, there will be a delay. In other words, it depends entirely upon him.

However, if the wish card appears in the pile of the ace of diamonds, it is a sign that there are factors affecting the realization of the wish over which the Questioner has no control. The card lying near the wish card may give a hint as to whether these factors are favorable or unfavorable. For example, if the ten of hearts lies next to the wish card, this is a sign that regardless of what the Questioner may do, everything will turn out for the best and his wish will be granted without any effort on his part. Or the appearance of the king of clubs would indicate that a loyal friend was going to act in the Questioner's interests.

If the wish card appears in the pile of the ace of hearts, it is a sure sign that the wish will be granted speedily and the Questioner will be very happy.

Time Divination. The Questioner hunts through the pack, silently concentrating upon his wish until he finds the wish card (nine of hearts). This he removes and lays on the table before him face down.

Still keeping his thoughts fixed on his wish, the Questioner shuffles the remaining thirty-one cards thoroughly and cuts them into two piles. The Seer removes the top and bottom card of each pile and discards them.

The Questioner places the two piles together again and re-shuffles the pack. He now cuts the pack into three piles and the Seer removes only the top card of each one and discards them.

Now the Questioner gathers up the three piles, shuffles them and cuts them once, without looking at the cut card. The Seer removes this cut card, discards it and puts in its place the wish card which has been lying in front of the Questioner. The pack is now joined together once more, and for a last time the Questioner reshuffles, this time thinking intently of his wish.

He gives the pack to the Seer who proceeds to deal out two piles of twelve cards each, face down. This done, the Seer first looks through the left-hand pile. If the wish card is in it, the wish will not come true within a year from the time. However, if it is not in this pile, the Seer begins to turn over the cards in the right-hand pile one at a time, counting as he does. The number at which the wish card turns up is the number of the months that will elapse before the wish is granted.

THE DECK OF 52 CARDS

When the full deck of fifty-two bridge or playing cards is used for fortune telling, there is no need to mark the cards as is done when only thirty-two are used. In the full pack of fifty-two each card has but a single meaning and no attempt is made to determine whether the card lies in reversed or normal position. As will be seen in the following table, the meanings for the full pack differ somewhat from those which obtain when only thirty-two cards are used.

THE MEANING OF THE 52 CARDS

CLUBS

ACE—The most favorable card in the deck. Wealth, prosperity, happy and tranquil thoughts.

TWO—Opposition to one's wishes, or a disappointment.

THREE—The Questioner is to be married thrice, with wealth in each case.

FOUR—Warning of impending evil, or a change in fortune.

FIVE—Wedding, with good prospects for the future.

SIX—Hard work in a business, with prosperity as a result.

SEVEN—Good luck, provided someone of the opposite sex doesn't interfere.

EIGHT—Overpowering desire for money, and gambling habits.

NINE—Unpleasant happenings because of the stubborness of some person, possibly a friend.

TEN—Wealth obtained unexpectedly.

JACK—A true and reliable friend of either sex.

QUEEN—A charming and affectionate woman, attractive to men.

KING—A man of generous disposition, true in love and very altruistic.

HEARTS

ACE—The house or home of the Questioner.

TWO—Great success, which will be delayed if there are evil cards near it.

THREE—Warning to the Questioner. There is danger of trouble as a result of lack of caution and prudence.

FOUR—A delayed wedding because of finicky tastes in the choice of a partner.

FIVE—A changeable and jealous nature. Inability to make up one's mind.

SIX—Friendliness and generosity, with a danger of being victimized by unscrupulous persons.

SEVEN—An unreliable, fickle person who may become a foe.

EIGHT—A festive occasion, good food and drink.

NINE—Wish card. It is usually the sign of wealth and position and honor. If surrounded by evil cards, however, it means temporary ruin.

TEN—A favorable omen, which cancels off bad cards near it, and reinforces good ones. It represents generosity and happiness.

JACK—Someone very close to the Questioner, of either sex— such as, a wife or husband, a best friend, a sweetheart, etc.

QUEEN—A tactful, lovable, fair-haired woman.

KING—An ardent, well-intentioned man who is more impetuous and hasty than he is wise. Likeable and good-natured.

DIAMONDS

ACE—A letter or money, sometimes a ring.

TWO—A love affair.

THREE—Disputes, either in the home (because of some ill-tempered person) or in business (lawsuits and litigation).

FOUR—Trouble and vexations.

FIVE—To a married person this indicates children who will be a source of great joy. Otherwise prosperity in business, or sudden tidings.

SIX—Unhappy end to an early marriage. Marrying a second time is to be discouraged.

SEVEN—A large loss connected with material things, such as wealth or property.

EIGHT—A wedding occurring late in life. The marriage may not be happy if unfavorable cards are near.

NINE—A surprise having to do with a sum of money. It may be good or bad, depending on surrounding cards.

TEN—Marriage to an individual who was raised in the country. Or a sizeable amount of money.

JACK—A relative or a close acquaintance of the Questioner. Headstrong, stubborn, not altogether loyal or reliable. Beware of his selfishness.

QUEEN—A vivacious coquette, who likes to attract the menfolk and has a way with them.

KING—A man whose temper is easily aroused and who is slow to forgive and relentless with those he decides to call enemies.

SPADES

ACE—Some kind of emotional relationship, as a love affair or a friendship, which may bring trouble. See list of Special Combinations.

TWO—A separation of some sort involving a change of place.

THREE—Faithlessness in love, with unhappiness for the Questioner.

FOUR—Envious disposition.

FIVE—Temper leading to quarrels.

SIX—Good plans and intentions meeting with failure.

SEVEN—Loss of a friend or loved one through a quarrel.

EIGHT—Warning of trouble unless the Questioner is very cautious. This may be connected with a difference of opinion with friends or relatives.

NINE—The card of bad luck.

TEN—Misfortunes. This cancels off the good cards next to it.

JACK—A well-meaning acquaintance who will not exert himself to help the Questioner.

QUEEN—A woman who likes scandal and will undertake nefarious business if properly bribed.

KING—A man with a great urge to get ahead in the world.

CARD GROUPS

The meanings of two, three or four of the same kind of card are the same with the pack of fifty-two cards as they are with the reduced pack of thirty-two. Therefore, in reading fortunes with the full pack, refer to the table at the beginning of the chapter under the heading *Meaning of Card Groups*.

SPECIAL COMBINATIONS WITH 52 CARDS

The following meanings apply only to card combinations which occur when the full pack of fifty-two cards is used. They are presented according to the four suits for rapid identification. It should be understood that these meanings apply only when the cards listed appear side by side.

CLUBS

KING—With the *Ace of Spades,* the King of Clubs represents a man who is active in politics.

EIGHT—With *Ace of Diamonds,* a business offer or proposition.

FOUR—With any *King* or *Queen* the four of clubs indicates that the person referred to by the King or Queen is going to suffer an injustice. With any *Jack* it indicates that the person referred to by that Jack is going to lose something.

TWO—With *two of diamonds,* an unexpected message.

HEARTS

ACE—When a heart card appears beside the Ace, a friendship is indicated. When hearts appear on both sides of the Ace, it indicates a love affair. When the Ace has diamonds on either side of it, money is indicated. When the Ace has spades on either side of it, quarrels are indicated.

NINE—With *five of spades,* loss of social position.

EIGHT—With *five of hearts,* a gift of jewelry.

FIVE—With *eight of diamonds,* a gift of money. With *eight of hearts,* a gift of jewelry.

FOUR—With any *King* or *Queen* the four of hearts indicates that the person referred to by the King or Queen has had a number of love affairs. With any *Jack,* it indicates that the person referred to by that Jack is going to marry presently. With the *Ace of Spades,* a child is to be born.

TWO—With *ten of diamonds,* a marriage bringing wealth.

DIAMONDS

ACE—With *eight of clubs,* a business offer or proposition.

TEN—With *two of hearts,* a marriage bringing wealth.

NINE—With any *King* or *Queen* the nine of diamonds indicates that the person referred to by the King or Queen will never realize complete success because of an inability to concentrate. With any Jack it means that the person referred to by that Jack is going to be made unhappy through his own actions. With the *eight of spades,* a bitter quarrel with a friend who has turned enemy.

EIGHT—With *five of hearts,* a gift of money.

SEVEN—With *nine of spades,* loss of money.

TWO—With *two of clubs,* an unexpected message.

SPADES

ACE—With *King of Clubs* the Ace of Spades indicates that the King of Clubs is a man who is active in politics. With *ten of spades,* a serious undertaking. With *four of hearts,* a child is to be born.

TEN—When a *club* card appears beside the ten of spades, trouble in business is indicated. When *clubs* appear on both sides of the ten, it indicates a grave business loss through theft, forgery or mismanagement.

NINE—With *seven of diamonds,* loss of money.

EIGHT—With *nine of diamonds,* a bitter quarrel with a friend who has turned enemy. If the eight appears next to the Questioner's card, he should be warned to abandon whatever plans he is now making.

FIVE—With *nine of hearts,* loss of social position.

THE SQUARE OF NINE

From the full pack of fifty-two cards the Questioner chooses one to represent himself according to the rules given at the beginning of the chapter under the heading *General Instructions.* The remaining fifty-one are now carefully shuffled and cut with the left hand into two packs. The Seer removes the bottom card of each of the packs and discards it. The Questioner now rejoins the two packs and shuffles them once more.

The Seer takes the cards and proceeds to deal out in a row three packs of five cards each. This done he lays the next card aside face down as part of the Surprise. He now deals off a second row directly beneath the first one and likewise containing three packs of five cards each. Again he lays aside a card face down for the Surprise. He deals out three more packs of five cards each in a third row which is placed directly beneath the second row. He now has a square formed of nine packs, each containing five cards (See Fig. 8).

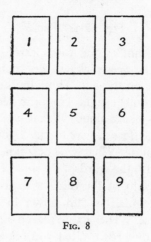

Fig. 8

There remain in the Seer's hand two cards. The top one he lays aside in the Surprise face down. The other one, which is known as the Indicator, he lays face up before him. If the Indicator is a heart, the Seer picks up the packs numbered 1, 5 and 9 in the diagram and discards the other packs. If the Indicator is a club, the Seer picks up packs 3, 5 and 7, discarding the rest. If the Indicator is a diamond, the Seer picks up packs 4, 7 and 8 and throws away the others. If it is a spade, he picks up packs 2, 3 and 6, discarding the rest.

In any case the Questioner's card which was previously chosen is now added to the three packs which have been picked up, and these sixteen cards are shuffled by the Questioner. The Seer then deals them out in a row on the table and proceeds to study their message. When this has been done, he turns over the three cards in the Surprise to ascertain what unexpected happening is going to affect the success and happiness of the Questioner. It should be remembered that in this method the meanings given for the full pack of fifty-two cards are to be used by the Seer.

THE SEVEN PACKS

The Questioner shuffles the cards carefully and cuts them into three packs. The Seer picks up the center pack and places it on top of the one on the left. These he then places on top of the one which was on the right. Now the Seer deals off the top card, face down, and says aloud, "What was." The second card is dealt off and laid face down to the right of the first card, the Seer saying aloud, "What will be." The third card is laid down in the row with the words, "To you." The fourth is placed face down to the right of the third with the words, "To your best beloved." The fifth is laid down in the row with the words, "Your house." The sixth, placed next to the fifth, is designated with the words, "What you hope for." The seventh and last in the row is laid down with the words, "A surprise."

With the row of seven cards now established, the Seer proceeds to deal off a second row of cards on top of the first seven, always moving from left to right, and this process is continued until the entire pack has been dealt off. There are now seven piles of cards and it will be noted that the first three piles on the left contain eight cards, while the remaining four contain only seven.

The Seer now spreads out the cards in the first pack on the left—"What was"—and proceeds to read their message, which naturally refers to the Questioner's past. In spreading out the pack, the Seer does so by first turning it face up and then dealing off the cards one at a time in a row from left to right. The

message is likewise read from left to right, the meaning of the
first card on the left being linked to the meaning of the second
card, and so on, as has been illustrated in the model readings
given in the early part of the chapter.

The messages of the other six packs are read in turn. The
second pack, "What will be," refers to the Questioner's future;
the third, "To you," to the Questioner himself at the present
moment. The fourth refers to the Questioner's sweetheart, the
fifth to his house, and the sixth to his wish. The last pack contains a message of a surprise which will unexpectedly affect his
fortunes.

THE FIVE MESSAGES

In reality this is but a variation of the preceding method, but
it is preferred by some students of cards. The full pack of fifty-
two cards is thoroughly shuffled by the Questioner, who then
cuts it with the left hand into two piles. The Seer removes the
top card of the pile on the left and the bottom card of the pile
on the right, and the Questioner then rejoins the cards and reshuffles them.

The Seer now deals off four cards and then takes the fifth
and discards it. He deals off four more and again discards the
fifth. This process is continued until the entire pack has been
dealt off. Now the cards are once more shuffled by the Questioner and then handed to the Seer who proceeds to deal off
five in a row face down and left to right. A second row is laid
down on top of the first five and so on until all cards have been
dealt out into the five packs, which are known—from left to
right—as "The Heart," "The Home," "The Hope," "The
Head" and "The Surprise."

Taking the first pack on the left—"The Heart"—the Seer turns
it face up and deals off the cards one at a time from left to right
in a row. Their message refers to the Questioner's sweetheart.

The next pack—"The Home"—is similarly dealt out and read, and it naturally refers to the Questioner's home. The third or "Hope" pack refers to the Questioner's wish; the "Head" pack refers to the Questioner himself at the present and the last pack concerns the unexpected event which will affect his future happiness and success.

QUESTIONING THE CARDS

The Questioner first chooses a card to represent himself according to the rules given at the beginning of the chapter under the heading *General Instructions*. This is laid in the center of the table face up. The remaining fifty-one cards are now thoroughly shuffled by the Questioner, who cuts the pack with the left hand into two piles of approximately equal size. The Seer takes the left-hand pack and from it deals off nine cards in a circle around the Questioner's card and face down. The Seer now joins the right-hand pack with the cards which remain in his hand and gives them to the Questioner, who shuffles them again.

This time there is no cut and the Seer takes the pack from the Questioner and proceeds to deal off a second circle around the first one. The second circle contains eighteen cards face down. The cards which remain in the Seer's hand are once more shuffled by the Questioner, after which the Seer takes them and deals all of them off in a third circle, face down and outside the two smaller circles.

There are now nine cards in the small circle, eighteen in the middle circle and twenty-four in the outer one. The Questioner now slowly turns over fifteen cards—selecting them at random —and as each card is turned face up the Seer reads its meaning, noting the connection which it has with the preceding card and the one which is turned up after it. In this way the Questioner picks out himself the message which lies waiting for him in the triple circle of cards.

THE THREE ANSWERS

The Questioner chooses three subjects about which he wants forecasts. A card is chosen to represent each of these subjects. Customary subjects and the cards which represent them are: *the home*—Ace of Hearts; *the. wish*—nine of hearts; *business affairs*—six of clubs; *the wedding*—five of clubs; *success in the future*—two of hearts; *happiness in the future*—ten of hearts; *the love affair*—two of diamonds; *words of warning*—three of hearts.

Let us suppose the Questioner wishes to learn what the future holds for him in regard to his love affair, his business and his home. From the pack of fifty-two cards he removes the two of diamonds, the six of clubs and the ace of hearts. These three Indicators he lays face down upon the table and the Seer mixes them up until the Questioner no longer remembers which is which.

Now the Questioner takes the remaining cards and shuffles them carefully. The Seer takes the pack and proceeds to deal out in a row seven piles of seven cards each, dealing from right to left. This done, the Seer takes the third and fifth piles and discards them. The remaining cards are gathered together and reshuffled by the Questioner, who then cuts them into three packs.

From the center pack the Seer removes the top card and discards it. From each of the two other packs the Seer removes the top and bottom cards and discards them. The remaining cards are now once more shuffled by the Questioner. Then the Seer proceeds to deal them out—right to left—into three piles.

Now the Questioner selects one of the Indicator cards, which are lying face down, of course, and places it above the center pile of cards. The other two Indicator cards he places above the remaining two piles in whichever order he chooses.

The Seer now turns over the Indicator card which is above the pile on the left. If this should happen to be the two of diamonds, it means that this pile of cards contains the message relating to the Questioner's love affair. The Seer deals off the cards from this pile in a row, moving from right to left, and proceeds to read the message, reading from *left to right*.

In like manner the Indicator above the center pile is turned face up to show the nature of the message in the center pile, and those cards are read in the same manner. So, also, the message contained in the remaining pile is studied.

The Four Stars

The Questioner chooses four subjects about which he wishes to obtain forecasts, removing from the pack of fifty-two the four cards appropriate to these subjects, as has been described in the preceding section. These four Indicator cards are laid out on the table face up, allowing plenty of space around each card.

The remaining cards in the pack are now shuffled by the Questioner and handed to the Seer. Choosing any one of the four Indicator cards at random, the Seer deals off three cards from the pack and places them beside it in a pile, face down. He now picks a second Indicator card and deals off beside it three more cards face down. The same is done for the third and fourth Indicators. Returning to the first Indicator, he deals off three more; then three for the second Indicator and so on. This process is continued until all the cards have been dealt out.

Now taking the pile of cards beside the first Indicator, the Seer proceeds to lay them out around the Indicator as follows: the first is placed face up above the Indicator, the second face up below it and to the left, the third face up below it and to the right. The fourth goes above the first, the fifth below and to the left of the second, and so on as is illustrated in Fig. 9, in which the card marked I stands for the Indicator.

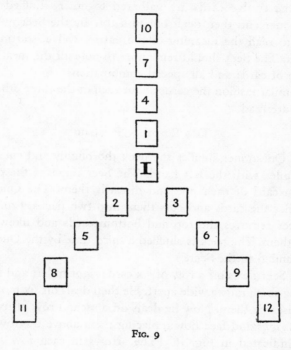

FIG. 9

In similar fashion a star is built up about the second Indicator from its pile of cards, and about the third and fourth Indicators from their piles of cards.

Now taking the first Indicator, the Seer reads off the messages of the cards. If the Indicator card happens to be the ace of hearts, the Seer notes the message regarding the Questioner's home which is contained in the top point of the star. This is composed of cards 10, 7, 4 and 1; then the message in the left point (cards 11, 8, 5 and 2), and finally the one in the right point (cards 12, 9, 6 and 3). The cards are usually read inward, from the end of the point toward the Indicator card.

When the messages of the three points of the star have been read, the twelve cards are gathered together, shuffled by the Questioner and then dealt out in a row by the Seer, who proceeds to read the meaning of the entire twelve, starting from the left. The Seer should remember to note all the meanings of groups of cards and all special combinations.

In similar fashion the cards about each of the three other Indicators are read.

THE EGYPTIAN PYRAMID

The Questioner shuffles the pack thoroughly and cuts it into three piles with the left hand. The Seer removes the top and bottom card of each pile and discards them. The Questioner reshuffles the cards and cuts them into two packs. From these the Seer removes the top and bottom cards and likewise discards them. The pack is shuffled a third time by the Questioner and handed to the Seer.

The Seer deals off a row of six cards right to left and face up, spacing them rather wide apart. He then deals off six more cards and discards them. Now he deals off a second row of five cards *left to right* and face down, placing them above the row of six, as is indicated in Fig. 10. (The arrows in each row show in which direction the deal is made.) After the second row is dealt off, he discards five cards.

The third row, of four cards, is placed above the second and is dealt *right to left*. After this four cards are dealt off and discarded. Next a row of three cards is dealt above this *left to right,* and then three cards are discarded. Two cards are then dealt off above and *right to left*. The next two cards are not discarded, however, but are laid aside face down for the Surprise. One more card is dealt out to form the top of the pyramid, and the card which remains in the Seer's hand is added to the Surprise, face down.

The Seer now proceeds to read the message of the pyramid, starting with the top card and proceeding down through the

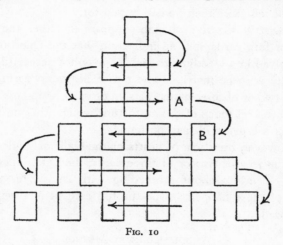

FIG. 10

rows, first right to left, then left to right, as is indicated by the little curved arrows at the ends of the rows in Fig. 10.

Care should be taken to note the meaning of any groups or special combinations which appear in the pyramid. Since each row is considered to be continuous with the row on either side of it, the possibility of special combinations in the end cards should not be overlooked. Thus in Fig. 10 if the card labeled A should happen to be the *eight of clubs* and the card labeled B should be the *ace of diamonds,* they would be considered as a combination (representing a business proposition), since the reading proceeds from left to right along the row of three cards and continues without break from right to left along the row of four cards.

It is considered a very good sign if the nine of hearts (wish card) appears in the pyramid. If it is found in the bottom row it is a sign that the Questioner's wish will be granted within a very short space of time. If it should happen to be the top card, then the Questioner is sure to have his wish come true and to receive even more than he had hoped for.

Likewise if the five of clubs appears in either the row of three or four cards, it is an indication that the Questioner will be involved in a wedding, though he may not necessarily be the one who is to be married. The ten of hearts appearing in the row of two or of three cards is a sign of great happiness to come and cancels off much of the misfortune which other unfavorable cards in the pyramid may portend.

If, however, the three of hearts or the eight of spades should be in the row of two or of three cards, the Questioner should be very cautious about proceeding with any of his plans. If either of these happens to be the top card, it is a warning to be heeded.

An Old-Country Method

A method which is often used among European fortune-tellers is as follows: The Questioner chooses a card to represent himself according to the directions at the beginning of the chapter. He then shuffles the full pack of fifty-two cards and cuts them in four packs. The Seer takes the pack on the right and puts it on top of the pack second from the left. These he places on top of the one which is on the left. Now the remaining pack is placed on top of these. The whole pack is spread out by the Seer face down on the table and the Questioner chooses seventeen cards at random and, without looking at them, hands them to the Seer. The rest of the pack is then taken up and laid aside temporarily.

Taking the seventeen cards, the Seer proceeds to deal them

out face up in the form of a cross, following the order which is indicated in Fig. 11. Special note is taken of any groups and special combinations.

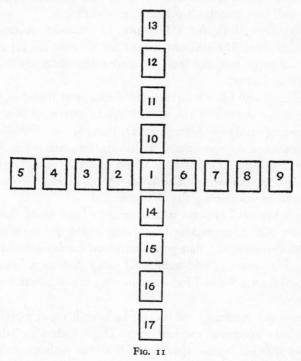

Fig. 11

If the Questioner's card is among these seventeen, it is a very lucky sign. However, aces detract from this good luck according to the number of them present. If one ace appears as well as the Questioner's card, the luck will not last very long. If two aces appear together with the Questioner's card, there will be a long delay before the lucky break occurs. If three or four aces appear in addition to the Questioner's card, the good luck is practically canceled off.

If the nine of hearts appears in either of the side branches the wish will be granted. If it appears in the upper branch of the cross, there will be a delay. If it appears in the lower branch, there will be obstacles hindering its realization.

Kings bring luck for a feminine Questioner, queens for a masculine one. The jacks of hearts and diamonds portend success and happiness, the jacks of spades and clubs are warnings of loss or failure.

The upper and lower branch should be read together, that is, the message should be traced by starting with card No. 13 and proceeding on down through 12, 11, 10, 1, 14, 15, 16 and 17. The side branches are considered as having separate messages, one being contained in cards 5, 4, 3, and 2; the other in cards 9, 8, 7, and 6, in that order. The latter group in some instances is regarded as containing the Surprise.

Whatever card appears in the center of the cross, that is, in position No. 1, is regarded as being especially significant. It should also be noted that even-numbered cards in the cross are lucky for women, odd-numbered ones for men. The odd-numbered ones are bad for women, the even-numbered unlucky for men.

When the meanings of the cards have been completely analyzed, the seventeen are laid aside. The remainder of the pack is now shuffled by the Questioner and cut with the left hand. The Seer takes the cut card and without looking at it places it face down on the table before him. Now from each of the two piles into which the cards have been cut by the Questioner the Seer takes the first four top cards. These, together with the cut card, total nine, and they are shuffled by the Questioner. The rest of the pack is discarded.

The Seer now deals out the nine cards face up to form the figure illustrated in Fig. 12, the numbers indicating the order in which the cards are laid down.

If the Questioner's card should happen to be among these nine, it is also a very lucky sign, though as before the aces detract from such a fortunate occurrence. Care should be taken to note any special combinations or groups. The card which is found in position 1 is of greatest importance. It is not consid-

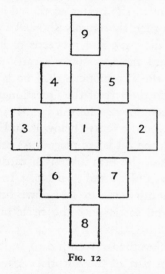

FIG. 12

ered lucky if any one of the jacks is found in position 2 or 3. The meaning of the cards is determined by reading them in sequence, starting with the top one, 9, and proceeding as follows: 4, 5, 3, 1, 2, 6, 7 and 8. It is a good sign if clubs or diamonds are found in positions 4, 5, 6 and 7. Spades in these positions are unlucky.

YOUR WISH WITH 52 CARDS

In addition to the methods of answering wish questions with the selected pack of thirty-two cards there are a number of ways to do this with the full pack of fifty-two. In summarizing these, it should be emphasized that none of these methods should be consulted more often than once a week.

The Twelve Months. The Questioner first chooses a card to represent himself according to the directions given at the beginning of the chapter under the heading *General Instructions.* This is laid face up in the center of the table. The remaining fifty-one cards are then thoroughly shuffled by the Questioner.

The Seer takes the pack and proceeds to lay out a circle of twelve cards around the Questioner's card as follows:

To the right of the Questioner's card he lays down the first card face down. To the left of the Questioner's card he places the second card.face down. The third card is placed above the Questioner's card and the fourth below it. In Fig. 13 is indicated the order in which the cards are placed. As can be seen by consulting this diagram, the fifth and sixth cards are arranged in a curve between card No. 1 and card No. 3. In the same manner the seventh and eighth cards are laid down between card No. 3 and card No. 2, and so on until the circle of twelve has been completed.

The Seer now takes the thirteenth card and lays it to one side face down to form part of the Surprise. After this is done the rest of the pack is handed to the Questioner, who shuffles it.

The Seer then takes the pack and deals off twelve more cards, laying them in the same order as before face down on top of the first circle of twelve cards. When this has been done the next card in the pack is likewise laid to one side in the Surprise.

Again the Questioner shuffles the pack and the Seer repeats the process, adding a third circle of twelve cards to the first two. After that he lays aside one more card for the Surprise, the Questioner shuffles the remaining cards in the pack for a last time and the Seer then deals them off around the circle for a fourth time.

We now have twelve piles of four cards each lying around

the Questioner's card. The pile which is numbered 3 in Fig. 13 stands for the month of January. Pile No. 7 is February, pile No. 8 is March, pile No. 2 is April and so on around the circle to pile No. 6, which is December. Beginning with January, the Seer

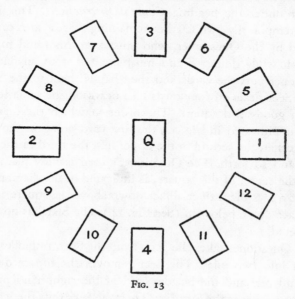

Fig. 13

turns over the cards in each pile until he locates the nine of hearts. The pile in which this card is found stands for the month within the coming twelve months during which the Questioner's wish will come true.

The three cards in the Surprise are now turned over and studied to discover what unexpected set of circumstances will lead to the realization of the Questioner's wish.

If it should happen that the nine of hearts is not to be found in any of the month-piles, it is a sign that there is no certainty that the wish will come true. The nine of hearts will be found in the Surprise, and the other two cards in the Surprise will indicate factors over which the Questioner has no control which may prevent him from realizing what he is hoping for.

The Aztec Star. The Questioner first chooses a card to represent himself according to the rules given at the beginning of the chapter under the heading *General Instructions.* This is laid aside temporarily while the remaining cards are carefully shuffled by the Questioner, who must keep his mind fixed on his wish while doing so and must not tell it to anyone. The Questioner cuts the cards and then hands them to the Seer.

The Seer deals off four cards face down on the table so as to form a good-sized square. The order in which these are laid down is indicated in Fig. 14, the first card going in the upper right corner, the second in the upper left, the third in the lower right, and so forth. The Questioner's card is now placed face up in the center of this square, as indicated in the diagram. The Seer now lays the fifth card face down above the square and the sixth face down below it. (See Fig. 14.) The Star has now been completed.

The Questioner takes the pack from the Seer, reshuffles it and cuts it into two piles. The Seer removes the top card of the left-hand pile and the bottom card of the right-hand pile and lays them aside as the Surprise. Then the Seer puts the left-hand pile on top of the right-hand pile and proceeds to deal off the cards face down onto the ones which form the Star, following this order:

First he puts one on the Questioner's card, then one on card No. 1, another on card No. 2, another on card No. 3, the next on No. 4, the next on No. 5 and the next on No. 6. After that he puts another on the Questioner's card, then the next on No. 1, and so on until the entire pack has been dealt off.

Now the Seer examines the seven cards which are piled on top of the Questioner's card. If the nine of hearts happens to be among them, it is a very favorable sign and indicates that the

Questioner's wish will be granted very speedily. If it is not in that pile, he then examines the other piles of cards until he finds it. If the nine of hearts is in the pile on card No. 1, it is a sign that there will be a long delay before the wish is granted.

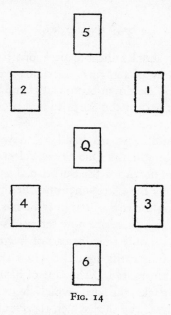

Fig. 14

If it is in pile No. 2, the wish will be granted but there will be trouble coming as a result of it. If it is in No. 3, the Questioner will not get his wish unless he is prepared to work very hard to obtain it. If it is in No. 4, he will have to be on guard against enemies who will do everything in their power to prevent him from obtaining his wish. If it is in No. 5, the wish will not be granted until the Questioner has mended a quarrel in which he has been involved, or is going to get into. If it is in No. 6, the wish will be realized as the result of some kind action on the part of the Questioner's friends or acquaintances.

If the nine of hearts is in none of these piles, it is very unlikely that the wish will be granted. The card will be found in the Surprise, and the other card with it will give a clew as to the factor which will operate to prevent the realization of the wish.

THE TEN PACKS

The Questioner shuffles the full pack of fifty-two cards. The Seer deals off a row of ten cards face down and then deals a second row of ten face down on top of them. He then lays the next card aside as part of the Surprise and proceeds to deal out ten more on top of the row.

The cards remaining in his hand are now spread out face down on the table and the Questioner selects two at random and lays them face down for the Surprise. The remaining cards are again shuffled by the Questioner and then the Seer proceeds to deal them out on the row of ten until he has run out of cards. It will be noticed that there are now ten packs of cards, but one of them will contain only four instead of five cards.

If this pack of four cards should contain the nine of hearts, the wish will not be granted. If the nine of hearts appears in any of the other nine packs, the cards which lie next to it should be examined carefully. If the card which represents the Questioner according to the rules given at the beginning of the chapter should lie next to the nine of hearts, the wish will be granted speedily. Otherwise there may be some delay, the nature of which will be indicated by the cards which surround the nine of hearts.

If it appears in none of these ten packs, then it is in the Surprise, and the other two cards in that pile will give a hint as to how the wish will be granted. When the nine of hearts turns up in the Surprise, it indicates that some unforeseen event is going to affect the wish.

V

Your Future in Your Dreams

FROM THE MOST ancient times people have been interested in finding out the hidden meanings of their dreams, and through the centuries a vast lore of dream interpretations has accumulated. Here follows some of the more common dreams with their traditional meanings.

It should be remembered that not all dreams have a special significance. Many dreams are merely things remembered from the preceding waking hours; thus if you have spent the day in your garden weeding the flower beds, it signifies nothing if you dream that night of flowers. The dreams which are significant and merit interpretation are the ones for which you cannot account by the ordinary process of memory. Thus any dream which refers to something that has not happened to you in your waking hours within the last week or so is likely to have a special meaning for you—a warning or a promise.

ABSTAINER—To dream that you refuse to drink any kind of alcoholic beverage is a forecast of excellent spirits and health.

ACCIDENT—To dream that you have an accident in which you are injured is a sign of a possible obstacle in plans you may have made.

221

ACHE—To dream that you have an ache or some slight pain is a sign of coming discomfort of a temporary nature.

ACORN—To dream of acorns is a very favorable sign. It signifies health, wealth and prosperity. To those who are in trouble it means that their fortunes will mend rapidly. To the person who is unmarried it indicates a happy marriage, with several children and the peace and joys of an ideal domestic arrangement. To the married person it foretells the birth of more children who will be a great credit to their parents. To merchants and those in business it betokens sound dealings and freedom from care. To dream that you are collecting acorns from beneath a tree indicates that your present line of endeavor will speedily be crowned with success despite any present hazards or obstacles.

ACQUITTED—To dream that you have been charged with some crime and have been acquitted in court means that the efforts of your enemies will come to naught and you will make rapid progress.

ACTOR—To dream of an actor or actress indicates a danger that your best laid plans will be upset through some frivolous or careless action on your part.

ADMIRED—To dream that people are admiring and praising you indicates that you have true and loyal friends. To dream that you are admiring or praising somebody means that your sweetheart or helpmate is true and sincerely devoted to you.

ADVICE—To dream that you are giving advice means that you are going to do something for which you will be greatly respected and honored by all those about you. To dream that advice is being given to you means that you will presently encounter obstacles but that you will be aided by the counsel of well-meaning friends.

AFFRONT—To dream that you have been affronted and have become angry because of this is a sign that you will have a quarrel with someone you love or that one of your debtors will make things unpleasant for you.

AGE—To dream about your age is a reminder that you must keep young in spirit.

AIRPLANE—To dream of an airplane overhead is a sign of a complete change; to dream you are riding in one is a sign that you should proceed very cautiously with the plans you are making.

ALE—To dream that you are drinking ale is a sign of an engagement leading to marriage; to dream that you are buying ale or that you see a large display of bottled ale is a sign of prosperity. However, if you dream you are drinking ale in a tavern or at a bar, it is a warning that you are surrounded by foes.

ALLIGATOR—To dream of an alligator or crocodile means that you have an underhanded and very dangerous opponent and should be on your guard.

ALMONDS—To dream that you are eating almonds means you may take a journey; if you enjoy the flavor of the almonds it is a sign you will find the trip profitable.

ALTAR—To dream that you are kneeling at the altar or that you are witnessing a marriage ceremony at the altar means that you must swiftly mend your ways.

ANCHOR—If you dream of an anchor in the water it is an unfavorable sign, signifying the miscarriage of your hopes and plans. To dream that the anchor is only partly in the water means that you are going for a trip by water. If you dream of an anchor which is not in the water it is a very favorable sign and foretells success and prosperity.

ANGEL—To dream of angels is a sign that you will be spared from harm and trouble. If you dream that you are with angels it is an augury of conviviality among pleasant acquaintances. If any of the angels offers you any word of advice, you should follow it immediately. To dream that you are an angel signifies an unexpected event.

ANGER—See *Rage*.

ANIMALS—To dream that you see a number of animals of different kinds means that your life will be filled with toil and hard work but that in the end you will know peace, security, and contentment.

ANTLERS—To dream of the antlers of a deer or moose is a sign that you are trying to undertake too many things at one time and must concentrate on only one or two, disregarding the others.

ANTS—To dream of ants means that you are going to face many worries and annoyances in a large city, where you will have to work hard and persistently if you wish to prosper.

APE—If you dream of an ape or monkey, be on your guard against an unexpected disappointment. If the monkey is sitting in a tree it is a sign of trouble and you should think carefully about what you have done recently to see if you have made any serious mistake which needs rectifying.

APPETITE—To dream that you see a man eating with a good appetite means you are going to have a wealthy friend.

APPLE—To dream of apples is a sign of coming success in some undertaking; to dream that you are plucking apples from a tree means that you will have a son who will be very rich.

APRICOT—To dream of apricots means success in love and a speedy marriage.

APRON—To dream that you are wearing a dirty apron is a sign that you are going to have some new clothes; to dream that you are mending an apron indicates a new love affair.

ARCH—To dream of a large memorial arch means you will achieve success through hard work; to dream you are walking under an arch is a warning of disappointments.

ARROW—To dream of shooting an arrow is a promise of coming pleasure; to dream an arrow hits you is bad, a sign that you have foes.

AUCTION—To dream of an auction means your business is going to improve.

AUTOMOBILE—To dream that you are riding in an automobile is a warning that you may become very poor.

BABY—To dream of a baby crying is an omen of coming trials and tribulations. To hear a baby laughing is a sign of loyal friends.

BACHELOR—To dream of a bachelor is the sign of a wedding in the offing. But if a woman dreams she is talking to a bachelor it means she will die either an old maid or a widow.

BACON—If you dream you are eating bacon it is a sign of sorrow because of quarrels.

BAGGAGE—If you dream that you have to look after a lot of personal baggage it is a sign of coming annoyances and troubles of a financial nature.

BAGPIPES—If you dream either of seeing or hearing these it means you will be very poor and that your marriage will be long delayed.

BALD—If you dream you are bald it means you will receive disappointing news.

BALLOON—This is a sign that hopes which you are now entertaining will not come off satisfactorily.

BANK—To dream that you are in a bank is a warning of hard times ahead. To dream that you meet a banker is a warning to proceed in your present plans with the greatest caution.

BANQUET—To dream that you are dining with friends at a lavishly set table is an omen of good things to come. If, however, the dream continues until you see the banquet table at the end of the meal, with the litter of empty plates and dirty dishes and with many of the chairs deserted, then it is a bad dream and a warning of unpleasantness to come.

BAREFOOT—To dream that you are barefoot is a sign that you should seek a change in the company you are keeping, for there are enemies about you though they seem to be friends.

BARREL—To dream of an empty barrel is a warning of failure; if the barrel is full, you are going to succeed in realizing one of your cherished plans.

BASEBALL—See *Sport*.

BASIN—To dream that food has been served to you in a basin and you are eating is a sign that you are going to fall in love but that it probably will be only a passing infatuation.

BASKET—To dream of an empty basket is a warning of failure, the same as is the dream of an empty barrel. If the basket is full, however, it is a sign that you are going to overcome an obstacle which confronts you.

BAT—If you dream of a bat flying about in the air over your head, it is a sign that you are imperiled by an unknown force. If you are in love it means that you have a dangerous rival.

BATTLE—To dream of a battle or a battlefield signifies an approaching quarrel with persons near you. If you dream that you win a battle, it is a very favorable sign.

BEADS—To dream that you are stringing beads is a sign of hard work ahead. To dream that you are wearing beads and that they break is a warning of discord. To dream that you are telling a rosary, however, is a very lucky sign.

BEANS—A dream about beans is unlucky. If you are eating them, it is a warning of trouble. If you see beans growing in a field, it is a sign of trouble involving your friends.

BEAR—A bear in a dream is a sign of worries and cares. If the bear chases you, you will be troubled by an enemy. If you kill the bear or elude it, it is a sign that you will overcome your troubles.

BED—If you dream you are making a bed, it is a sign that you will presently change your present occupation.

BEEF—A dream about beef is a forecast of prosperity and contentment, though it does not necessarily indicate great wealth.

BEER—See *Ale*.

BEES—To dream of a bee or a hive of bees is a sign of hard work bringing happiness and honor. To dream that you are attacked by bees is a warning that your work will not be easy and that you will face several handicaps but will prosper in the end.

BEG—To dream that you are begging is a very favorable sign and indicates the reverse: that you will never be in want. To dream that you are giving money to a beggar means that a person who poses as your friend will try to cross you, but that you will outwit him.

BELLS—To dream of bells is good or bad, depending on the sound the bells make. If they are merry and joyous, as sleigh bells, it is a lucky portent. It means promotion in business or a happy marriage. However, if they are alarm bells or tolling bells, think before you act.

BELOVED—If you dream that your beloved or sweetheart is happy and smiling, it is a sign of faithfulness. If your sweetheart appears sad or sickly, it is a sign of duplicity.

BET—To dream you are placing a bet is a sign that you are about to undertake something which involves a risk to your personal safety. To dream of winning a bet is a sign that you will suffer a financial loss of some sort.

BICYCLE—To dream you are riding a bicycle with ease is a sign of difficulties overcome. To dream that you are pedaling as hard as you can is a warning that an attempt to defame your character will be made. To dream of seeing someone on a bicycle is a caution against taking risks, regardless of how safe the outcome may seem to be.

BILLIARDS—To dream of a billiard game is a warning of trouble to come through your own carelessness.

BIRDS—To dream of birds is usually a sign that the situation in which you now find yourself will be changed for the opposite. To dream that you are feeding birds with brilliant feathers indicates that you are to receive an honor.

BITTER—To dream that you are eating something with a bitter taste is a sign of trouble.

BLAME—To dream that you have been blamed for something you did not do is a sign that you will triumph over your enemies and will witness their downfall.

BLIND—To dream of seeing a blind person indicates that your friends will come seeking your help. To dream that you are blind means that you are going to be in need of help soon.

BLOOD—To dream that you are bleeding means strife.

BLUEJAY—To dream of a bluejay is a sign of an approaching marriage. To dream of a pair of bluejays means that you will be married twice.

BOIL—To dream that you are afflicted with a boil is a sure sign of coming success. If you suffer from a number of boils, your eventual triumph will be all the greater.

BONES—If you dream of seeing dried bones it indicates that you are going to receive some money. If you dream of seeing a skull with the bones it is a sign that you are going to receive money from a will.

BOOKS—To dream that you are reading a book indicates that you will achieve fame. To dream that someone is giving you a book is a sign that you will soon be courting and that it will end in a happy marriage. To dream that you see books on a shelf is a sign of a happy future.

BOTTLE—If you dream that you are drinking from a bottle, it is a warning that you should watch your actions carefully lest you be led into evil-doing. If you dream of a filled bottle, it is a sign that you will enjoy success and happiness; if the bottle is empty, you must be on guard against enemies.

BOW AND ARROW—If you dream that you are shooting with a bow and arrow and that you hit what you have aimed at, then it is a very good sign and indicates you will obtain your wish. But if you do not hit what you aim at, it means that there are many obstacles between you and your wish.

BOWLING—To dream that you are bowling is a warning of severe hardships and losses to come. To dream that you are watching others bowl means that your friends are going to be sorely troubled.

BOX—If you dream you are presented with a box and you open it to find it empty, it is a very unlucky sign. On the other hand, if you find something in it which pleases you, it is a very favorable omen regarding the immediate future.

BOXING—This is not a favorable dream. It portends business worries and losses.

BRACELET—To dream that someone is putting a bracelet on your arm is a sign that you are going to fall in love presently with a stranger. If you dream that you are wearing a beautiful bracelet it is an indication that you will marry a wealthy person if you are single, and if you are already married, it indicates that your spouse will come into possession of a large sum of money.

BRANCH—To dream that you are looking at tree branches which are filled with leaves, blossoms or fruit is a sign of every good thing coming to you in due course of time. To dream of bare branches warns of coming poverty.

BREAD—If you dream you are eating bread it means that you will escape unpleasantness which may affect others near you.

But if you dream you are eating dry or stale bread, it is a warning to be cautious about your present plans.

BREAKFAST—See *Meal*.

BREATH—To dream that you are panting and out of breath is a warning not to overwork.

BREEZE—To dream that you feel a gentle breeze blowing is a very fortunate sign, especially for those in love.

BREW—To dream that you are brewing beer or making wine is a forecast of a visit by some friend whom you have not seen for a long time. It also betokens happiness which will come unexpectedly.

BRIDGE—To dream that you are passing under a bridge either in a boat or a car is a sign of troubles to come which will not, however, be of long duration. To dream that you are walking or riding over a bridge is a portent of sure success. If you see water flowing beneath the bridge as you pass over it, the dream signifies that it will be some time before you realize complete success.

BROOM—To dream that you are sweeping with a broom means that you are going to have to make amends for something you have done.

BUGLE—If you dream you are blowing a bugle, it is a very good sign and indicates that you may expect increasing good fortune. To dream, however, that you hear the bugle blown is an omen of a quarrel.

BUILDINGS—Dreams about buildings vary in meaning, depending on the kinds of buildings you dream of. To dream of new buildings is an indication of a change of occupation. To dream of run-down and dilapidated ones is a sign of discord. If you dream of factories or rows of shops it is a sign that you are about to engage in some new business activity. To dream of rows of homes is a sign your domestic life will prosper and bring you much contentment. To dream of skyscrapers is a warning that your aspirations may be too high and that you may never succeed in reaching the goal you are striving for.

BULL—To dream of an angry bull is a warning of coming trouble. If the bull is chasing you it is a sign the trouble will come soon, and pass quickly.

BULLDOG—To dream of a bulldog is a sign that some person whom you mistrust is in reality one of your most loyal friends. But if you dream that this dog bites you or is chasing you, it means you have good reason to mistrust someone who seems to be a friend.

BUNDLE—If you dream you are carrying a bundle, it is a warning of business losses of some sort. But if you dream you have received a bundle as a gift, it is a sign that a friend is going to call and tell you something which will benefit you greatly.

BURDEN—If you dream you are weighed down with a heavy load or burden it is a sign that you are going to work very hard to achieve any sort of success whatsoever. If you dream that you are helping somebody with his burden, it is a sign your friends are going to ask your aid in some affair.

BURGLARY—To dream of a burglary or burglars is a sign you are contemplating some action which will bring discredit upon you.

BURN—To dream that you have received a burn is a sign of very good fortune. If you dream that you see a house burning, it is an indication that you are going to make a considerable fortune.

BUTTER—If you dream of butter, it is a very favorable sign and indicates happiness in your love affairs and means that you are going to win in any dispute which may arise. If you dream that you are spreading butter on bread it means that your children are going to bring you great happiness. If you do not have children, it means that a member of your immediate family will bring you great happiness.

BUTTERFLIES—To dream of butterflies is the sign of happiness to come.

BUTTERMILK—If you dream that you are drinking buttermilk, it is the sign that you are going to have a quarrel with someone you love dearly.

BUTTON—If you dream that you have lost a button, it is a promise of good news.

CABBAGE—If you dream that you are eating cabbage, it is a sign that an enemy who is jealous of you is going to try to do you harm. If you dream that you see cabbages growing, it means that you will lose some money.

CAGE—If you dream that you see a bird in a cage, you are going to marry soon. If you dream that you see an empty cage from which a bird has flown, it is a sign that your lover will desert you for another love. If you dream that someone is letting a bird out of a cage, it indicates an approaching elopement.

CAKE—To dream of a birthday cake is a very fortunate sign. If the candles are lighted it means health and prosperity all your life long. If you dream that you are cutting the cake, it is a sign that your luck will temporarily desert you.

CALAMITY—This is a dream which has an opposite meaning. If you dream that a calamity has befallen you, it is a sign that one of your friends will receive a promotion very soon. To dream of a calamity in business is a sign of prosperity.

CAMEL—If you dream of a camel with one hump, it means that burdens will press down upon you. If you dream of a camel with two humps, it indicates that you are going to have many troubles, but through courage and intelligence, you are going to win out in the end.

CAMERA—If you dream that you are taking pictures with a camera, it is a sign that you are soon going to change your present line of work.

CAMP—If you dream that you are camping and having a good time, it means that you are never going to be successful in love. However, if you dream that you are camping and it is raining and you are not having a good time, it is a sign that you will enjoy a happy married life.

CANARY—If you dream that you hear a canary singing, it is a sign that you will marry a person who is devoted to you and who will make your home life a very happy one.

CANDLE—If you dream that you are blowing out a candle, it is a forecast of rejoicing. (See *Cake*.)

CANNON—If you dream that you hear a cannon fired, it is the sign that you are going to have a quarrel with your loved one. It may also mean that you will have news from someone who is in the military services.

CAPTURED—If you dream that you have been captured by the police or by soldiers, it is a sign that you will be misunderstood. It is also a warning of marital troubles.

CARDS—To dream that you are playing cards is a sign that you will die a widow or a widower. If you dream that you are telling your fortune by cards, pay special attention to the significance of them, for their meanings will come true.

CARNIVAL—If you dream that you have gone to a carnival, it means that you are going to be careless and will lose money in business deals. It also indicates that you are going to mistreat your friends.

CARVE—If you dream that you are carving meat or a fowl at table, it is a sign that you will obtain great wealth through your marriage.

CAT—It is a bad omen to dream of a cat because it means that friends or loved ones are going to prove treacherous and unfaithful. A cat with her kittens, however, indicates happiness and contentment.

CATERPILLAR—A dream about a caterpillar is a warning that an enemy is going to try to wreck your plans.

CATHEDRAL—If you dream that you are in a cathedral, it means that you are going to receive some money through a will. It is also a sign that something very good will come to you from someone connected with a church.

CHAIN—If you dream that you are tied up with a chain, it means that you are going to suffer temporary setbacks. If you dream that you are freeing someone who is tied with a chain, it means that you will overcome severe obstacles which will confront you in business.

CHAIR—If you dream that you are sitting in a rocking chair, it means that a baby is to be born. If you dream that you are taking your ease in a fan-backed chair, it indicates that your present plans are going to succeed.

CHASM—To dream that you are standing on the brink of a chasm is the sign that you must think carefully before making a change.

CHEAT—If you dream that you are cheating someone, it is the sign that you are going to be known for your honesty. If you dream that someone is cheating you, it means that you can count on the loyalty of your friends in trouble which is to come.

CHECKERS—If you dream that you are playing checkers, it is a warning that you lack powers of concentration and that you must settle down and work very diligently if you wish your plans to succeed.

CHEESE—If you dream of cheese, it signifies unfaithfulness on the part of the one you love.

CHERRIES—If you dream of cherries, it is the sign of a disappointment, especially in love.

CHESTNUTS—If you dream of chestnuts roasting on a pan, it is a sign that good things are going to come your way after a certain amount of disappointment.

CHICKENS—If you dream of a flock of chickens, it is a sign of impending change.

CHILDREN—If you dream of children, it is a sign that you will have success in business and that your married life will be very happy.

CITY—If you dream that you are lost in a big city, it is the sign that your present plans are going to undergo an unexpected change.

CLOCK—If you dream that you are looking at a clock to see what time it is, it is a warning that you are paying too close attention to details and that you may miss a great opportunity through lack of imagination.

CLOTHING—If you dream that you are wearing new clothes, it is a sign of poverty and want. However, if you dream you are wearing old clothes, which are ragged and torn, it means that some day you will have a great fortune. If you dream that you are making clothes, it signifies that a child will be born.

CLOUD—If you dream that you see clouds in the sky, it is a sign that discord will come soon but will pass rapidly.

COAL—To dream that you are throwing coal on the fire is the sign that you will have much work to do which will bring you money in large quantities.

COFFEE—It is a very good sign if you dream that you are drinking coffee, for it indicates that you are going to find happiness and contentment in a very short time. If you see someone else drinking coffee, it is a warning that your future happiness may be marred by something which you are about to undertake.

COLD—If you dream that you are cold, it indicates that you have many warm friends who will always come to your aid in time of trouble. If you dream that you are suffering from a cold, it is the sign that you will receive a long-looked-for letter.

COLLECT—If you dream that you are collecting anything, such as fruit or vegetables from a field, it is an indication of great prosperity to come. If you dream that you are collecting old clothes, etc., it is a warning to avoid quarrels.

COMET—If you dream of seeing a comet in the sky, it is a warning that the nation is in grave peril. It means that there may be war.

COMMUNION—To dream that you are having communion in church is a very good sign and means that all the troubles which you will have will pass away very quickly.

CONCERT—To dream that you are at a concert is a warning that you are going to be involved in a serious quarrel.

COOK—To dream that you are cooking is a sign of a merry party at which love matches will be made.

COW—If you dream that you are milking a cow, it is a sign that you are going to prosper in business.

CRAB—To dream that you are pinched by a crab at the seashore is a warning to avoid travel by water.

CRAMP—To dream that you are seized with a cramp indicates that your luck will change for the better.

CRIPPLED—If you dream that you are crippled, it is the sign that you are going to move to a distant city.

CROW—To dream of a crow is a warning of bitter enemies who are going to try to harm you. If you dream that you catch the crow or shoot it, it is the sign that you will overcome them and that they will be unable to do you any harm.

CROWN—To dream that you are wearing a crown is the sign that you are going to be promoted.

CUCKOO—If you dream that you hear a cuckoo call, it is the sign that you are going to be disappointed in a love affair.

CUPBOARD—If you dream of an empty cupboard, it is the sign of money troubles.

CUSHION—If you dream that you are making a cushion, it means that you will spend an old age surrounded by comfort and material wealth.

DAGGER—To dream of a dagger is the sign of a quarrel in which you will be the loser.

DANCE—If you dream that you are dancing, it is a very lucky sign. If you dream that you are toe dancing, it is a warning that you have set your ambitions too high for the present.

DANDELION—To dream that you see dandelions growing is a warning that a distant friend is going to write to you for advice.

DARK—If you dream that you are lost in the dark, it is a sign that you will presently need the assistance of your friends. If you dream that you are in the dark but that you see a distant light shining, it means good news coming from afar.

DEER—To dream of deer indicates you are too timid in the pursuit of your beloved.

DENTIST—If you dream that you are going to the dentist or are in the dentist's chair, it is the sign that you are going to resist evil. If you dream that you are leaving the dentist's chair, it means that the worst of your troubles are over.

DESERT—To dream that you are wandering on the desert is a warning of a troublesome journey.

DESERTED—If you dream that you have been deserted by your friends, it means disappointment in the very near future.

DIAMOND—If you dream that you find a diamond, it is a warning of trouble. If you dream that someone is giving you a diamond, it means that someone holds evil thoughts against you; but if you dream that you see diamonds, it is the sign of the best possible luck coming your way.

Dice—If you dream that you are playing with dice, it is the sign that you are going to undergo great changes in your fortunes.

Dinner—If you dream that you are eating dinner, it is a warning of difficulties to come. If you dream you are preparing dinner, it means that you will have a happy home life.

Dirt—If you dream that your clothes are covered with dirt, it means that your reputation is going to suffer from some action of yours. If you dream that you are smothered by dirt, it is the sign that you will triumph over your enemy.

Ditch—If you dream of falling into a ditch, it is the sign to make all plans carefully. If you dream that your automobile has plunged into a ditch, it is a warning of changes in business.

Dog—It is a very good sign to dream of dogs. If they are barking and snarling, it means that you are going to overcome great obstacles. If they are friendly and wagging their tails, it is the sign that you will be very happy soon.

Donkey—To dream of a donkey is an indication that a friend is going to prove untrue.

Dove—If you dream of a dove, it is the sign of the greatest prosperity and good fortune.

Drink—To dream that you want a drink but cannot find any water is the sign that you are going to be alone and unaided in time of trouble. To dream that you have obtained a drink of water is the sign of much happiness to come.

Drive—To dream that you are driving an automobile foretells prosperity and financial gain. To dream that you are driving a horse is the sign of a marriage.

Drown—If you dream that you are drowning, it is a sign that your character is being besmirched by a close friend.

Drum—To dream that you hear a drum beating is a warning of a grave crisis for the nation.

Drunk—If you dream that you are drunk, it is a sign that your wastefulness and careless habits will lead to your downfall.

Duck—To dream that you see a duck flying is the sign of wealth to come. To dream of a duck swimming in the water is the sign of peace and contentment.

Dumb—If you dream that you are dumb and cannot speak, it means that you are going to fall into great disgrace.

Dust—If you dream that you are dusting the house, it is a sign that you are going to have disappointments. If you dream that you are choked with dust, it is a sign of a temporary setback in business.

Eagle—If you dream that you see an eagle flying high in the sky, it is the sign that you are going to prosper in your present undertaking. If you dream that you see an eagle sitting in a cage, it is a warning that your enemies are plotting your downfall.

Earthquake—To dream you are caught in an earthquake is the sign of a grave decision to be made.

Eat—If you dream that you are eating with friends at a big banquet table, it means that you will receive great honors from your community.

Eclipse—To dream of an eclipse of the sun or the moon indicates that a friend of the opposite sex is planning a long trip.

Egg—To dream that you are eating an egg is very unlucky. To dream that you find a nest full of eggs is a very good sign, for it means that you will have a happy marriage and contented old age together.

Elephant—To dream of an elephant means that whatever troubles may befall you your health will always be sound and you will be able to overcome all obstacles.

ELEVATOR—To dream that you are going up in an elevator is the sign of honors to come. To dream that you are descending in an elevator is a warning of trouble.

ELOPE—If you dream that you are eloping, it means that you are going to be disappointed in your first love.

ENVY—To dream that you envy someone is the sign that a rival in love is going to be defeated by you. To dream that you are envied means that you will be much admired by those around you.

ERMINE—If you dream that you are wearing ermine, you may expect honors and great public acclaim.

ESCAPE—To dream that you are making an escape is the sign that you are going to be in serious trouble soon but that you will come out all right in the end.

EXPLOSION—To dream that you hear a loud explosion is a warning of an important change. To dream that you see an explosion means that you will lose some valued possession.

FACE—If you dream that you see your own face in a mirror, it means that some secret which you are keeping is going to be found out. If you dream that you see many strange faces, it indicates that you are going to change your occupation.

FACTORY—To dream that you are working in a factory means that your financial worries are over for the time being.

FAIL—To dream that you have failed in business or in love means that quite the contrary will happen.

FALL—If you dream that you are falling, it indicates a loss of position or property.

FAN—To dream of a fan is a very good omen. It means that you are going to have some enjoyable experience.

FARM—If you dream that you are working on a farm, it is a sign that you will enjoy very good health. If you are sick at the present time, it indicates a rapid recovery.

FAT—If you dream that you are fat, it indicates that you are going to have good health for most of your life.

FATHER—If you dream of your father, it is a sign that all will be well with you. If your father is dead it means that you will encounter trouble in which someone near you will render you assistance.

FEAST—If you dream that you are at a feast, it is a sign that you will prosper in your present undertaking.

FEATHER—If you dream of feathers that are brilliantly colored, it means that you are going to hear good news. If the feathers are black or dirty, the news will be dull. (Also see *Fan*.)

FIELD—If you dream that you are walking through a beautiful green field, it means that your wish is going to come true. If you dream that you are walking through a newly plowed field, it means that you are going to achieve success through hard work. If you dream that you are lying down in a field, it means that you will make new acquaintances.

FIG—If you dream that you are eating figs, it is a sign that you are going to receive an unexpected gift.

FIGHT—If you dream that you are in a fight, it means success in business and in love.

FIRE—To dream that you are building a fire is a very good sign. To dream that you are warming your hands over a fire means that you are going to find some very lucrative work. To dream that your house is on fire is a warning of friction.

FISH—To dream that you see fish swimming in the water means new business opportunities. If you dream that you are fishing and can catch nothing, it is the sign that you are not going to succeed in your present undertakings. If you dream that you have caught a fish, it is the sign of prosperity.

FLOAT—If you dream that you are floating in the air, it is a warning that you lack decision. If you dream that you are floating in the water, you should think twice before undertaking any journey.

FLOOD—To dream of a flood is a very favorable sign and means that your personal affairs will turn out well.

FLOWERS—To dream that you are picking beautiful flowers is the sign that you will succeed in anything which you undertake in the next few days. To dream that you see faded or withered flowers means that your wish is not going to come true.

FLY—To dream that you are flying in an airplane means success in business. To dream that you are annoyed by flies and are swatting them indicates that you are going to be plagued with many trivial and petty annoyances.

FOG—This is a sign that your affairs are in a very uncertain condition and that you must proceed with extreme caution, lest you fall into great difficulties.

FOOD—To dream that you see a table laden with food is a sign of prosperity and happiness.

FORLORN—To dream that you are sad and forlorn means that you are going to make a financial sacrifice.

FORT—To dream that you see a fort is a sign that you are going to be very strong and self-reliant in the face of trouble.

FOUNTAIN—To dream that you see a beautiful fountain bubbling with water means that you are going to come into a good inheritance.

FOX—To dream that you see a fox means that there is someone who is trying to outwit you in love or in business. This person may appear to be a friend.

FRIENDS—If you dream about your friends and it appears that they are sick or in trouble, it means that they are in need of your help. If you dream that you are with your friends and they are happy, it means that you are going to have a very happy love affair.

Frost—Any dream in which you see frost is a warning.

Fruit—To dream that you see fruit growing on a tree means good health and material prosperity.

Game—See *Sport*.

Garden—If you dream that you are working in a garden, it means that you are going to have much useful work to do which will bring happiness to a great number of people.

Garter—To dream that you are losing your garter is the sign that you are going to have petty troubles and disappointments.

Ghost—If you dream that you see a ghost, it is a sign to watch your relationships with friends and dear ones. If the ghost should speak, you should pay special attention to whatever it says.

Giant—If you dream that you see a giant, it means that you are going to be confronted with a great obstacle which will require all your strength to overcome.

Giraffe—To dream of a giraffe is a harbinger of great good fortune and success in all your personal affairs.

Girl—If you dream that you are talking to a girl, it means that you are going to be very happy in the near future.

Glasses—To dream that you have broken your glasses means that you are going to suffer a slight upset. If you do not wear glasses but dream that you are wearing them, it is a warning of discord because of a misunderstanding.

Goat—If you dream that you see a goat, it means that your enemies are plotting to undo you, but that you will be able to overcome them if you will keep your head and not let fear weaken your will.

Gold—To dream of gold is a warning that you should beware taking chances in business. If you are in love, it means that you should be careful that you do nothing to arouse the jealousy or suspicion of your lover.

GONG—To dream that you hear a gong sounding means caution.

GOOSE—To dream that you see a goose is a sign that one of your friends is going to do something very foolish. Beware of giving any unfounded information.

GRAIN—To dream that you see a field of grain growing is the sign of prosperity and happiness.

GRASS—If you dream that you are cutting the grass, it is the sign that you are going to do well in business. The longer the grass, the greater will be your success.

GUITAR—To dream that you hear a guitar playing means that your lover is true.

GUNSHOT—To dream that you hear a gunshot is a warning that you will have news of trouble at a distant point.

HAIL—To dream that it is hailing is an unhappy sign. It means that your business affairs will not prosper for a while.

HAIR—To dream that you are combing your hair is a warning that your loved one is thinking of someone else. If you dream that your hair is gray, it means that you are discouraged. If your hair is snarled, it is a sign that you are going to get yourself into trouble by talking too much.

HAM—To dream that you are eating ham is one of the luckiest signs possible.

HAMMER—If you dream that you are using a hammer, it means that you are going to have prosperity in your business life. If you dream that you hear a hammer pounding, it means that you are going to have temporary setbacks from which you will recover quickly.

HAND—If you dream that your hands are tied, it means that you are going to have difficulty in getting out of trouble. If you dream that your hands are dirty, you must beware lest you are led into some wrongdoing.

HANGING—To dream that you are going to be hanged is a very

good sign and indicates that you are going to receive a certain amount of money.

HARM—To dream that someone has harmed you means that you are going to have a disagreeable quarrel with one of your friends. To dream that you are harming someone indicates that one of your closest friends is going to pick a fight with you.

HAT—To dream that you have a new hat is a sign that your most cherished wish is coming true and that your business affairs are going to prosper.

HAY—To dream that you are raking hay is an excellent omen and indicates that you are going to have a very pleasant surprise.

HEAVEN—To dream that you have gone to Heaven means that your life will be very happy and free from trouble.

HEDGE—To dream that you are clipping a hedge means that you will have difficulties which will be speedily overcome.

HELL—A dream of adversity, signifying possible business loss.

HERD—To dream of driving a herd of cattle indicates success in your present undertaking.

HERMIT—To dream you have become a hermit means temporary failure in business and unpleasant home conditions, followed, in a short time, by great wealth and happiness.

HILL—If you are climbing a hill in your dream but do not reach the top, it is a sign you will work hard for everything you get and rewards will be few. In matters of love, something will happen at the last minute to prevent marriage.

HIRE—To dream you are hiring someone means possible injury to that person, if you do not use care in your relations with him. If you are seeking a position, it indicates prosperity.

HOME—To dream of home denotes happiness in your present surroundings, continued health and financial success. It indicates a happy marriage and several gifted children.

Honey—To dream of eating honey means sweetness will enter your life. You will have a long and happy life, a successful marriage based upon deep and lasting love, and a gradual increase in business growth that will bring financial success.

Horn—To dream of blowing a horn means success in love and business. To dream only of hearing a horn denotes quarrels, financial troubles and embarrassment through friends.

Hornet—If you are stung by one in your dream, beware of false friends who will cause you trouble.

Horse—If you dream of riding a white horse you will be married in the near future, or will hear of the marriage of a close friend. If you are thrown from a horse in your dream, you will have unpleasantness around you. To ride a horse indicates happiness in the near future, but seeing a black horse in a dream foretells trouble.

Horse Shoes—To dream you are playing this game denotes an uncertain future, with business and financial reverses.

Hospital—Dreaming that you are visiting in a hospital denotes a business promotion.

Hotel—If you dream of residing in a hotel, it denotes unsuccessful undertakings in the near future.

Hounds—To dream you are hunting with hounds indicates an unhappy marriage. Conditions in general will be unfavorable.

House—To dream of building a house means a profitable return on investments or a salary increase. Affairs of the heart will end in a wealthy marriage.

Hummingbirds—Seeing a flock of these birds in a dream foretells travel, with business or professional success. To see a dead hummingbird means an unsuccessful journey.

Hunger—To dream of being hungry foretells you will attain a place of honor and wealth through your own efforts and genius. If you are a lover, your loved one will undertake a journey of great length before your marriage.

HUSBAND—To dream you have a husband means failure of your desires. Dreaming you love the husband of another indicates complete disregard of others. For a widow to dream she has a husband indicates a happy and prosperous marriage at an early date.

HYMNS—To sing hymns in a dream foretells happiness, prosperity and success. Your loved one will be everything you desire.

ICE—Dreaming of ice in any form indicates hardships, financial and business worries, failures and quarrels. It foretells an unhappy love and broken engagement.

ICICLES—If the icicles are hanging, it means good fortune. A marriage of wealth will be yours and your children will attain great success.

INFANCY—To dream you are an infant again denotes bad fortune. Dreaming of your own infancy indicates good business conditions and happiness in courtship and marriage. To a married woman it means unsettled conditions.

INJURY—To dream of injuring yourself or of being injured by another implies that just the opposite will occur. All your plans will materialize in love and business and any attempt by another to harm you will prove futile.

INK—To use ink in a dream indicates favorable business conditions, with advancement; if spilt, and the hands are soiled, you will receive unfavorable news of business and personal natures by letter.

INSULT—Dreaming of being insulted foretells misfortune. You will be separated from a loved one through a quarrel or slight misunderstanding. This condition will continue for some time, if you do not change your mental attitude.

IRON—To dream of iron indicates a rise to wealth and position through your own endeavors and speculation in business; a marriage with a person of strong will and spirit.

ISLAND—If the island in your dream is barren, it portends the loss of your beloved. If the island is green, attractive and flowers are in evidence, your lover will be fickle, but you will soon meet and marry another person who will bring you great happiness.

ITCH—To dream your skin is itchy indicates unhappiness and adverse conditions.

IVORY—A dream of good fortune to the lover, with much beauty and sweetness entering his or her life. To the farmer it foretells a rich harvest. To the business or professional person it indicates a successful and profitable career.

IVY—To dream of ivy means that the good things of life will cling to you as the ivy clings to the wall. Your husband or wife will remain close to you; your home will be a center of happiness; your business will prosper and friends will be devoted to you.

JAM—To dream you are eating jam foretells a temporary upset. If you are sharing it with another, beware of a false friend or lover. If you are eating it in the presence of a group, it means kind friends will be ready and eager to aid you in any trouble. To dream of making jam is a sign you will participate in a wedding ceremony.

JEALOUSY—To display jealousy in your dream indicates troubles and anxiety. In business your affairs will undergo changes from unforeseen causes. You will experience disturbances in money affairs due to the failure of another. To dream you are the object of another's jealousy indicates misunderstandings and altered relations, which will eventually prove beneficial to you.

JEWELS—To see them in a dream is a good sign. To be given jewels denotes great affection and an early and happy marriage. To dream of counting jewels means you are counting the good things that will come to you in many ways. Your children will be healthy and talented; you will attain wealth and an enjoyable life in your chosen work.

JOB—To dream of getting a job indicates good fortune; to dream of losing a job is a sign of misfortune.

JOY—A dream of health and of wealth, which you will receive through an unexpected legacy from a distant relative.

JUDGE—To dream you stand before a judge charged with a crime portends misfortunes, if he convicts you. If you are freed, it is an omen of good fortune. To dream you are a judge foretells your advancement to a position of prominence and financial security.

KEY—To dream of many keys indicates riches as the result of a flourishing business. To dream you give a key denotes a marriage; to find or receive one, the birth of a child. To lose a key denotes disappointments.

KING—To dream of speaking with a king means you will advance to a position of honor and dignity. If he is unfriendly, expect misfortunes. To the young, it foretells a future mate of wealth and position.

KISS—To dream your lover kisses you with affection is a sign he is true to you. To dream of kissing one whom you should not denotes a false friend. To see another kiss your intended indicates a rival.

KITE—To dream you are successfully flying a kite and it rises high and steadily is a sign you will rise above your present position to one of honor; some administrative post will be yours. In love it is a good dream. It foretells travel; good farming and business. If the string breaks and the kite flies away, it becomes a dream of adversity.

KITTEN—To dream of being scratched by a kitten indicates your loved one is possessed of an unpleasant disposition, and that only unhappiness can result from marriage.

KNIFE—To dream of sharp, shiny knives denotes enemies. You will have disappointments in love, and losses in business.

KNIT—To dream of knitting denotes deceit in those who seem to love you.

LACE—To dream of wearing lace indicates some extravagance in which you will indulge. If a young man dreams his loved one is adorned with lace, it means she will want an elaborate home.

LADDER—To dream of ascending a ladder, or of reaching the top of a ladder, foretells a bright future. To the lovers it means attainment of their heart's desire. To the business person, it indicates independence, with wealth, honor and position. If, however, you should become dizzy upon reaching the top of the ladder, it indicates you will be unable to adjust yourself to the success you have attained and eventually will return to your former station. If the ladder should break, or you should fall, it means disaster to your present hopes.

LAKE—To dream of a smooth, clear, glassy lake denotes a happy pleasing life, success in business and a position of honor. It shows success in love and matrimony, and agreeable family life. If the water in the lake appears dark, muddy or disturbed, it indicates trouble.

LAMBS—For a young woman to dream of lambs indicates a marriage with a gay, light-hearted person. Her children will be healthy and of good disposition. For a young man, it shows his future wife will be young and beautiful, but inexperienced in the art of home making. For married persons, it shows great happiness through their children.

LAMPS—To carry a bright lamp indicates you will be successful and highly esteemed in your chosen profession. If the lamp light is dim and flickering it foretells unhappiness. If the light goes out it means delay in achieving your hopes and plans. To see many bright lamps foretells a party, or wedding.

LAND—To dream of possessing land is a good sign. It foretells wealth and independence.

LARK—To hear the singing of a lark denotes good health and prosperity. If not married, you will marry a person of means. You will have several children, at least one of whom will be a musician or vocalist.

LATE—To dream that your lover is late indicates he is a person cool and calculating in his actions. He will not be very affectionate.

LAUGHING—To dream of laughing excessively foretells disappointment. If you are in love, be careful of your actions or you are likely to be jilted. Laughter is frequently a sign of tears.

LAUREL—Dreaming of laurel means victory, pleasure and prosperity. If a married woman dreams of smelling laurel it foretells the birth of a child. To a young person, it indicates a speedy marriage.

LAW—To dream of being involved in a lawsuit or litigation denotes difficulties and business reverses. Be careful of your affairs after such a dream. Do not become involved in any new enterprise, enter into a partnership, or lend money. Do not make large purchases at this time or you will regret it.

LEAP—To dream you are leaping over a barrier indicates you will easily overcome any obstacle to your advancement. To a lover, it denotes many obstructions will be found in your path, but you will attain your heart's desire.

LEASE—To dream of leasing a house or other building shows great business success. You will marry soon and be happy in that marriage.

LEAVES—To see trees covered with fresh green leaves means your affairs will prosper, and you will have business success. If blossoms and fruit appear among the leaves it indicates a happy marriage with many children. If the leaves are dry and withered it means disappointments in love.

LEG—To dream of having injured your leg foretells a marriage of poverty, with a person of indolent habits and intemperate ways. If a young man, your wife will be a poor home manager.

LEGACY—If you dream of receiving a legacy, it is a sign that the wealth of your intended is only a pretense, to impress you and insure your marriage.

LEMONS—To see lemons growing signifies travel, and marriage to a person you will meet while traveling.

LEND—This is a dream that foretells losses.

LEOPARD—To dream of leopards means you will travel in a foreign land, where you will marry and stay for the remainder of your life. You will have hardships and adverse conditions for a while, but will overcome them and attain prosperity.

LETTER—To send one indicates you will soon do a kind and generous act. To receive a letter means unexpected news from old friends, or gifts.

LIE—If you dream that you have told a lie, you will meet with true and loyal friends.

LIGHT—To dream of light means happiness. Your hopes will be realized. In love you will attain your desire. To see many bright lights, indicates an event of great joy is close at hand.

LIGHTHOUSE—A dream promising better things for you in the future. A promotion, with prosperity, is just ahead.

LIGHTNING—To dream of lightning alone is favorable. It indicates success in present ventures, advancement, and a happy marriage. If accompanied by storm or rain, it is an unlucky dream.

LILACS—To dream of lilacs indicates an unexpected good fortune.

LILY—To see one of these lovely flowers augurs well. Your marriage will be successful; business conditions will prove favorable. If the flower appears withered, you may hear unpleasant news.

LIMP—To dream of limping means your path will be full of difficulties and disappointments.

LINEN—White linen means news of a surprising and pleasant nature. Colored linen indicates you will inherit money. Soiled linen is an omen of disappointments.

LION—To dream of lions denotes greatness. You will attain a position of trust. Your marriage will be to a person of intellect, and will be a happy one.

LOCK—If you are faced with locked doors, cabinets, etc., and have no keys, it implies difficulties will beset you. If, however, you unlock them, it is a sign of a smooth road to success ahead.

LOTTERY—Beware of treacherous friends who seek to ruin you in business and to interfere in your home life.

LOVE—To dream of loving and of being loved indicates you are surrounded by well-wishing friends, who will aid you in anything you may undertake. To dream of failure in love means you will have great success with the person you hope to win. To dream of loving friends is a sign of domestic happiness and success in business.

LUCK—To dream of being lucky is an omen of disappointment. Be careful of your actions, and be sure your head governs and not your heart.

LUMBER—To dream of searching through stacks of lumber, and of finding the object of your search, is a sign of unexpected wealth. To be surrounded by lumber through which you have difficulty in finding your way, indicates misfortune.

LUNCH—See *Meal*.

LUXURY—This is a dream of contrary, indicating poverty, losses, and jealousy.

MACHINE—To dream of being among machines indicates an industrious nature, which will bring you ultimate wealth.

MAGIC—To dream of magic means a change for the better, in many ways. Watch for a false friend who will seek to harm you.

MAGNET—If you see a number of magnets, it indicates trouble ahead, if you are not careful. If you see a magnet in use, you will soon have a dangerous rival.

MAID—To a man this indicates a marriage.

MANNA—A dream of hope and sweetness that will follow any troubles in your life.

MAP—To dream of maps foretells many years of travel in foreign lands. If the maps are colored, it indicates you will return wealthy.

MAPLE—To admire a maple tree indicates a long life. To be sitting under one is a sign that you should not be careless. To see numerous trees, all thriving, is a sign you will receive money.

MARIGOLDS—This is a sign of success in your undertakings, happiness in love and marriage, and advancement in business and social spheres.

MASK—To see a person wearing a mask is a sign of insincerity in someone close to you.

MAY POLE—To dream of dancing around a May pole, or of seeing others dancing around one, foretells great joy. If a widow has this dream, it indicates she will soon marry again.

MEADOW—To dream of walking through a meadow is a sign of happiness in the immediate future.

Meal—To prepare a meal foretells a busy home life, with many children.

Measles—To dream of having measles is a sign of good health, business improvement, and good fortune, which will come to you from an unexpected source.

Medicine—A good dream. If the medicine has a bad taste you will have some slight unpleasantness.

Melons—Travel in a foreign land. If not married, you soon will be, and will have lasting love and happiness.

Microscope—A sign you will soon discover that a trusted friend is deceitful. If you look through a microscope, you will be separated from a loved one, but will rejoin him soon.

Midget—To dream of seeing one denotes good health, strength, and an improvement in circumstances that brings you independent means.

Milk—To drink milk denotes joy; selling it, sorrow. To dream of milking a cow foretells prosperity.

Mirror—To dream of looking into one means business failure unless you mend your ways. Avoid confiding your affairs, as someone near you is working against your interests.

Miser—An unhappy dream, foretelling a gradual loss in circumstance.

Misfortune—To dream of having misfortunes denotes a change of fortune for you that will bring with it the comforts of life.

Monastery—A dream of peace, and freedom from worries.

Money—A dream of general prosperity. To find it means a sudden advancement through business or marriage. To count it means your marriage will be blessed with numerous children.

Moon—A full moon foretells happiness and success in marriage. A new moon brings good fortune in business, industry and farming.

MOTHER—To dream of talking with your mother indicates comforts that will come as a pleasant surprise.

MOTHS—Beware of dishonest associates, as someone is trying to undermine your position.

MOUNTAIN—To dream of climbing one denotes a life of toil and struggle for every good thing you attain. To see green covered mountains indicates true, generous friends.

MOURNING—As you mourn in a dream, so shall the good things of life be yours. Much comfort, health, and prosperity follow such a dream.

MOUSE—Look for a series of misfortunes resulting from the gossip of enemies.

MULBERRIES—A good dream foretelling wealth, honors and a happy marriage.

MUSHROOMS—To dream of picking them is a sign of riches that will come to you gradually.

MUSIC—To dream of hearing music foretells a long and happy life, with a marriage of great harmony. It is a sign of affectionate friends and many well wishers.

MYRTLE—To dream of myrtle indicates an agreeable life, with pleasing events and circumstances throughout. To a married person, it indicates a second marriage late in life.

NAME—Changing your name in a dream is a sign of spinsterhood.

NECKLACE—To dream you are wearing a necklace of value indicates a speedy marriage to a person of wealth and position, which will bring you great happiness.

NEST—Dreaming of birds' nests is a sign of marriage and domestic happiness. If the nest holds broken eggs beware of failures.

NETTLES—To see them is a good sign, indicating good health and prosperity. To be stung by them indicates disappointment.

NEWSPAPER—To dream of reading one foretells you will soon have news that will result in a change of employment. This change will lead to gradual ownership of your own business.

NIGHT—To be walking in the night foretells delays in accomplishing your purpose.

NIGHTINGALE—To dream of hearing one is a sign that good fortune awaits you. Everything to which you turn your hand will result favorably. You will be admired and loved for your sweet nature.

NIGHTMARE—You are under the influence of another, and must break this influence or disaster will result.

NUTS—Seen in clusters they denote happiness and success. To crack them is a sign of temporary disappointment.

OAK—To dream of a strong tree foretells a lifetime of steady growth, in which your business will steadily improve, your family life will prove well rooted in love and your friendships will prove as numerous as the leaves on the tree. If the tree appears stunted or withered, your future may be clouded.

OATS—To walk through a field of ripe oats indicates marriage with an ardent and sincere person. Oats in any form are a good sign for the traveler. They are a sign of financial improvement.

OCEAN—Happiness and satisfaction will follow a dream in which the ocean appears calm. If it is rough or stormy, beware of disturbing influences.

OFFICE—To dream of being forced from office indicates a loss of affection. It is also a sign of loss of property.

OLD MAN—To dream of being courted by an old man is a sign of financial success.

OLD WOMAN—To dream of courting one foretells success in worldly affairs.

OLIVES—To eat olives in a dream indicates a change of occupation, in which you will be associated with government officials. This new position will prove beneficial in every way. To gather olives denotes a peaceful home life, and contentment in marriage.

ONIONS—To slice or cut them in a dream is a sign of domestic quarrels. To eat them foretells the recovery of a treasured article.

OPERATION—To dream of an operation denotes a complete recovery from an illness.

OPPONENT—To dream of meeting with an opponent is a sign you will overcome some obstacle to your happiness. It indicates a prosperous future.

ORANGES—To see them foretells a trip to some sunny clime with a group of good friends.

ORCHARD—To gather fruit in an orchard foretells you will inherit money or property. If the fruit is green, it will be in the distant future.

ORGAN—To be near an organ and listen to its music is a sign of happiness, prosperity and a fortunate marriage.

OVEN—To dream of using an oven indicates success in the immediate future. If, however, you burn what you are baking, it is a sign of quarrels, temporary losses, and misunderstandings, caused by a jealous friend.

OVEREAT—To overeat in a dream is a sign of exaggerated conceit. To see another overeat indicates lasting happiness.

OWL—Seeing this bird in a dream denotes failure to your present hopes. To hear him hoot means poverty.

OYSTERS—To eat them in a dream is a sign you will need to cultivate patience, as all your plans will be slow to mature.

PACKAGE—To dream of carrying a package denotes a change in circumstances for you, and disappointment in love. To receive one is a sign of good fortune.

PAIN—To dream of being in pain is a sign of great benefits

coming to you unexpectedly. The future is favorable to expansion in business and any new undertaking will prosper.

PAL—To dream of a pal denotes true and lasting friendship.

PALACE—To live in a palace foretells a rise to a position of wealth and honor, and great happiness through your children.

PALM TREE—To see these graceful trees in a dream foretells a future rich in the material and spiritual things. It predicts the attainment of moderate wealth, through successful speculation, good health, and a long life.

PAPER—If you dream of paper that is white and evenly folded, it is a sign of happiness and the attainment of your wish through the affections of a friend. If the paper is soiled, blotted or wrinkled, it is a sign of troubles and anxiety that will prove costly to you.

PARK—To dream of walking in a park is a propitious dream, indicating true friendship, flourishing business, health and happiness. To walk with another is a sign of a speedy marriage.

PARROTS—To see numerous parrots in your dream indicates a journey to some foreign place, where you will marry. To see a bird of very bright feathers is the sign of a gay and talkative friend.

PARTRIDGE—A dream of ill omen.

PASTRY—To eat pastry in a dream denotes a wedding invitation soon. To dream of making pastry foretells your marriage to a person of means.

PATH—Walking in a well-defined path signifies an upturn in business and increased happiness. If the path appears rough and overgrown, it is a sign of disaster to your plans.

PAWNBROKER—To dream of visiting one denotes losses. If you seek an elective office, you will be unsuccessful.

PEACHES—To see them in a dream is favorable, indicating happiness in love, success in trade and a life rich in friendships.

PEACOCK—To dream of a peacock with feathers spread denotes security in your present position. To the young it is a sign they will marry for love and will attain social position.

PEARLS—A dream of happiness, signifying honors and wealth that will come to you as a result of your own industry and ability. To dream of wearing pearls indicates a marriage of wealth.

PEARS—To dream of this fruit is a sign you will soon be elevated above your present position in business. It is a sign of happiness in a marriage based on true love.

PEAS—To dream of growing them foretells good fortune in love; to eat them is a sign of social and financial gains.

PENNY—To receive a penny indicates a loss of money. If the penny is new and bright, the loss will prove temporary.

PERFUME—A favorable dream, indicating success in all present undertakings.

PHEASANTS—To see these birds denotes a gift of money or an inheritance. If they fight or fly away, you risk the loss of this money through the courts.

PICTURES—To dream of pictures denotes troubles through the actions of deceitful and false friends, who are working against you.

PIES—See *Pastry*.

PINE—A dream of lasting happiness, foretelling a life in which every effort meets with success.

PINEAPPLES—This dream is associated with marriage. If unmarried, you will soon meet your future mate. If married, you will receive a wedding invitation that results in increased happiness to you.

PISTOL—To dream of firing a pistol foretells a steady rise and growth for you in all your undertakings. Your marriage will be blessed by a child who will achieve prominence.

PLENTY—Dreaming of plenty is a sign your present plans will succeed and you will have prosperity throughout your life.

PLOWING—To dream of plowing is a sign of happiness and contentment in the marriage state. You will achieve independence through industry and perseverance.

PLUMS—Ripe plums foretell better things to come; green plums are an omen of unhappiness.

PLUNGE—To dream of plunging or jumping indicates there are obstacles in your path that must be overcome before you attain your desires. To those in love, it is a sign of parental objection to their marriage.

POCKETBOOK—To dream of finding a full, fat pocketbook foretells great happiness, a marriage that brings property to you.

POND—See *Lake*.

POVERTY—A dream of contrary, foretelling the gift of money, and a fortunate occurrence.

PRAYERS—To dream you are at prayers denotes health and great happiness. A kind and loving heart.

PREACH—To dream you are preaching indicates your rise to a position of honor, through a benevolent act.

PRESIDENT—To dream of meeting the President is a sign of coming honors. If he proves unfriendly, your plans will be altered.

PRISON—This dream of being confined in a prison is a sign of greater freedom to you, through which you will enjoy many of the good things of life. It is a dream foretelling that joy and gaiety will enter your life.

PROMOTION—To dream of being promoted is a favorable sign, indicating your ability to win out in anything you undertake.

QUAILS—To see them in a flock signifies trouble. Be slow to start a quarrel.

QUARRELS—This is a sign of impediments in the path to your

success. However, you will overcome these difficulties and succeed in your endeavors, if you have patience.

QUEEN—To dream of seeing a queen indicates an unexpected advancement, which will come as the result of your own efforts. To those in love, it is a sign of marriage to a person active in government affairs.

QUICKSAND—A forewarning of danger to you as the result of your own indiscretion, and hasty conduct.

QUIET—To dream of a deep quiet surrounding you denotes the end of troubles for you, and the beginning of a life of contentment.

RABBITS—To dream of chasing them indicates you are surrounded by enemies, but you will be able to avoid involvements by using care. If a rabbit runs toward you, look for an early visit of a dear friend.

RACE—To dream of participating in a race is a sign of swift and sure success in business matters; you will win the one you love, easily.

RAGE—To be in a rage at someone indicates that person to be the most loyal of friends.

RAIN—Heavy rain, accompanied by high winds, foretells troubles and generally upset conditions. A gentle rain is a sign of happiness and prosperity.

RAILROAD—To see one indicates a journey for you, or the arrival of a dear one.

RAINBOW—An indication of change, but for the better.

RATS—To dream of rats denotes trouble, which will be caused by a designing person, who appears to be your friend. In marriage, it is a sign that someone is trying to undermine your happiness and peace of mind.

RATTLESNAKE—To see one is the sign you have an enemy. If you tread upon one, it signifies you will be able to overcome your enemy. If you are bitten by one, beware of troubles.

RAVENS—These birds are a sign of trouble that will come to you through an injustice.

REAPING—To participate in a harvest, or see workers reaping is a most favorable dream. It denotes prosperity, success in matters of finance, and contentment and happiness in love.

RESTAURANT—To dream of being in a restaurant means that you will be exposed to the malice of enemies. If you are drinking, someone will seek to deceive you through flattery.

RICH—Dreaming you are rich indicates you will have a meager existence for many years. Independence will come to you very late in life.

RISE—To dream of rising signifies you will attain your ambitions.

RIVER—A muddy river denotes difficulties; a clear river, with calm surface, indicates great happiness and prosperity.

ROBBED—To dream you have been robbed is a bad dream, indicating losses.

ROBIN—An improvement in your luck.

ROSES—To dream of full, fragrant roses denotes happiness, success, and commercial prosperity. If the roses are wilted, it indicates troubles and reverses.

ROW—To dream of rowing foretells you will be offered a position of great responsibility, which, should you accept it, will bring you fame and fortune.

RUG—To dream of rugs denotes advancement to a position of wealth.

SAD—To dream you are sad signifies you will soon have cause for great joy. To dream you are in the company of others who are sad signifies you will soon rejoice over their good fortune.

SAGE—This herb denotes honor and advancement, the result of wisdom and carefulness.

SAILING—To be sailing on smooth waters denotes prosperity; rough waters denote misfortunes.

SAILOR—To dream you are a sailor denotes a journey to a distant place.

SAINTS—To dream of them denotes a life of peace.

SATAN—A dream foretelling deep troubles, the result of bad habits, and easy ways.

SCHOOL—To dream you are the head of a school denotes an unfavorable change in conditions for you.

SCYTHE—An indication of injury from enemies, and disappointment in love.

SEASHORE—To dream of bathing at a seashore foretells business successes.

SERVANTS—To dream of servants denotes an early association with persons of wealth and influence.

SHADOW—Dreaming of shadows is an indication of quarrels with a friend. It also signifies loss of money through lending.

SHEAVES—If you dream of gathering sheaves, it is a sign of wealth, acquired through your own enterprise.

SHEEP—To see them in numbers is a sign of happiness and prosperity; scattered, is a sign of hardship. To shear sheep foretells a marriage of wealth.

SHIPS—To see one indicates a journey; if the ship is in distress, the journey will be unsuccessful. To a married woman, it predicts the birth of a male child.

SHIPWRECK—A sign of misfortunes.

SHOES—To dream of being without shoes indicates a life of comfort and honor. New shoes signify a journey; if they hurt or pinch, the journey will be unsuccessful.

SHOOTING—To dream of shooting game is a sign of happiness, and promotion in business. To shoot a bird of prey signifies you will overcome your enemies.

SHOPPING—A sign of good trade, comfortable circumstances and domestic happiness.

SICK—To dream you are sick means a great temptation will soon confront you.

SILK—To see silk is an omen of good fortune; to wear it foretells great personal happiness.

SILVER—To dream you possess silver foretells poverty. If you have many silver coins, it denotes business profits.

SIN—To dream you have sinned denotes approaching troubles; to have resisted sin denotes a successful and happy life ahead.

SIREN—An indication of danger and worry at hand.

SLANDER—To dream you have been slandered means increased respect.

SMILE—To be greeted with smiles indicates good luck in many ways.

SNAILS—To dream of snails is a sign of unpleasantness, resulting from the actions of designing friends.

SNAKES—Snakes denote enemies seeking your ruin. To the lover, snakes denote rivals. To kill a snake in your dream shows your ability to outwit your enemies.

SNOW—To see snow on the ground in a dream indicates prosperity and happiness. To be in a snowstorm indicates there will be difficulties ahead, but they will be overcome.

SOAP—To dream of soap is an indication of troubles, which will be solved readily, if you apply yourself.

SOLDIERS—To dream of being a soldier foretells a series of changes.

SOUVENIR—To dream you are given a souvenir is a sign of a joyous surprise. To dream you are giving souvenirs denotes improved conditions, and an enlarged circle of friends.

SOWING—If you dream of sowing, it would be well to weigh the value of those around you, as someone that you know is not worthy.

SPADE—To dream of digging with a spade indicates there is something in your life you are trying to hide.

SPARROWS—To dream of seeing one sparrow foretells troubles, which will prove costly to you. A flock of sparrows denotes a journey.

SPIDER—To see one is a sign of extreme good luck.

SPINNING—If you dream of spinning, beware of new friends, as they will bring you only troubles and worries.

SPORTS—To dream of participating in sports, and winning, indicates misfortunes. To lose at sports is a sign of sure gain in the near future.

STABLE—To dream of one is a sign of happiness, through the visit of an old friend.

STAIN—To dream you are striving to remove a stain denotes a threat to your happiness.

STAR—Dreaming of stars means happiness. The brighter the star, the greater your happiness will be.

STEALING—The sign of a gift, which will bring you great happiness.

STEEL—Steel, in any form, is a sign that much strength will be needed to attain your ambitions.

STIRRING—This dream is an indication of temporary quarrels, and confusion. The faster you stir, the longer this condition will last.

STORE—To dream you are working in a store denotes comforts and moderate means.

STORM—This dream indicates troubles and losses in the future, but all will be overcome.

STREAM—See *River*.

STYLE—To dream of striving for style indicates a possible extravagance. Neatness in style denotes a warm and loving heart.

SUN—To dream of a clear bright sun is an indication of success in financial matters, and affairs of the heart. A rising sun foretells news. An overcast sun signifies trouble and changes.

SUPPER—See *Meal*.

SWAMP—To dream of being in a swamp denotes unhappiness and difficulties. If you struggle through the swamp, you will attain moderate comforts in your old age.

SWIMMING—For one to dream of swimming with his head above the water means that he will have success in whatever he undertakes; but, if he is swimming with his head under water, trouble is just ahead.

TARGET—If you dream that you are shooting at a target and make a good hit, you will have success in your undertaking. If, however, you dream that you miss the target, you will have difficulty and may be delayed in reaching the goal for which you are struggling. For one to dream that he is merely watching others shoot at a target means that he has a great many friends in whom he is interested. He is an inspiration to these friends.

TAXI—If you are hailing a cab and getting into it, you will soon go on a long journey during which you will experience many complications and disappointments. If you are driving the cab, you will soon have a position of importance through which you will meet a handsome and wealthy person of the opposite sex with whom you will be very happy.

TEA—To dream of drinking tea means that you will very soon have an experience which will possibly cause worry. But, if you take precautions, you will avoid this.

TEACHING—To dream that you are being taught means that you will soon be in a situation where you need advice and help. It may concern marriage or business problems. If you dream that you are teaching, a friend will be in this situation very soon and will need your instruction and help.

TEAR—A dream of tearing paper is a good sign. It means that all your worries and troubles will soon be over.

TEARS—To dream of crying means that there is great happiness ahead for you. Your troubles will soon be over and you and your friends will celebrate your great good fortune.

TELESCOPE—To dream of looking through a telescope means that you will very soon receive news from far away. It will have considerable influence upon your future.

TERROR—Fear or terror in a dream means that someone is trying to plot your downfall.

THEATER—To dream of attending a place of entertainment foretells great happiness for you. If you are hesitant in leaving the place, you will have a happy and long marriage. This is always a good sign.

THIMBLE—To dream of a thimble is a warning that you should not be too ambitious.

THIN—For one to dream that he is getting thin is a good sign. It means that he will have good fortune and will prosper in his undertaking.

THIRST—If you dream that you are thirsty and drink clear water, it means that you will experience good fortune. If the water you drink is muddy, you will have hard luck.

THORNS—Thorns in a dream mean that care and difficulties are ahead for you.

THREAD—If you dream of thread, be careful lest your friends involve you in some intrigue the results of which will be bad for you. Should the thread break, you may lose some money before long. If the thread is tangled, your affairs will also be tangled.

THUNDER—To dream of seeing lightning and hearing thunder near at hand means that you are soon to find yourself in a difficult situation. If the lightning and thunder are heard at a distance, you will be successful in overcoming your enemies and those who wish to do you harm.

THYME—A dream of thyme means that a lover will have success in his love. To all others it means prosperity.

TOADS—If a businessman dreams of a toad, it means that he has a low and mean competitor who is trying to destroy his business. For a lover to dream of a toad means that his beloved is undecided and inconstant and is open to flattery from others.

TOOTHACHE—To dream that you have a toothache means that you will soon experience great joy in some unexpected event. If you dream of cutting a new tooth, you will very soon move to a new home or be placed in a new position.

TRAIN—Should you dream that you are riding on a train, you will be tied down to one place, possibly because of marriage and your family. You will not be able to travel. If, however, you merely see a train or hear a train whistle, you will very soon make a change in your residence or possibly take a journey to a far place.

TREES—To see a tree in full bloom or full leaf in your dream means that you will have much prosperity and good fortune. To dream of climbing a tree means that you will have continued difficulty in reaching your goal.

TRIP—To dream of taking a trip indicates that you will soon make a change in your residence or business. If the dream trip is pleasant, your change will be for the good. If the trip is difficult, your change will not be good.

TROUT—A dream of trout in clear water means that you will have great prosperity in your business.

TURKEY—The turkey is a bird of great show. Thus, to dream of him means that you will experience instability in trade and a great front without much to back it up.

UNFAITHFUL—For one to dream that a friend or partner is unfaithful means that this friend or partner is most faithful and true. But to dream that you are unfaithful means that you will soon be put to the test and your faithfulness to some friend will soon be tried.

UNIVERSITY—To dream that you are in a university or attending one means that you will attain a place of prominence and respect. You will lead the scholarly.

VINEGAR—A dream of vinegar means that there will be many stinging and hard words in your life. Beware of antagonizing those about you unless you want an argument.

VIOLIN—If you dream of hearing violin music, you will soon be among friends who are enjoying dancing and other amusements. If, in your dream, you are dancing to violin music, you will soon have great prosperity and happiness and your love will be true and satisfying.

VOICE—To hear many voices in conversation means that you will soon take part in some joyous event.

VOLCANO—This is an evil dream. If you are scheming something to get the better of another, the scheme will blow up.

VULTURE—If, in your dream, you see a vulture the meaning is that someone is trying to worry you. If you are in love, some rival is trying to steal your lover.

WAGON—To dream that a wagon filled with provisions comes to your house means that you will be befriended by someone in time of need. If you dream of driving a wagon belonging to someone else, you will soon experience unhappiness. If the wagon is your own, you will be advanced in your position.

WALKING—If you dream that you are walking on a clean street or sidewalk, you will have happiness and good luck. If you are walking in dirt, your luck will be disappointing.

WALL—A wall is a symbol of a barrier. If you dream of a wall between you and a friend or lover, there are many barriers between you and that person. You will have to overcome them before you are successful. If you dream that you are walking on a wall, you will engage in a new enterprise. If you finally come down from the wall without falling, you will succeed in the enterprise.

WAREHOUSE—To dream of a warehouse is good. It means prosperity and happiness. For a businessman, it means success in his enterprises. For a lover, it means marriage to one with great wealth. For the farmer, it means good crops and a well filled silo.

WASH—To dream that you are taking a bath or washing yourself means that you are worried about matters which will soon be cleared up. If you dream that you are washing clothes for someone else, you will live a life of toil for others.

WATCH—If you dream of a watch, you will have much prosperity and wealth. Your business will succeed, and you will be happy in your marriage. But, if during the dream the watch stops, beware lest your luck change.

WATER—Clear water means happiness, prosperity, and good luck. Muddy water means unhappiness and ill luck.

WEALTH—Often a dream of wealth means that you will never have wealth.

WEEPING—To weep in a dream means that you will have much joy.

WHALE—To dream of a whale means that someone whom you are interested in will go on a sea voyage.

WHARF—To dream that you are standing on a wharf means that you will receive some good news from abroad very soon.

WHEAT—For one to dream that he sees a field full of ripe wheat means that he will have wealth and prosperity and a happy life. If a sailor dreams of a field of wheat, he will retire from the sea and live in wealth and be happy for the remainder of his life.

WHISKY—This means drunkenness and is a warning for you to avoid liquor.

WINDOW—If you dream that you are peering through a window, you have many worries about friends. But these worries are not justified. Your friends are true to you and will prove it in the end.

WINE—This is a dream of prosperity and happiness. As wine is the symbol of good health and hilarity, a dream of drinking wine means that you will be with friends and will be happy. Any trouble which you are experiencing now will soon pass and you will be happy.

WOLF—To dream of a wolf means that you have sly and unprincipled enemies who will do anything to cause you harm. Beware of trusting them.

WOUND—To dream that you have been wounded means that you will have prosperity and be happy in your love.

WREATH—If you dream that you are crowned with a wreath, you will have success and happiness and will rise to heights of fame and prominence. Your friends will give you proper recognition for the work you are doing. You will come into wealth and have the respect of your fellows.

WREN—To dream that you see wrens flying means that you will receive good news from afar.

WRITING—If you dream that you are writing, you should be careful what you write and to whom you write.

YOUNG—If you dream of young people, you will be happy.

ZEBRA—If you see a zebra in your dream, be on the alert, careful and observing.

ZEPHYRS—This is a dream of happiness and contentment.

VI

Your Fate in Magic Tables

For centuries Magic Tables have been used as a means of telling fortunes. All Magic Tables are in reality diagrams of which each important part has a meaning. We give here the fourteen Magic Tables which contain the most valuable information for people of our time. In some cases we have reproduced the Tables in exactly the form in which they have appeared through all the years. In other cases we have modernized the Tables so as to make them of special value to present-day users. By consulting these Tables you will find the answers to a great many questions about which you have undoubtedly been wondering.

THE SECRETS OF THE SUN

To learn the secrets of the sun and their meaning for you, hold a long pencil in the right hand with the point hanging downward over the diagram. Now close your eyes and have someone turn the picture around three times on the table beneath the pencil point, finally placing the book so that the tip of the pencil is pointing approximately at the center of the diagram. With your eyes still closed trace in the air above the diagram a small square, then wave the pencil back and forth three times and set the point down on the diagram. The ray of the sun which the pencil touches *or the one which is nearest to the tip of the pencil* contains the number giving the key to your forecast. Consult the Key below for the message of this number. Do not consult this powerful charm more often than every 42 days.

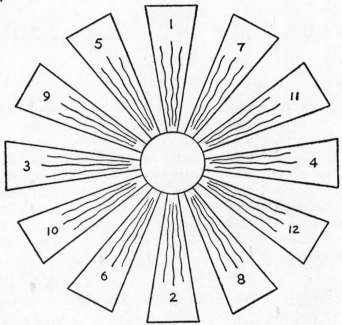

Key to the Secrets of the Sun

1—You will receive an unexpected sum of money.
2—You will find a valuable article and will receive a fine reward for its return.
3—You will realize a gain in connection with business.
4—Loss of money or jewels.
5—A sum of money from a distant relative.
6—You will receive a gift of jewelry.

7—You will suffer loss by theft, but that which is stolen will come back to you.

8—A bonus or a raise in pay.

9—Considerable wealth coming mysteriously.

10—A loss through an investment.

11—A large sum of money coming in a letter.

12—Alter your plans or you will suffer financial setbacks.

THE LUCKY CLOVERS

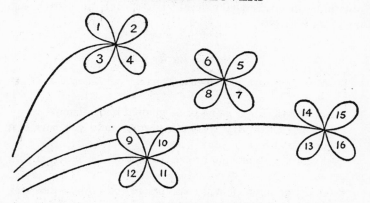

To learn what Lady Luck holds in store for you, place this diagram before you on a table. Now take a long pencil and hold it by the eraser end in your right hand, letting the point hang downward over the four lucky clovers. Now close your eyes and wave the point of the pencil around in a circle over the picture, repeating aloud:

> Lucky clovers, answer me.
> Tell me what my luck will be.

Now with eyes still closed set the point of the pencil down on the picture and open your eyes. The clover leaf which the pencil point is touching contains the number which gives the key to your forecast. Consult the following table for that message. For example, if the pencil should touch the leaf numbered 5, then the message below which is numbered 5 is intended for you. If the pencil does not touch one of the leaves the first time, you should repeat the entire process again. You may try a third time, if you get no results the second time. If, however, after three tries you have failed to touch any of the lucky clover leaves, it is a sign that the time for questioning is not ripe and you should wait a day before consulting the clovers again. If you do succeed in obtaining an answer, you should not consult the clovers again for at least 37 days.

Key to the Lucky Clovers

1—You will have a change of fortune within the next ten days.

2—Your wish is not going to be granted immediately.

3—Do not expect any change in fortune until you have first made a change in your plans.

4—Everything is favorable to an immediate realization of your wish.

5—A disappointment will come before you achieve the thing you desire.

6—Do not lay too great store in the plans you are now making.

7—There is an unexpected good break coming to you.

8—Beware of a situation which will seem to be very favorable to you.

9—A misunderstanding or quarrel is standing between you and your wish.

10—A surprise is in store for you which will change everything you have planned.

11—Do not give up hope if you meet with temporary disappointments.

12—All is not well; do not expect an immediate streak of good luck.

13—If you have any plans, pursue them with vigor. The time is ripe.

14—There is trouble ahead unless you are very discreet in regard to your wish.

15—Do not try to rush things. Everything is going to turn out for the best.

16—The best of luck is with you or will appear soon.

THE TREE OF LIFE

To consult the mystic diagram of the Tree of Life, first take a long pencil in your right hand by the eraser end, letting the point hang downward over the picture. Now close your eyes and have someone turn the picture around three times on the table beneath the point of the pencil, finally placing the book so that the tip of the pencil points approximately toward the center of the Tree. With your eyes still closed you now wave the pencil back and forth slowly twice and then set the point down on the diagram. If it touches a leaf, you trace down to the twig on which the leaf grows and then trace the twig to its branch. The number of the branch will indicate the number of the message for you in the Key below. If you do not succeed in touching a leaf the first time, you may repeat the process twice more. If you do not succeed on the third try, it is a sign that the time is not ripe for consulting the mystic Tree and you should wait a day before questioning it again. If you do receive an answer, do not consult the Tree again for 37 days.

Key to the Tree of Life

1—You will avoid a threatened illness.
2—Take care of yourself while you are traveling.
3—There will be an improvement in your health in the near future.
4—A journey as the result of a quarrel.
5—Take care lest you go too fast a pace.
6—A minor illness in your immediate family.
7—You will have good health if you guard against excesses.
8—Watch your diet carefully for the next 13 days.
9—A friend who is sick is going to recover soon.
10—There is going to be disillusionment because of overindulgences.
11—A long and healthy life.

THE SIXTEEN PYRAMIDS

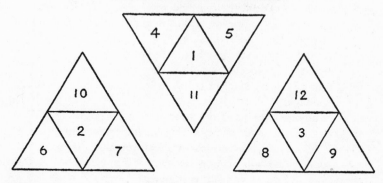

Since the days of the ancient Egyptians, the pyramid has been a symbol of secret knowledge. To share in the wisdom typified by these sixteen pyramids take a long pencil and hold it in the right hand with the tip pointing downward over the diagram. Close your eyes and have someone rotate the diagram beneath the point of the pencil five times. Now with your eyes still closed, set the pencil down on the diagram. The pyramid which the pencil touches will contain the number giving the key to your forecast. Consult the key below for the message of this number. If you do not touch one of the pyramids the first time, you may try twice more, repeating the entire process each time. If you fail after three tries, do not consult the pyramids again for twenty-four hours. If you do obtain an answer, do not try to obtain information from the pyramids again for the space of 37 days.

Key to the Sixteen Pyramids

1—Trust in your hunch; it is good.
2—Beware the advice of a well meaning friend.
3—If you are planning some action, delay it for a few days.

4—Seek advice before you proceed with your project.

5—You should think over your recent actions carefully.

6—Do not let yourself be tempted into taking a hasty step.

7—You must apologize or make amends for an unfriendly word you have uttered.

8—An unpleasant duty lies ahead; do not shirk it.

9—Beware of unexpected benefits. They may bring sorrow.

10—From an enemy you are going to learn something to your advantage.

11—Let no one sway you from your present purpose.

12—You are in danger of neglecting an important duty.

13—Abandon your present schemes lest you meet failure.

14—A dark cloud will bring great joy.

15—Fear will beset you soon; conquer it.

16—You are going to offend a friend if you continue with present plans.

THE WHEEL OF FORTUNE

If you wish to find out what Fortune's ancient wheel holds in store for you, take a pencil in the right hand by the eraser end and hold it point downward over the diagram. Close your eyes and have somebody turn the diagram around three times beneath the point of the pencil. Now with eyes still closed, set the point of the pencil down on the diagram. The numbered circle which is nearest to the pencil point contains the number of the message for you. Consult the Key which appears below. If the pencil point is near a spoke of the wheel, the number which appears in the circle at the end of that spoke is your number.

Key to the Wheel of Fortune

1—An unexpected sum of money coming in connection with business.

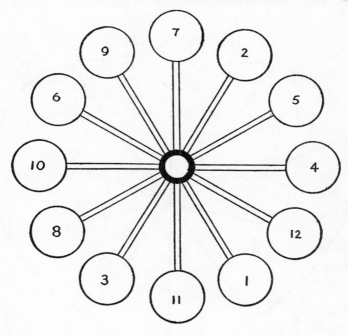

2—A loss which will result in a great blessing.

3—Beware of requests for a loan coming from an acquaintance.

4—Small risk, small gain; great risk, great loss.

5—Now is the time to venture boldly, for the return will be worth the effort.

6—An investment is going to prove worthless.

7—You will have a change of fortune.

8—You are overlooking an opportunity to make money which lies near at hand.

9—Do not take the advice of friends in your financial plans.

10—A loss of money in a crowded place.

11—Financial aid is coming as a surprise in an hour of great need.

12—You will receive something of benefit from a distant place.

THE MAGIC HEART

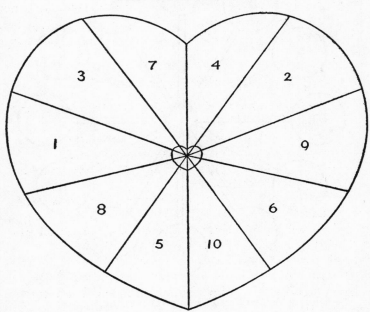

To consult this old charm regarding matters of love and romance, take a long pencil by the eraser end and hold it point downward over the diagram. Now close your eyes and have someone turn the diagram around three times beneath the point of the pencil. When that is done, repeat, while your eyes are still closed, the old charm:

> Oh, magic spell, lend me your art
> To know the secrets of the Heart.

Now set the point of the pencil down on the diagram and open your eyes. The section of the Heart which the pencil touches contains the number of the message for you, which lies in the

Key below. If you do not touch any part of the Heart with the pencil, you may try twice more, repeating the entire process each time. If you fail on the third time, however, the time is not ripe and you must not consult the charm for 24 hours. If you do obtain an answer you should not consult the Heart again for 90 days.

Key to the Magic Heart

1—A romance with a person of dark complexion and merry disposition is in store.

2—You are going to quarrel with your sweetheart.

3—Expect a surprise in connection with a love affair.

4—Be on your guard against becoming jealous without cause.

5—A wedding in the near future.

6—Beware lest you reveal a confidence and ruin another's romance.

7—You will meet someone soon whose love is true and lasting.

8—A passing infatuation.

9—A love affair with one who is not worthy.

10—You will meet a stranger at a party; it will be love at first sight.

THE SACRED EAGLE

Of special interest to travelers, this occult symbol may be consulted by taking a long pencil by the eraser end and holding it in the right hand so that the point hangs downward over the diagram. Now close your eyes and have someone turn the diagram around twice beneath the point of the pencil. Then repeat aloud:

> Messengers of storm and night,
> Help me read the future right.

Now set the pencil point down on the diagram. If you do not touch any numbered area on the Eagle—either the feathers or the body or head, you may try twice more, repeating the entire process each time. If you fail on the third try, do not question the symbol again for 27 hours. If you do touch one of the numbered areas, study the Key below for the message represented by that number.

Key to the Sacred Eagle

1—You are about to make a long journey.

2—Beware of a friendly stranger you will meet while traveling.

3—You will acquire a friend during a trip.

4—You are going to make a journey across water.

5—If you are planning a trip, postpone your plans a day.

6—In the midst of a journey, you will be called to return.

7—In the next three days do not travel in the company of more than two friends.

8—Unexpected news, leading to a hasty trip.

9—Look for a tall, dark person of the opposite sex when you travel again.

10—A friend is going away for a long time.

11—You will meet good luck at a gathering place for travelers.

12—A surprise awaits you on your next pleasure trip.

13—A business errand which will turn out unexpectedly.

14—Delays in connection with travel.

15—A honeymoon trip.

THE TABLETS OF THOTH

6	11
1	4
8	10

9	5
7	3
12	2

To learn the wisdom of these ancient Tablets, which some believe have been handed down from the days of the sages in old Egypt, take a long pencil by the eraser end and hold it point downward over the diagram. Now close your eyes and have someone turn the diagram around four times beneath the point of the pencil. Set the point of the pencil down on the page and open your eyes. If you do not touch any part of the tablets the first time, you may try twice again, repeating the entire process each time. If you fail on the third try, do not consult the tablets again for 24 hours. If the pencil does touch any part of the tablets, that section will contain the number of your message. Consult the Key below for the meaning of the number, and do not consult the tablets again for 25 days.

Key to the Tablets of Thoth

1—A child will be a great help to you.
2—Seek to improve yourself; a great opportunity is coming.

3—Guard against carelessness lest it be your undoing.

4—Trials are coming; be steadfast and all will end well.

5—Do not let baseless gossip sway you in your purpose.

6—You are going to be sorely tempted to do evil.

7—Heed the words of your friends.

8—A stranger is coming who will bring aid in time of trouble.

9—Be careful of what you say.

10—Beware of unexpected proposals.

11—The best of life still lies ahead for you.

12—Guard against worry. It alone can defeat you.

THE SECRETS OF THE STARS

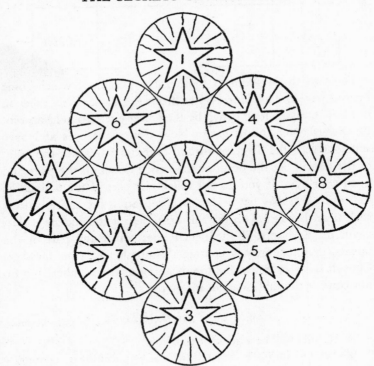

To obtain an answer from this unique charm, hold a pencil in the left hand with the point hanging downward over the diagram close your eyes and have someone who is a friend move the diagram back and forth three times beneath the point of the pencil. Now, with eyes still closed, rotate the point of the pencil slowly three times as though you were tracing a small circle in the air. Now set the pencil down on the diagram. If it touches a star or the halo surrounding the star, the number will indicate which message in the Key below is meant for you. If you do not succeed the first time in obtaining a message, do not consult the charm for two days. If you do obtain an answer, do not consult the charm for the space of five months or your hopes will never be realized.

1—With your help and advice another is going to achieve great success.
2—Within 30 days someone in your family will receive an honor.
3—Beware lest a willful act of yours offend a friend.
4—A change in your daily life will bring unexpected financial gain.
5—You will achieve local fame after you have reached the age of 55.
6—Something of great benefit to you is now being done without your knowledge.
7—The hour of your greatest opportunity approaches.
8—A chance which you believed you missed is going to return.
9—A lucky star will be over you for about fifteen days.

THE BIRD OF PARADISE

This charm from the ancient East contains advice and guidance regarding marriage problems. To consult it hold a long pencil point downward over the diagram. Now close your eyes

and have some unwed person turn the diagram around three times in either direction. Then set the point of the pencil down on the diagram. The feather which it touches in the bird's tail will contain the number of your message. See the Key below. If you do not succeed the first time, you may try again, repeating the entire process. If you fail a second time do not attempt to obtain further answer, but put the charm aside for the space of a week. If you do obtain an answer, you should not consult it again for 45 days. If you should do so sooner, the answer will be false.

Key to the Bird of Paradise

1—You will be happily wed for twoscore years or more.
2—Guard your marriage lest a shrew should your happiness undo.
3—A friend is going to prove a traitor in a love affair of yours.

4—Faithlessness is going to test your power to forgive.

5—A newcomer in the family circle.

6—A marital ship is going aground on the rocks of jealousy.

7—Hold fast to your marriage vows whatever betide.

8—A third party is going to menace your home.

9—An erring helpmate will return.

10—Honor is going to crown your marriage soon.

11—You are going to live long with your partner.

12—When things look darkest, happiness will suddenly return to your home.

THE CHARMED CIRCLE

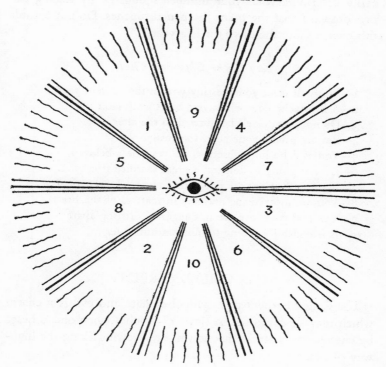

Advice for those not yet married is contained in this mystic circle in which the eye represents the spirit of eternal wisdom.

To consult the charm take a long pencil in your right hand and hold it over the diagram with the point hanging downward. Now close your eyes and have some person who is also not married turn the diagram about to the left twice. Now set the point of the pencil down on the diagram. Whatever ray of the Charmed Circle it touches, that will be the number of the message for you which lies in the Key below. Since the rays are considered to extend outward from the center into indefinite space, no matter where your pencil touches the page you can easily determine what your number should be by tracing the rays outward past the point the pencil touches. Do not consult this charm more than five times a year.

Key to the Charmed Circle

1—You will meet your destiny within the present year.
2—A heartache now will save a heartbreak later on.
3—Do not let yourself be hurried to the altar.
4—Beware giving your heart too easily.
5—You will be long absent from your best beloved.
6—Love is going to demand a great sacrifice from you.
7—If your affections are not at first returned, be patient.
8—You are too retiring and shy in matters of the heart.
9—You and your love are in danger of drifting apart.
10—A friendship is going to blossom into love.

THE COILED SERPENT

The Coiled Serpent as a symbol of hate and evil is a charm which may be consulted in times of trouble when one is beset by enemies or is afraid that storms are brewing along the highway of life.

To find a message with this old spell, take a long pencil in the left hand and hold it so the point hangs downward over the diagram. Close your eyes and have someone turn the diagram

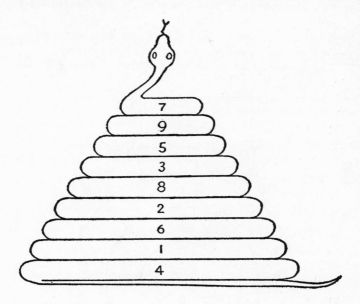

about three times beneath the point of the pencil. Now set the point down on the diagram. The coil which the point touches contains the number of the message for you. Study the Key below for the words of the message. If you do not obtain an answer the first time, do not try to consult the charm again for 36 hours. If you do obtain an answer, you should not consult it again for at least 90 days.

Key to the Coiled Serpent

1—An enemy will be defeated by his own mischief-making.
2—You are going to win a faithful supporter in a former foe.

3—You are going to have cause to hate, but you must not yield to this passion.

4—A chance to defeat a rival is coming very soon.

5—In a forthcoming quarrel you must be the first to try to make peace.

6—If you give way now, you will have your own way later.

7—Despite good intentions you are making an enemy.

8—You are not going to be happy until you forgive a great wrong.

9—Your hour of triumph will come within the month.

THE MYSTIC CIRCLES

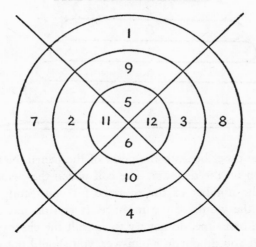

This is one of the most powerful and mysterious of the occult divining charms. Dealing as it does with the World Beyond and its connection with us among the Living, it should never be consulted more than once every full moon.

To consult this charm, take a long pencil and hold it in your left hand, with the point hanging downward over the diagram.

Now close your eyes and have someone revolve the diagram beneath the pencil point three complete turns to the left. At the same time you must repeat aloud the following:

Mystic orbs of earth and sky
Hear my plea and give reply.

Now set the point of the pencil down on the diagram. The numbered section of the charm which it touches will contain the message destined for you. Consult the Key below for its meaning. If you do not succeed in touching any part of the diagram on the first try, *you should not attempt to consult the charm again for another 24 hours*. To do so, it is said, will anger the Spirits of the Circles and will bring you very bad luck.

Key to the Mystic Circles

1—A message is coming to you from the Beyond.
2—Within two nights you will receive an important warning in a dream.
3—A loved one is trying to guide you in some undertaking.
4—For the next fortnight you will have no luck with charms or psychic spells.
5—You should follow the strong hunch which will come within 72 hours.
6—A fortune teller is awaiting you with an important message.
7—Do not carry a mirror for the next 10 hours.
8—If you hear a voice in the night, do not be afraid, but listen carefully.
9—On your next journey you will meet with an occult adventure.
10—A message awaits you at home.
11—Have faith in your loved ones.
12—The next time you feel sad or melancholy, keep some fresh flowers near you.

THE DIAMOND

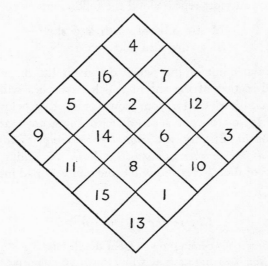

The diamond, with its cold, brilliant fire, has long been associated with the mind as a symbol of intellectual powers, and so it is only natural that the Diamond Charm should be used to answer questions relating to matters of the mind, thought and the making of decisions. To consult this charm for guidance in daily affairs, hold a pencil by the eraser end in the left hand so that the point hangs downward over the diagram. Close your eyes and have someone turn the diagram around three times beneath the pencil point. Now set the pencil down on the page. The section of the diamond which the pencil point touches contains the number of the message for you. Consult the Key which appears below. If you fail on the first try, you may consult the charm only once more, repeating the entire process as described above. If you fail the second time, you should not attempt to obtain a prediction for at least 29 hours. In case you do receive an answer from the charm, do not consult it again for the space of 33 days, lest you disturb its magical powers.

Key to the Diamond

1—A sudden inspiration will be the turning point of your life.

2—You have an unsuspected gift for mathematical studies.

3—If you wish to forge ahead, you must discipline your will power.

4—You are letting a feeling of inferiority handicap you unnecessarily.

5—You should broaden your taste in reading.

6—Do not underestimate the importance of your original ideas.

7—Keep your opinions more to yourself or you may arouse antagonisms.

8—When a friend comes asking advice, do not hesitate to be completely frank.

9—Study your thoughts closely, for you are unconsciously trying to deceive yourself.

10—You have great powers of concentration, but they need to be developed.

11—You will have to make a decision soon; do not let others sway you.

12—Now is the time to begin studying the subject you have always wanted to learn.

13—You are spending too much time in idle conversations.

14—Remember: a brilliant mind, like a gem, needs polishing.

15—You are letting trivial details block your path to true mental power.

16—Do not be afraid of the company of the wise and learned; you will learn much from them.

THE CROSS AND THE CIRCLE

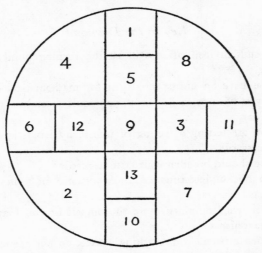

To consult this charm relating to the home and family, hold a long pencil in the left hand, with the point hanging down over the diagram. Close your eyes and have someone turn the diagram around twice beneath the point of the pencil. Now set the point of the pencil down on the diagram. The numbered section which it touches contains the number of your message, which appears in the Key below. If you do not touch any part of the diagram, you may try twice more, repeating the entire process each time. If you do not succeed the third time, the time is not ripe and you should not consult the charm again for two days. If you do obtain an answer, do not seek another until 27 days have passed.

Key to the Cross and Circle

1—A visit of a distant relative is approaching.
2—An addition to the family—by marriage or birth.

3—There will be a family quarrel unless you act hastily to prevent it.

4—A wedding.

5—Among the in-laws there is going to appear a trouble maker.

6—Guard against jealousy, which may harm the family circle.

7—A divorce within the year among your acquaintances.

8—Anxiety in the family caused by a slight illness.

9—A sudden exchange of messages among distant kin.

10—A proposal long awaited is going to take place.

11—Gossip is threatening the family's peace.

12—A confirmed bachelor is suddenly going to turn shy suitor.

13—A youth is going to bring great honor to the family.

THE CIRCLE AND THE STAR

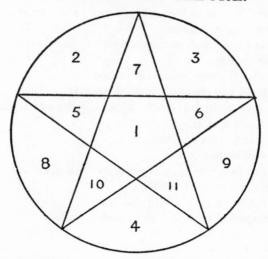

This gentle old charm is of particular interest to parents and all those who have children among their immediate relatives. As can be seen, it is related to the preceding charm of the Circle and Cross, which deals with the family and home.

To consult this spell, hold a long pencil in the right hand, with the point hanging downward over the diagram. Close your eyes and have a friend turn the diagram around four times beneath the point of the pencil. Now set the point down. Whatever section of the diagram it touches, there you will find the number of your message, which is contained in the following Key. If you do not succeed the first time, you may try once more, repeating the entire process as before. But if you fail a second time, do not consult the diagram again for three days or it will not be favorable to the children in your home. If you do obtain an answer, do not again consult the charm for 34 days.

Key to the Circle and the Star

1—A child yet to be born will grow up to be a lover of beauty, with artistic leanings.

2—Guard the health of children under three carefully for the next six days.

3—Within the year twins will be born.

4—A child will show unexpected promise.

5—Beware a fretful child; it is a judgment against the mother's temper.

6—Recovery from an illness.

7—A visit by the stork.

8—A child's questioning is going to reveal a hidden truth.

9—Greatly improved health.

10—A birth to a couple long childless.

11—Unexpected news of a child born to friends.

THE COIN AND CARDS

Forecasts regarding money and prosperity may be made with a pack of cards and a coin as follows:

From a pack of cards the Questioner removes the Ace of

Clubs, the King of Diamonds, the Jack of Hearts and the Jack
of Spades, the five of clubs and the two of diamonds. These six
cards are laid face down upon the table and mixed up so that
the Questioner no longer can tell which is which. They are then
arranged, face down, in the pattern illustrated below, allowing
about an inch of space between the cards.

The Questioner now takes either a penny or a dime, shakes
the coin in his hand and lets it fall from a height of about a foot
upon the cards. The card upon which the coin falls *or nearest
which the coin falls* is now turned face up, after the Questioner
has first been careful to note whether the coin has landed heads
or tails up. The Key given below will reveal the significance of
the toss.

For example, if the coin falls tails up on or near the Ace of
Clubs, the Questioner will find his forecast listed below as *Ace
of Clubs* (*Tails*).

If the coin should fall equally near two or more cards, it is a
sign that the time is not ripe for questioning and the Questioner
should not seek an answer for the space of 18 hours. If he does

obtain an answer, he should not again consult the coin and cards for 37 days.

Key to Coin and Cards

ACE OF CLUBS

(Heads)—Beware severe losses through reckless use of your money.

(Tails)—A gift of considerable value from a stranger.

KING OF DIAMONDS

(Heads)—Enter into no financial transactions for the next two days.

(Tails)—A raise or bonus is coming unexpectedly.

JACK OF SPADES

(Heads)—Loss because of theft or carelessness on your part.

(Tails)—A quarrel over a trifling sum of money.

JACK OF HEARTS

(Heads)—An unexpected sum of money which will bring responsibility.

(Tails)—Be on guard against some well-meant advice regarding your finances.

FIVE OF CLUBS

(Heads)—Another will intrust you with a valuable property.

(Tails)—It would be wise to save up now for a rainy day that is coming.

TWO OF DIAMONDS

(Heads)—A talent you have overlooked is going to prove very profitable to you.

(Tails)—Within a month or two you are going to have good luck in regard to money.

THE WISHING RING

In order to consult the Wishing Ring, the Questioner must first take a small piece of cardboard and cut out a pointer in the shape illustrated above. A hole is made in the center of the pointer (as is indicated) and a pin is thrust through this. The point of the pin is now placed in the center of the Wishing Ring where the lines all meet. Holding the pin upright with

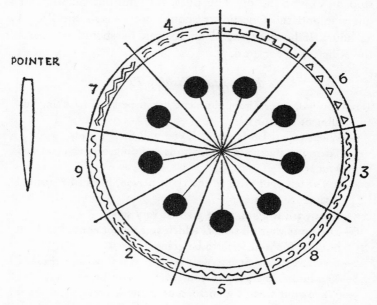

POINTER

a finger of the right hand, the Questioner is now able to spin the pointer about with the left hand. The hole in the pointer should be large enough to allow the pointer to spin freely on the pin.

When seeking advice on his wish, the Questioner does as has been directed above and then closes his eyes. He now repeats aloud the following:

> Spirits of the Wishing Ring
> Tell me what the Fates will bring.

Still keeping his eyes tight shut, he now flicks the end of the pointer with his finger so that it spins around on the pin. When it has come to a stop, he opens his eyes. The section of the Ring to which the pointer is turned contains the number of the message, which is found in the key below. If the pointer should stop on one of the dividing lines, the time for questioning is not ripe and the Questioner should not consult the Ring for 24 hours. If he does obtain an answer, he should not consult the Ring again for 49 days.

Key to the Wishing Ring

1—You will meet disappointment if you persist in seeking fulfillment of your wish.

2—When your wish is granted, you will find it a joy.

3—There is an acquaintance who is standing between you and your wish.

4—If you tell your wish to the right person, it will be granted instantly.

5—Your wish is going to be granted very soon.

6—You must wait till factors which you cannot control make it possible for your wish to be granted.

7—You have a long time to wait yet before your wish is realized.

8—The future in regard to your wish is very uncertain.

9—When your wish is granted, a dear one is going to be made very sad.

THE FOUR KINGS

(And Their Advice to Women)

An old method by which a girl may obtain advice on matters of the heart involves the use of dice and a pack of new cards. The Questioner first shuffles the cards thoroughly and then lays the pack face up on the table. Then she begins to remove the cards one at a time from the pack until the first King appears. This she places face up on the table before her; then she continues to remove more cards from the pack until the second

King appears. This is placed to the right of the first King. The process continues and when the third King appears, it is placed below the first King. The fourth King is placed below the

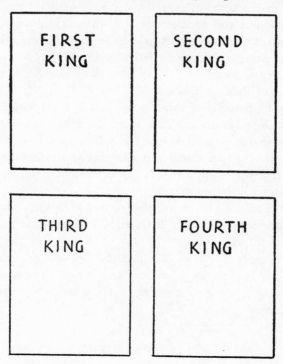

second King, so that the four Kings form an oblong as is illustrated above. As soon as the fourth King is turned up, the rest of the cards are discarded. The Questioner now takes a pair of dice, shakes them and tosses them on the table. The one which turns up with the higher number of spots is selected, the other discarded. If a pair is rolled, the Questioner tosses the dice once more, choosing the one with the higher number. If a pair is rolled on the second toss, too, it is a sign that the time for questioning is not ripe and the Questioner must wait a day before trying to obtain an answer again.

However, once one of the dice has been successfully selected by this method, the Questioner takes it in her hand, blows gently upon it and then drops it from a height of about 18 inches upon the four cards which lie face up on the table. The King upon which the die falls contains the key to the Questioner's reply. Below are listed the three meanings possible with each of the four cards.

It is to be noted that only the two-, four- and six-spot on the die have any significance. Thus if the die falls upon one of the Kings with the one-, three- or five-spot uppermost, it has no meaning for the Questioner and she must again blow on the die and drop it upon the cards. If the die rolls off the cards, she must also try once more.

There is no limit to the number of times the Questioner may repeat the process until the two-, four- or six-spot has turned up on one of the four Kings.

After a reply has been obtained the Questioner should not consult the four Kings again for the space of sixty days.

Following is a list of meanings for the individual cards and spot combinations:

Key to the Four Kings

KING OF CLUBS

Two-Spot—If the two-spot falls uppermost on the King of Clubs it is a sign that the Questioner may be tempted to consider a jolly, friendly young man as a prospective husband but that it will be very unwise to marry him.

Four-Spot—If the four-spot falls uppermost on the King of Clubs it is a sign that the Questioner is in danger of putting trust in the promises of a fickle lover.

Six-Spot—If the six-spot falls uppermost on the King of

Clubs it is a sign that the Questioner will meet a shy, dark suitor who is much worthier than he seems.

KING OF DIAMONDS

Two-Spot—If you look deep enough into two dark eyes you will see sorrow ahead for both of you.

Four-Spot—An attentive suitor will offer wealth and comfort, but he can offer little real love and devotion.

Six-Spot—You are going to be faced with a difficult choice between two men.

KING OF HEARTS

Two-Spot—A love affair with a dark man which will bring tears.

Four-Spot—A charming companion is going to prove to have an uncontrollable temper.

Six-Spot—A gay, reckless affair of the heart is going to sweep you off your feet soon and very unexpectedly.

KING OF SPADES

Two-Spot—Beware the flattery of a tall blond stranger.

Four-Spot—An old friend is going to propose marriage unexpectedly.

Six-Spot—You must resist a suggested elopement or hasty marriage, otherwise you will be unhappy the rest of your life.

THE FOUR QUEENS

(*And Their Advice to Men*)

A man may obtain advice on matters of the heart with the dice and a pack of cards in much the same manner that is described in *The Four Kings*. However, the man shuffles the pack and then removes the four Queens (instead of the Kings) in the order in which they appear, as has been noted. The Queens are laid out on the table in the same order as the woman sets out the four Kings.

The man then selects one of the dice as has been described in the preceding section and, after blowing upon it, drops it from a height of about 18 inches on the four cards beneath. The Queen upon which the die falls contains the key to the Questioner's reply.

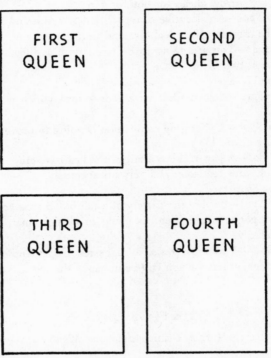

Below are listed the three meanings possible with each of the four cards. It should be noted that when the Questioner is a man, only the one-, three- and five-spot on the die have any significance. Thus if the die falls on one of the Queens with the two-, four- or six-spot uppermost, it has no meaning for the Questioner and he must again blow on the die and drop it upon the cards.

If the die rolls off the cards, he must also try again, and there is no limit to the number of times he may try until either a one-, three- or five-spot has turned up. After a reply has been obtained, the Questioner should not consult the four Queens again for the space of sixty days.

Following is a list of meanings for the individual cards and spot combinations:

Key to the Four Queens

QUEEN OF CLUBS

One-Spot—Beware a brunette flatterer.

Three-Spot—An older woman, loyal and true, will help you in time of trouble.

Five-Spot—An affectionate young girl will offer you her heart; do not break it.

QUEEN OF DIAMONDS

One-Spot—You will meet a blonde who will offer her love in vain.

Three-Spot—You will become infatuated with a dangerous, dark stranger.

Five-Spot—A love affair that will bring you good fortune is near.

QUEEN OF HEARTS

One-Spot—An older woman is plotting mischief against you.

Three-Spot—You are going to be spurned by a girl with auburn hair.

Five-Spot—There is a jealous woman with whom you can never be completely happy.

QUEEN OF SPADES

One-Spot—A fair-haired woman will bring joy to your life.

Three-Spot—There is disappointment awaiting you regarding a brunette younger than you.

Five-Spot—Be on your guard; a husband hunter may get her clutches on you.

VII

Other Ways to Tell
Your Future

TEA LEAVES

THE PRACTICE of looking into a teacup to discover, from the shapes left by the tea leaves, what is to happen in the future is very old. Many, many thousands of years ago people believed that ringing bells would drive away evil. This led to the belief that one could find inside a bell tokens of the future. So men began to study the inside of bells and to predict the future from what they found there.

Then the ancient Chinese realized that a teacup was much like a bell inverted. So they began to study the inside of teacups from which the tea had been drunk and in which a few leaves were left in interesting patterns and forms. Now, after many centuries, the reading of tea leaves in order to predict the future has spread throughout the world and there is hardly a place where this ancient practice is not known.

The method of reading tea leaves is very simple and a little practice will make one proficient. First, use a teacup that is plain on the inside. Cups with designs painted or grooved on the inner surface are of no value since they force the leaves to take unnatural shapes. Second, the cup must have a handle since the handle plays a part in the reading.

After the one whose fortune is to be read has drunk the tea, all but a few drops, he must take hold of the handle and rotate the cup three times. The cup should always be held in the left hand, and the cup rotated to the left. Then, turn the cup upside down on a saucer, allowing the leaves to fall into place in the cup. Permit the cup to drain thoroughly. After this, turn the cup over and begin reading at the left side of the handle and proceed around the cup.

There will be leaves on the side of the cup and all the way down the cup to the bottom. Those forms which appear higher up on the cup indicate what is to happen in the near future, while those further down in the cup indicate more distant happenings.

When you examine the cup, you will notice that the leaves have taken certain more or less well defined shapes. Each shape, each pattern made by the leaves has a meaning for the life of the one who has drunk the tea.

It is not necessary that someone else do the reading. The one who has drunk the tea may read his own fortune.

While drinking the tea, the drinker should make a wish. Then, keep this wish in mind while drinking the tea and while preparing the leaves for reading. Then, just as the cup is turned straight up, look quickly into it and the first pattern or form which you see will contain the answer.

After many years, readers have developed a definite set of meanings for the forms discovered in the cup. The following is such a list:

ABBEY—No need for worry.

ACE—of Clubs, a letter; of Diamonds, a present; of Spades, a large building; of Hearts, happiness.

ACORN—Success.

AIRSHIP—Journey that you don't expect; it may mean disappointment.

ANCHOR—Your worry will soon pass.

ANGEL—Good tidings.

ANKLE—Not stable, ambitious but do not understand.

ANT—Industry. Will work hard and succeed.

APPLES—Success in business.

APRON—You will soon make a new friend.

ARAB—Some friend is not true.

ARCH—You will take a long journey to foreign parts.

ARROW—You will receive a letter bearing bad news.

ATTIRE—You will change your life for the better.

AXE—Trouble will be surmounted.

BABY—There is a series of troublesome happenings ahead.

BAGPIPES—There will be trouble in home and business.

BALL—Someone whom you know is connected with sports.

BALLOON—Your trouble will not last for long.

BARREL—You are going to a party.

BASIN—There is trouble in your home, perhaps serious.

BASKET—An empty basket means money worries. A full basket means a present.

BAT—You will take a journey and find disappointment.

BATH—You will be disappointed.

BAYONET—Someone will make a sharp remark about you.

BEANS—Your poverty will cause much trouble.

BEAR—Your delays will cause trouble.

BEEHIVE—Your business will prosper.

BEETLE—You are involved in some difficult undertaking.

BELL—You will receive some unexpected news. Many bells indicate a wedding.

BELLOWS—Your plans will meet with reverses.

BIRD—You will receive some good news very soon.

BIRD CAGE—You will have happiness in love.

BIRD NEST—Your home will be happy.

BISHOP—Good fortune is on its way.

Boat—You will receive a visit from a friend.

Book—An open book means success while a closed book means delay.

Boot—You will have success in your venture.

Bottle—Be careful or you will be sick.

Bouquet—You are happily in love.

Bow—Beware of scandal.

Box—If open, trouble connected with love will soon pass. If closed, something that is lost will be found.

Bracelet—Marriage is impending.

Branch—If with leaves, there will be a birth. If without leaves, there is disappointment ahead.

Bread—Do not waste your substance or you will be in trouble.

Bridge—You will have an offer that will bring success.

Broom—Some friend of yours is false.

Buckle—Disappointment lies ahead.

Bugle—To succeed you must work hard.

Building—You are to move to another place.

Buoy—Do not give up hope. All will turn out well.

Butterfly—Frivolity and innocent pleasure.

Cab—You will have a disappointment.

Cabbage—A business associate is jealous of you.

Cage—You will have an offer of marriage.

Car—Good fortune is in store for you.

Cap—Be careful. There may be trouble ahead.

Cart—Your business venture will be most successful.

Cat—You will have a quarrel and your business should be watched against crafty enemies.

Cattle—Prosperity will be yours.

Chain—There is an engagement or wedding ahead.

Chair—An unexpected guest will arrive.

Cherries—Your love affair will be happy.

Chessmen—Beware of difficulties which are ahead.

CHIMNEY—Proceed in what you are about to do with great caution.

CHURCH—There is some ceremony ahead.

CIGAR—You will make a new friend.

CIRCLE—You will achieve your end and bring your work to perfection.

CLAW—You have a hidden enemy who is after you.

CLOCK—You are thinking of the future.

CLOUDS—Trouble lies ahead. If there are dots around the clouds, the trouble will be over money.

CLOVER—Prosperity and happiness will be yours.

COAT—You will be parted from a friend.

COFFEE-POT—A slight illness is in the future.

COFFIN—Watch out for trouble.

COIN—Some obligations in business will meet with success. You will be able to pay your debts.

COLLAR—Your success will depend upon others. You will have to depend upon others for your happiness.

COMB—You have a false friend.

COMET—Something unexpected will happen.

COMPASS—There is travel and new work ahead for you.

CORKSCREW—Don't be so curious. It will bring trouble.

CRAB—You have an enemy.

CROSS—You will be asked to make some sacrifice for those you love, and you will make it gladly.

CROSSED KEYS—You will have success in business and love.

CROWN—Your wish will come true.

CRUTCHES—You will receive help from a friend.

CUP—Success will follow your efforts.

CURTAIN—Your secret is in good hands and will be kept.

DAGGER—Danger lies ahead. Beware of being too hasty.

DAISY—You will be happy in your love.

DANCER—There is disappointment ahead.

DEER—There is some dispute in which you are involved.

DESK—You will receive a letter containing news.

DEVIL—Evil influences are around you.

DOG—You have a true friend.

DISH—There is a quarrel at home.

DONKEY—You will succeed through patience.

DOVE—Everything will turn out well.

DRAGON—There is a sudden change in store for you.

DRUM—You will take a trip concerning new work.

DUCK—That speculation will bring you luck.

DUSTPAN—You will receive strange news about the home life of a friend.

EAGLE—There will be a change for the better.

EAR—You will receive some unexpected news.

EAR-RINGS—Look out for a misunderstanding which will cause you some trouble.

EGG-CUP—The danger which you are in is passing.

EGGS—You will receive news of a birth.

ELEPHANT—You can trust your friend.

ENGINE—Some hasty news is on the way.

EYE—You will overcome the difficulty which besets you.

EYEGLASSES—You will receive some startling news.

FACES—You will attend a party with many friends present.

FAN—There is a flirtation in progress.

FEET—You must make an important decision.

FENCE—Success is close at hand.

FENDER—Beware of the person whom you dislike or fear.

FINGER—Pay strict attention to that to which the finger points.

FIREPLACE—This has to do with your home.

FLAG—There is danger ahead, perhaps a quarrel.

FLY—You will be hounded with petty annoyances.

FONT—You will receive news of a birth.

FORK—You have a false friend.

FOUNTAIN—Much success is in store for you.

FOX—Someone in whom you trust is your enemy.

FROG—Through a change or a move you will have success.

FRUIT—Prosperity is in store for you.

GALLOWS—Be careful, social failure is ahead.

GARDEN ROLLER—Difficulties lie in the immediate future.

GATE—You may proceed with confidence as all will be well.

GEESE—You will have unexpected visitors and will enjoy their visit very much.

GIRAFFE—Think twice before you act. You may experience trouble if you act thoughtlessly.

GOAT—You will receive news from a sailor.

GRAPES—Much happiness is in store for you.

GRASSHOPPER—You will receive news from a friend.

GREYHOUND—Good fortune is in store for you.

GUITAR—You will be happy in love.

GUN—There is a quarrel in the future.

HAMMER—Your wish will come true if you are persistent and do not give up too easily.

HAND—This denotes friendship and success in your undertaking.

HANDCUFFS—Trouble lies ahead unless you are careful.

HARE—An absent friend will return.

HARP—You will be happy in love.

HAT—You will enter a new occupation and be successful.

HAWK—You have a friend who is jealous of you.

HAYRICK—Don't act before you think carefully.

HEAD—There will be new opportunities for you.

HEART—You have a friend in whom you can trust.

HEAVENLY BODIES—These are symbols of good luck and success.

HEN—There is happiness at home.

HIVE—Success will follow your business venture.

HOE—You will have to work hard for success.

HORSESHOE—There is much good luck in store for you.

INITIALS—Letters of the alphabet are initials of friends.

JUG—This symbol means that good health is ahead.

KEY—You may expect good fortune. All doors will be opened to you.

KNIFE—Watch out for a broken friendship. Perhaps a lover will leave you.

LADDER—You will experience a promotion.

LINES—These indicate journeys. Wavy lines indicate uncertainty and possibly disappointment.

NUMBERS—These signs indicate time, number of days before an event will happen.

OAR—There is a small worry in your life.

OWL—Beware of scandal. It will involve you.

PALM TREE—You will be happy in love and marriage.

PILLAR—Your friends will help you in times of trouble.

PIPE—This symbol represents thoughts.

RAILWAY—You will go on a long journey.

RING—There is an engagement or marriage in your future.

ROCKS—You will experience some slight difficulty.

SAW—Strangers will interfere with you and cause trouble.

SCISSORS—You will quarrel with your husband or wife.

SHIP—Your journey will be successful.

SICKLE—You will have disappointment because of one you love.

SNAKE—You have an enemy.

SPADE—You must work hard for success.

SQUARE—This means comfort and peace.

STAR—*See* Heavenly bodies.

STEEPLE—You are in for a slight delay of good luck.

SWORD—There is some minor unhappiness just ahead.

TENT—You will take a journey.

TOWER—You will be offered a good opportunity. Do not let it slip.

TREES—There will be a change for the better.

TRIANGLE—This means mystery and hides things.

VIOLIN—You will be in a large group of gay people.

WALKING-STICK—A visitor is coming to see you.

WHEEL—If it is complete you will have good fortune. If it is broken, you will experience disappointment.

WORMS—Look out for scandal. It is near at hand.

WREATH—Happiness lies just ahead, perhaps a wedding.

Reading the tea leaves requires imagination and the ability to relate symbols into a pattern. Each form or outline has a meaning, but this meaning is also related to other meanings. For example, the symbol of a marriage may be discovered in the cup. Nearby may also be letters and numbers. These have to do with the marriage and may be the initials of the one you are to marry and the days which will elapse before the marriage. A good reader attempts to tie up the meanings of many symbols into a connected and meaningful fortune.

Practice will make you more proficient in this work and you can become "the life of the party."

HANDWRITING

Handwriting has long been studied to discover the hidden character of the writer. Even though the person whose character you are studying may attempt to hide the facts of his character or even to disguise his writing, it is impossible to succeed since some little fact will be so revealing that the character is discovered.

To analyze someone's handwriting, take anything the person

has written and apply a few simple rules to it. For example, let us take a word from a letter written by a friend. First, draw a straight line under the word and parallel to the top of the page on which it is written. If the word follows the line closely, the friend is level-headed, even-tempered, and average. If, however, the word runs up and away from the line, your friend has great strength of character and is able to succeed in many things better than the average man or woman. But, if the word runs down and across the line, or even dips into the line, your friend is one who often misses good chances for success. He is never quite there when the opportunity comes.

Now, let us analyze this word more closely to uncover your friend's hidden characteristics:

1. *Downstrokes thicker than upstrokes.* He worries over little things.

2. *Capital separated from word.* He is easygoing and generous. Capital joined to word: he is practical. If all letters are separated from each other: he takes life easy and has some artistic interests, possibly some talent.

3. *Loops of letters are pointed.* He is practical and possibly broad-minded.

4. *Letters rounded.* He is pleasant and affectionate.

5. *Each letter properly formed.* He is very tidy and works and lives by method.

6. *Loops joining letters come down to line.* He has sound judgment. If the loops are at the top of the letter, he lacks judgment.

7. *Letters slope backhand.* He has much artistic feeling.

8. *Many flourishes.* He is kind, one who makes you feel at home almost at once.

9. *Bottom of word blacker than top.* He is scientifically inclined and has talent for inventing things.

10. *Line under signature*. He thinks well of himself and may be conceited.

Not only does a word show one's character, but the general appearance of a whole page of writing is very revealing. If, for example, the writing is big and wide, if the letters are large and cover a great deal of space, the writer is a generous person with a kind heart. If, however, the letters are small and crowded together, the writer is narrow-minded and stingy. If his writing is average, he is just an average individual, generous at times and close at others.

Also, the general slope of the letters is revealing. If the letters slope to the left, the writer is artistic and loves beautiful things. If the letters are straight up and down, he is very determined, knows what he wants, and will not be easily turned from a course of action. But, if the letters slope to the right, the writer is one who enjoys being unhappy, looking on the gloomy side of life.

Again, the capitals in a page of writing show much about the character of the writer. If the writer prints rather than writes his capitals, he is highly critical, will pick people and things to pieces, and is often very cruel in this. If the writer uses old forms of capitals, those which have gone out of fashion, he is possibly old-fashioned, living largely in the past. He may also be critical of modern youth, holding that the good old days and the ways people acted then were good and should be returned to.

If the person crosses his "t" with a line running over the whole word, he has strong likes and dislikes. If he crosses the "t" low down near the word, he is not kind. If the cross is a curl rather than a straight line, he is secretive.

Now, as we look at the page of writing as a whole, getting

its general impression, we can discover some character traits which are most revealing as regards the writer:

ACTIVITY—Regular handwriting with medium to moderately thick letters standing upright. The words just tend to rise above the line.

AMBITION—The words follow a line of steady rise from the line.

AMIABILITY—The letters are rounded softly and there are many flowing curves and slopes.

CALMNESS—Each word is clear and uniform and the letters are open and rounded. The line is straight and even. The capitals are small and well formed.

CANDOR—The writing is open and rounded and the lines are straight. Letters are plain and frank with no curves and frills.

CAUTIOUS—The writing is precise and every detail is cared for. Punctuation is carefully attended to. Each letter is standing straight, but is close to the next one.

CONSCIENTIOUS—All details are carefully attended to. Punctuation is clear and accurate.

COURAGE—The line shows rising slope clear across the page.

ECONOMY—Each letter is formed carefully and, at times, there is a marked economy in making each letter. Only enough stroke is used. The writing is angular with no flowing words or spreading letters. Letters are short to avoid waste of paper and ink.

ENTHUSIASM—There is dash and fire in the writing and the line rises from the page and flows along.

ENERGY—Letters are angular rather than curved; the writing ascends from the line. The letter "t" is barred low down and the stroke moves downward.

GENEROSITY—The final marks of each word are turned up and

rounded. The final "y" is given a broad curve. Capitals are large and generous.

HUMILITY—Small writing free from any flourish or deep lines.

IMAGINATION—Capitals are large and original in form. Often the handwriting is hard to read and the letters are irregular and slightly angular.

INDOLENCE—The letters are rounded and consist of many curves which have no real connection with the word. Often letters are only half formed and toward the end of a word the writer drops into a half scrawl. The writer gives the impression that he is too lazy to form his letters accurately or to finish a word.

INTUITION—Letters in the signature are disjointed and in general letters are angular.

JUDGMENT—Here words may be joined in a complete sequence. There are many flourishes and curls which have no meaning but stand out on the page.

MELANCHOLY—The words run down below the line. Letters are rounded and often they look lazy. Words may not be finished and letters may not be closed.

OBSTINACY—Clear, readable writing which is not at all pretty to look at. The letters seem to be formed by much labor. Words tend to curve upward and return to the original level.

ORIGINALITY—This is best seen in capitals. These are formed in strange ways and never conform to the standard.

PERSEVERANCE—The writing is angular and runs in straight and rigid lines across the page. The capitals are conventional and the small letters are well formed and well marked.

PRIDE—Letters are large and the capitals emphasize this largeness. Look for a flourish under the signature.

SELFISHNESS—The writing is angular and compressed.

SENSITIVITY—Letters slope and curve. There is no stiffness to the letters and no angularity.

SENSUOUSNESS—The lines of the signature are heavy. This is relieved at times by less heavy lines.

TACT—The letter lines are fine and tend to stand upright. The loops are usually small and the lines are straight.

VANITY—Writing is ornate and full of flourishes which have no meaning. The capitals are over-elaborate.

VERSATILITY—The letters are of different shapes and sizes and tend to become spear-shaped in the loops. The letters are well rounded and each is completely formed.

WILL—The "t" is crossed with a heavy bar and there may be a short bar beneath the signature. The downstrokes are firm and there is a slight angularity to each letter.

DICE

To make predictions from dice you should use three dice and should shake them well in a cup or other container. As the dice are tossed out they will fall with certain meaningful faces up. After each throw, add the numbers on each face together, and the total will have meaning for you.

Should the same number come up twice in succession, you will receive news from abroad. If the dice fall off the table on which they are being thrown, you will be involved in an argument which may come to blows if you are not careful. If one of the dice lands on top of another and remains there, it means that you will receive a present.

When you have added the figures on the three faces of the dice, you will have a meaningful number. Here is the meaning:

THREE—You will receive a pleasant surprise.

FOUR—Something is about to happen which you have been hoping for.

FIVE—You will soon meet a stranger who will prove to be a good friend in time.

SIX—You are going to experience a loss of property.

SEVEN—You will be involved in scandal.

EIGHT—You will be reproached for something you have not done.

NINE—There is a wedding in which you will be involved in some capacity. It may be your own.

TEN—This indicates that there is a christening just ahead at which something very important to you will happen.

ELEVEN—Perhaps you will receive a large inheritance.

TWELVE—Very soon you will receive a letter.

THIRTEEN—This means that sighs are in store for you.

FOURTEEN—You will soon have a new admirer. He may fall in love with you.

FIFTEEN—You must be careful or you will be drawn into a plot or some trouble for which you are not responsible.

SIXTEEN—You will take a pleasant journey.

SEVENTEEN—Very soon you will either be on water or you will have some dealings with those who are on the water. The result will be to your advantage.

EIGHTEEN—Almost immediately there will be something very good happening to you. You will rise in life, make good profit, or have something which you want very much.

Another way of using dice to predict the future is to draw a circle on the table with chalk and count only the dice which remain within the circle after the throw. The circle represents the individual's life and any number which falls out of it does not apply.

Many people have used only two dice and found the results very interesting. When only two dice are used, the thrower should shake them well in a box or cup and then toss them onto the table or the floor. Each time the dice fall, the thrower should make note of the numbers facing up and write them down. Three throws should be made in this manner.

Then the thrower adds the two numbers shown in each throw. For example, should he throw three and two the first time, he would have a number 5; six and two the second time, he would have the number 8; and one and three the third time, he would have the number 4.

After each throw, the thrower should make use of a set of dominoes and select all the dominoes from the set which add up to his number. In the first case mentioned above, the thrower would select 5—blank, 4—1, and 3—2. With these dominoes before him, the thrower should then refer to the table in the next section, that dealing with dominoes, to discover what the dominoes mean. The meaning of each domino should be written down and the entire significance of the various meanings studied for a general meaning.

DOMINOES

To predict from dominoes, the individual should turn all the dominoes of a set face down on the table and shuffle them well.

Then draw one domino from the pack, lay it aside, and shuffle again. Then draw another domino and shuffle. And then draw a third domino.

Now, turn your three dominoes over, face up, and study their meaning. The meaning of each domino is:

BLANK-BLANK—You will experience disappointment.
ONE-BLANK—Beware! Your enemy is after you.
TWO-BLANK—You are worrying about something.
THREE-BLANK—You are in for some trouble. If single, it is concerned with love; if married, it is concerned with money.

FOUR-BLANK—You will experience a slight disappointment, possibly a postponement of something you are interested in.

FIVE-BLANK—Think carefully before you answer what you are asked. A hasty answer may bring trouble.

SIX-BLANK—You are involved in a scandal.

ONE-ONE—You will soon meet a stranger.

ONE-TWO—An old friend will soon come to see you.

ONE-THREE—The answer to the question you are asking is decidedly "No." You know the question.

ONE-FOUR—Be careful. You are in danger of trouble over money.

ONE-FIVE—You will soon have a new friend.

ONE-SIX—There is a wedding in the near future. You will be involved in it.

TWO-TWO—Your wish will come true. You know what it is.

TWO-THREE—You will soon make a change. It may involve your work or just a journey for a short time. In either case the outcome will be good.

TWO-FOUR—You are trusting someone who is not to be trusted.

TWO-FIVE—You have a friend in whom you can trust. He is true to you.

TWO-SIX—You will have good fortune in all you undertake. This is an excellent sign.

THREE-THREE—You will soon receive a sum of money.

THREE-FOUR—If you are single, this means that you will have a happy love affair. If you are married, you will have happiness in your home life.

THREE-FIVE—Someone who is in a position above you will give you help in time of need.

THREE-SIX—You are soon to receive a present.

FOUR-FOUR—You are to have some relationship with a big building.

FOUR-FIVE—There is a surprise in store for you.

Four-Six—You will be involved in a quarrel.

Five-Five—You will make a change which will bring you much good fortune.

Five-Six—A loved friend will be the source of some gaiety and happiness.

Six-Six—There is great happiness in store for you.

After you have drawn three dominoes and found what each one means, average the meanings and you will be able to draw general conclusions which will be the real message for you. Never draw more than three dominoes and never draw more than once in a moon. If you do, the other drawings will be meaningless as far as you are concerned.

FIRE

There are fortunes in the fire.

Modern progress has given us many comforts and conveniences, but where it has taken away the fireplace with its glowing embers and bewitching tongues of flame, it has robbed us of a source of much fun.

For the fire has meaning and messages which we can discover if we are patient and understanding.

If you and your friends want to know the messages from the fire, wait until the flames have died down and left only a bed of glowing coals. Then spread a handful of kitchen salt over the coals and seat yourselves before the fire and wait until the crackling and the flames have died down.

Do not talk to each other while you are watching. Just sit quietly and wait. A word or a discordant sound may destroy the mood and break the magic charm of the fire.

After you have studied the fire for a short time certain shapes and figures should take form more or less clearly. These have meaning for you and your future. Here are some of the figures and their meaning:

A BUILDING: This building may have steps in front of it or may be faced with pillars. If there are steps, count them. Steps indicate some good event to happen. They mean that your wish will be granted. When the coals are bright red, your wish will come true quickly. If they are dark and lifeless, there will be a delay.

If the house has pillars, there is a love affair, either yours or that of a friend. If the pillars are clear and easily distinguished, either a former lover will return or you will have a new love very shortly.

The building always means happiness. But should the building collapse while you are looking at it you can expect a change in the work you are doing or a move to some other place.

TREES: You may see either a well defined tree or merely a few branches of trees. In either case there is here a promise of great business success or better than average happiness in love.

FRUIT: If the fruit you see, whatever kind of fruit it is, is in a basket or lies around as if already picked from the tree, you will have worry due to a love affair. But, if the fruit is still hanging from the tree, the trouble will soon pass and will be followed by the happiness indicated by the tree, for fruit cannot always remain on the tree. In time it falls and leaves only the tree of happiness.

A FACE: Faces are the most common figures found in the fire. Often you will recognize a face as that of someone you know. However, if you cannot recognize it, be sure that very soon you will meet someone whose face resembles in a striking manner that seen in the fire.

Study the face carefully to see whether or not it is bright or dull. A bright face means happiness resulting from some act of the person whom the face resembles or someone closely related to this person. If, however, the face is dull, you can expect the person whose face it resembles to be the center of some trouble, either directly or indirectly.

Perhaps you see more than a face. At times you will see a whole figure. If this is the case, the happiness or trouble will be delayed, depending upon the dullness or brightness of the figure.

ANIMALS: Animals are common figures in fire. If you see a dog in the fire, you have a true friend. If the figure is that of a cat, you can expect great happiness either in your business or your job. If the figure is a horse, you will soon take a journey. The horse may be running. If so, the journey is to take place very soon. If you see a cow, you may be sure that someone is thinking about you right now. If the animal you see is either an elephant, tiger, lion, or some other animal of the forest, you will receive some news from a great distance.

A SHIP: This means that either you or a friend will take a journey very soon.

A WINDMILL: Always a windmill means change, for its turning arms are constantly changing position. If the windmill is bright the change will be for the good; if it is dull, the change will be for ill.

FLOWERS: Often figures of flowers will appear in the coals. These are not good signs, for they betoken disappointment. If, however, a flower is seen near any symbol that indicates a journey, it simply strengthens the meaning of the journey and emphasizes the parting that must take place at the beginning of a journey.

HAND: If the hand is reaching out, you can know that someone dear to you needs your help.

FLYING EMBERS: Often, while you and your friends are studying the fire, it will crack or a piece of wood will explode and throw cinders out on the hearth. They have a meaning for the one in whose direction they fall. Examine the cinder carefully to see what shape it resembles. If the shape is that of a cradle, look for a new birth or possibly an offer of marriage. If the shape resembles a purse, there is money coming to you. If you can see in it the shape of a bird, know that a letter is on the way to you. These are all good signs. But if the shape is that of a dagger, watch out for a quarrel.

MOLES

Moleosophy, the study of moles and their meaning, is based upon the ancient art of Astrology.

As we have seen in the section dealing with Astrology, many ancient people, and many living today, have held that each part of the body is dominated by a sign of the Zodiac. The particular sign influences this section of the body so that it determines its fate and future.

The signs of the Zodiac and the parts of the body which they dominate are:

Aries . .	the head and face
Taurus . .	the neck and throat
Gemini . .	the arms and shoulders
Cancer . .	the chest and stomach
Leo . .	the heart and back
Virgo . .	the abdomen
Libra . .	the lumbar regions
Scorpio .	the groin
Pisces .	the feet and toes
Capricorn .	the knees
Aquarius .	the legs and ankles
Sagittarius .	the legs and thighs

If a mole appears in any of these areas of the body, it is supposed to indicate that this part and its Zodiacal Sign are dominant in the life of the person in question. Therefore, since very early times it has been the custom to study the body, discover the location of each mole, and make predictions about the character and the future of the person having the moles.

Moles, as we must remember, are birthmarks, coming with the birth of the person in question. Thus, they are not to be tampered with except under the care of a competent physician. To attempt to remove one without this advice and aid may mean serious trouble and even death.

Further, it has been found that moles may change their size during the lifetime of the person having them. This indicates that the dominance of the particular part of the body is either increasing or decreasing. Then they may change color. When the mole is on the body of a man, a change of color means a change of fortune. To become lighter means good luck, but to become darker means trouble and great disappointment. If the color of a mole on the body of a woman changes, no significance is to be attached to the fact.

If a mole is raised, like a wart, it is a good sign, whatever its color.

The meaning of moles is:

ARM: If a mole is found on the right arm, it means that the person will have trouble in his early life but this will clear up and his later years will be full of happiness and contentment. Should the mole be near the elbow, this prophecy is far more certain.

If the mole is under the right arm, the person will have much difficulty and the odds against him will always be great. But, if the mole is under the left arm, it means that the person will have to work hard, but will succeed and have wealth and position.

BROW: If a mole is found on the left brow, it means that the person is careless with his money and is in danger of becoming a spendthrift. Further, the person is headstrong, has a stubborn disposition, and, if he dissipates, he is in danger of developing brain trouble. Thus, he must live a normal, quiet life or he will have great trouble.

If the mole is on the right brow, it means that the person has marked talent and can go far. Therefore, he should begin all important business ventures or life projects in either April, July, or August.

CHEEK: Should there be a mole on the right cheek, it is a sign of success in life. If there is a mole on the left cheek in addition, this success will come only after much hard work and struggle against odds. If the mole is only on the left cheek, the sign is not good. Success will not come.

CHIN: A person with a mole on his chin is highly gifted with artistic ability in addition to much common sense. He can make the best of opportunities so that good fortune will follow him and increase throughout life.

EYEBROW: To have a mole over either eyebrow is an excellent sign. These people will have an early and very happy marriage. But they must guard against being struck by lightning.

FOREHEAD: A mole in the middle of the forehead means that the person is dominated by Mars and must be on guard constantly lest he show tendencies toward cruelty and evil temper.

HAND: A mole on the right hand or right wrist means that the person will be successful in his business. If the mole is on the left hand or wrist, the person has a decided artistic disposition.

JAW: If the mole is on the left side of the jaw, it means that the person is inclined to be critical. A mole on the right side of the jaw indicates that the person may face danger either from fire or water.

KNEE: If the mole is on the right knee, the person will have a happy marriage. If it is on the left knee, he has a bad temper.

LEG: One who has a mole on the left leg is lazy and will try to dodge work. But if the mole is on the right leg, he is full of energy and will persevere until he succeeds.

LIP: A mole on the lower lip indicates that the person is quiet and studious and lives a very peaceful life. As he grows older his fortune will improve.

NECK: A mole on the front of the neck means that the person has an artistic temperament. If it is anywhere else on the neck, it means that he will be highly successful and may come into unexpected riches.

NOSE: If one has a mole on the right side of his nose, he will be a great traveler or will be keenly interested in traveling. Thus, he should avoid occupations which tie him to one place or to a desk in an office. He will succeed best in a job that keeps him on his feet. An out-of-doors job will be much better for him.

If the mole is on the left side of the nose, the person may be untrustworthy and changeable. However, he will be fortunate and successful. He should be careful lest he fall and injure himself.

If an individual has two moles close together he will have two serious love affairs and may be married twice in his lifetime.

When two moles exactly balance each other, such as moles on both knees, both cheeks, or the like, the meaning is that the person is a dual nature. One nature is constantly fighting the other. In almost every case the person will be under the influence of the dual signs of Pisces or Gemini.

LUCKY CHARMS

Belief in charms, mascots, amulets and the like is as old as man himself. As far back as we know people are found who wrote strange words, made peculiar marks, or carried some item on their person to ward off evil or bring good luck.

This belief is widespread among us today. Everywhere people carry a lucky coin, a rabbit's foot, or some token for luck. In some quarters certain objects are constructed to ward off evil or to invite good fortune.

The right charm to use has been studied by a great many people and long lists of such items come to us from the gypsies, the Indians, and others. Some of these are:

ABRACADABRA: This is an ancient word which early people wrote on parchment or burned into bark and carried on their person, usually fastened around the neck. Its chief function was to protect the wearer from evil spirits and the "evil eye." Usually the word is written in the following manner—

ABRACADABRA
BRACADABR
RACADAB
ACADA
CAD
A

So written, it spells the word across the line or down the left side and up the right side.

ACORN: For a long time people have been known to carry a dried acorn, believing that it would give them youth. Also, many believe that it will cause a lover to return and repent of leaving his beloved.

ANCHOR: The anchor is regarded, especially by people who

live along the seashore or make their living on the sea, as a bringer of safety, hope, and good luck.

ANGLES: A right angle, like the letter "L," is the harbinger of learning and deep understanding for those who are scholarly.

ARROW-HEADS: The arrow-head is a protection against evil, especially the "evil eye." It is usually worn about the neck, and one that is found is better than one which the wearer makes himself.

AXE: An axe-head, carved from an attractive piece of stone, is believed to be a charm against evil. Usually it is worn about the neck either on a string or chain.

BADGER TOOTH: Since the times when playing cards were invented, players have worn a badger tooth in order to have luck at the game.

BAMBOO AND SERPENT: From ancient times comes this complicated symbol. Usually it consists of a circle around the edges of which are inscribed numerous triangles, one following another around the circle. Across the circle lies a bamboo stick of seven sections crossed by a serpent. This charm is supposed to bring skill in learning and is worn by students.

The circle represents eternity, a never-ending thing. The triangles, having three sides, represent the Trinity. The bamboo stick has seven knots to represent the seven stages of wisdom through which the scholar must pass to attain perfect knowledge. And the serpent has always been a symbol of wisdom and knowledge. Added together, all these bring luck and success to the student who wears the charm.

BANGLES: When one accepts bangles from another and wears them, he becomes the slave of the giver. Lovers give bangles to their beloved and acceptance signifies that the beloved will always remain the willing slave of the lover.

BEADS: Coral beads are worn by children as protection from the "evil eye" or from disease.

BEES: A great deal of jewelry consists of the figure of a bee or of several bees worked in with precious stones or shaped from precious metals. When worn, this charm brings great success in business. The wearer will be energetic, will persevere, and will be successful in any enterprise in which buying or selling is involved.

BELLS: That the ringing of bells will frighten away evil spirits is an ancient belief. In some places church bells are tolled when evil approaches. Out of this belief came the custom of wearing small bells or replicas of bells in order to ward off evil and trouble.

BULL: The bull is a symbol of strength, power, and determination. Thus, to wear a replica of a bull, especially his head, will bring these qualities to the wearer. He too will be powerful, strong, and determined.

CATS: Black cats are not, as has often been believed, symbols of evil. Rather, they bring good luck. However, they must be treated kindly. It was believed in ancient times that black cats were companions of witches. If treated badly, they would bring the curse of the witch upon those so treating them. Therefore, people like to have a black cat about. If he is treated well, he will bring good luck and fortune to his owner.

CAUL: This is the covering found on the head and face of some children at birth and is considered a most lucky charm. It is supposed to bring good fortune to the child born with it and also to be a source of luck to anyone possessing it. In ancient times midwives used to sell the caul at a high price. It is especially valuable as a protection against drowning.

CLOVER: The four-leaf clover has long been considered a source of much luck. According to tradition, one leaf of the clover brings fame, another wealth, a third a faithful lover, and the fourth good health. All these being good, the clover is a symbol of luck and good fortune.

COAL: If found, coal is a symbol of good fortune. But it means nothing if bought in the normal way. It is said that if a dark man carrying a piece of coal is the first person to cross the threshold after 12 midnight on New Year's Eve, the house will have good luck during the whole new year.

CORNUCOPIA: To wear a replica of a cornucopia, a curved horn out of which are flowing fruits and flowers, will bring happiness and prosperity and wealth.

DOLPHIN: This is a mythological fish-like being whose replica is worn by those wishing for success in music, literature, or painting. Its influence on these arts is said to be great.

EVIL EYE: Belief in the "evil eye" is very old. It is held that some evil eye is constantly watching every individual to discover ways of bringing harm and trouble to him. To protect oneself from this danger, pieces of polished stone or metal on which is etched an "evil eye" are worn. One eye is said to frighten away the other and protect the person.

EYE: The symbol of the eye is derived from the symbol of the sun. As the sun is the sign of intelligence, the symbol of God, it is believed to possess great power to bring fortune and prosperity. The early form of this symbol was a circle with a spot in the center. Later this became the eye and is believed to carry the same influence and power as the sun. Thus, a wearer of such a symbol will have good luck and great wisdom since he is under the protection of the sun or the all-seeing eye of God.

FISH: Because of its great fertility, the fish is a sign of wealth and prosperity. Thus, many people wear little carvings of fish as a means of insuring wealth and good luck. The ancient Hebrews, along with other peoples, adopted the fish as a religious symbol and it has come down to the present in various religious rites.

HAND: The figure of the hand is a symbol of the good qualities of hospitality, generosity, strength, and goodness. Usually the hand is that of Fatima, the daughter of the prophet Mohammet, and the wearer of the symbol is supposed to be endowed with the qualities represented by the hand.

HEART: Early people believed that the heart of man would be weighed at death and its weight would determine whether or not the owner was admitted into heaven. Later it became the symbol of love. Now lovers give a symbol or small replica of the heart as a pledge of love and fidelity. To wear it means that the wearer accepts the pledge of love in all sincerity.

HORSESHOE: This is the most universal good luck charm known. It is used everywhere and is always suspended with the horns up to keep luck from spilling out.

KEY: A key unlocks a door. Thus, the key is the symbol of ability to unlock the doors to those things which people want. A symbol of one key means that the wearer can unlock the door to life. Usually we see three keys worn together. In this charm the keys stand for love, wealth, and health and the wearer is believed to be able to unlock the doors to these.

KNOTS: The knot ties things together. Thus, for generations the knot is the symbol of unity. We have the "lover's knot" and many other knots worn to symbolize that there is an unbreakable bond between the wearer and someone else.

LADYBIRD: The ladybird is a bearer of good fortune. But this lasts only so long as no harm is allowed to come to the ladybird. Many people wear jeweled symbols of the ladybird in order to have the good luck which the ladybird will bring and at the same time avoid doing the ladybird any harm.

LYRE: Apollo was the god of the lyre. Thus, if a jeweled lyre is worn, it is supposed to bring to the wearer the qualities which he most desires.

OWL: The owl is the symbol of deep knowledge and wisdom. Thus, the bird is associated with these traits and those interested in learning often wear a replica of the owl.

PENNIES: The ordinary penny is not a source of good luck, even though many people carry lucky pennies. The only penny that has lucky powers is one bearing the date of a leap year. If one of these is carried on the person, it is supposed to bring good fortune.

PIG: The pig of itself is not a symbol of good fortune. But if the image of the pig is mutilated in some way, it is believed that this damage will absorb any danger which might come near the wearer. Thus, very often people wear small jeweled or metal pigs with tail, leg, or some other part of the body broken or damaged.

RING: The meaning of the ring is that of unending eternity. It is the perfect circle which has no end. Thus, if worn, it signifies that a vow made is to be kept for eternity. The wedding ring has this meaning.

SERPENT: The serpent has for generations been thought of as the source of knowledge, wisdom, and a means of healing from disease. Therefore, small images of serpents are worn by many who wish to excel in either the arts of learning or those of healing.

SHAMROCK: This is a symbol of good fortune and is worn, either in the natural state or in the form of a symbol, by many people to bring fortune and prosperity.

SWASTIKA: Although this symbol has been adopted by the present German ruling party and has fallen into disrepute in many quarters of the world, its ancient meaning should not be lost sight of. The word itself comes from the Sanscrit and means "purveyor of good fortune." Thus, it is a symbol of luck and prosperity and has been used by many peoples and many individuals to bring this good fortune.

TAU: This consists of two straight lines, one vertical and the other horizontal. People wear this symbol to ward off diseases of the skin.

Many people make and carry their own charms. This is perfectly permissible. If, in some experience, an object seems to be connected with your success, it is permissible to make this object your charm and the source of good luck. Often an heirloom, which has brought good fortune to the family, will be passed on to the child and will bring continued good fortune. Such an object may be anything or things in any combination. Indeed, it is possible to find almost everything used in some form as a symbol of luck and happiness.

OUIJA BOARD

A B C D E F G H I J K L
M N O P Q R S T U V W X Y Z

GOOD BY

OUIJA

PLANCHETTE

The Ouija Board has been used both as a toy and as a means of receiving messages or answers to questions.

A great deal of discussion has taken place as to whether or not the messages and answers are authentic communications from the spirits of the dead. Many Spiritualists and investigators into the occult have held that the board is a means for making direct contact with the dead and that the messages which are spelled out are from these dead.

Others have held that the messages are not true messages, but are the result of muscular tension and unconscious direction of the hand.

Whether or not either group is correct, the Ouija Board is a source of much enjoyment and the messages can cause much merriment when a group is assembled for a pleasant evening.

The Ouija Board consists of a flat board approximately eighteen inches wide and thirty inches long, with a very smooth surface. On the surface the letters of the alphabet are printed, beginning on the left with "A" and running in two arched rows across the board. At the bottom of the board is the sentence, "Good By." More complicated boards may have other sentences in addition to the one suggested.

There is also a small planchette or three-legged table about one inch high and shaped in the form of a heart about six inches long. Near the tip of the planchette is a round hole about the size of a half dollar and covered with transparent material. In the center of this hole is an opening through which a pin is suspended. The table is equipped with felt pads on each leg to make movement as easy as possible.

To use the board, two people sit facing each other and rest the board on their knees. Then each puts the tips of the fingers of both hands on the planchette. To make the board work most accurately, there must be complete quiet. Further, the party asking the question must concentrate on the question he wishes to ask. Do not tell your question to anyone. You may write it down on a piece of paper and hide the paper where no one will see it. The other party working with you should not know the question.

Usually you will have to sit quiet and concentrate for about five minutes. Do not consciously push or pull the planchette.

Permit it to move of its own accord. After a while it will begin to move over the letters on the board and will stop every now and then directly over a letter. The letter indicated will be directly under the pin in the planchette. As it moves it will spell out the answer to your question.

It is not well for one to work for more than a half hour with an Ouija Board since the concentration necessary may cause a headache or other physical discomfort.

TABLE TIPPING

Table tipping or table turning was for many years the chief evening diversion at many parties or gatherings of young and old.

To accomplish this strange phenomenon, a group of people would gather about a small, light table and rest the tips of the fingers of both hands on the table. Usually the fingers would be spread out with the thumbs touching and the little fingers of each hand touching the little fingers of those on both sides of each person participating. This "completes the circuit."

Then everyone should remain quiet and make every effort to exert no force to move the table. Frequently the group would sing together. If the experiment was successful, the table would begin to move more or less violently about the room so that the group would have to follow it.

This phenomenon has been investigated by a great many people since it was used for a long time by mediums and others claiming that the movement was caused by the spirits of the dead and that certain movements were messages from these dead. The results of these investigations have shown that the table moves because of unconscious muscular pressure exerted by those taking part. Under strong concentration people will tend, purely unconsciously, to push the table. Since they are all concentrating on the same thing and each trying not to push the table, it is usual that they will all push in the same direction or someone who is more "heavy handed" than the others will unconsciously push the table even though the others do not co-operate.

To get the most fun out of this, usually the group agrees that movement in one direction will mean "Yes" and in another will mean "No." Then they agree upon a question to be answered, arrange themselves, and begin to concentrate. All questions asked should be answerable with a simple "Yes" or "No."

CRYSTAL-GAZING

Crystal-gazing is an ancient and widely practiced art. Through its use many strange things have happened. Crimes have been solved, lost articles found, hidden facts in the lives of people have been uncovered, and unrealized aspects of one's relationships with others have been revealed.

Though crystal-gazing has been used with some remarkable success in piecing together the facts of the past, its chief use both by professional seers and others is to look into the future and discover what is about to happen or what may happen unless precautions are taken.

The first requirement for successful crystal-gazing is for the person to be highly sensitive and receptive. Many people are not at all receptive and no amount of effort will make them competent in this art. Others differ in degrees of receptivity. A small few have the gift necessary for success in this art.

Fundamental to success here is ability to concentrate so that everything about you is completely shut out from your thinking. Without perfect concentration one will be unable to discover anything in a crystal. Differences in ability to concentrate mean differences in ability to read the crystal.

The second prerequisite is to have a clear crystal in which to gaze. The crystal should be about the size of a baseball or slightly larger. And it should be perfect and clear. Crystals with even slight blemishes or bubbles are valueless since the blemish will distract the gazer and make complete concentration impossible.

The gazer should seat himself so that light, whether full light or subdued light, comes from his back. Never sit looking into the light. He may hold the crystal in his hand or rest it on a table in a suitable cup or stand about two inches high. It is best to cover the table with black cloth and to have a black curtain a foot or two behind the crystal. This helps in concentrating.

Then the gazer should seek to put everything out of his mind except the problem with which he is concerned. There should be no noise in the room. The slight moving of a chair, loud breathing, the crackling of the fire, or any other even slight noise will distract and make complete concentration impossible.

To think of anything else than the problem in hand will make success impossible. Close the mind to everything else, shut out all other thoughts, all other ideas. Try to forget where you are and what is about you. In this way you will induce a mild form of self-hypnotism in which you are completely wrapped up in your problem. Gaze steadily at the crystal without batting an eye or making any movement of the muscles of the body.

To be proficient in the art of crystal-gazing requires much practice. At first you will not succeed. You will become restless and cannot help but move slightly. But after you have practiced several times, you will gain proficiency in the art so that you can control your body, your eyes, and can shut out all other factors except your problem.

As you gaze in the crystal and your concentration becomes complete, after a time you will see the clear crystal becoming cloudy. It will be as if a milky cloud has floated into the crystal.

This is the sign that the spell is operating. Then this cloud will begin to change color. It usually becomes red, and then green, and finally will become completely black as your concentration is complete. This black color in the crystal serves as a shade or curtain behind which is the information you wish to gain. It is hiding it from you, but the information is there.

The final stage is when this black cloud rolls away as if a curtain were lifted. Then you will see in the crystal what you are looking for. Often the rolling away of the black curtain will be so startling that you are awakened from your trance and the message is lost. If this happens, wait a while and try again. It may take a number of sittings before you are able to resist the shock of the revelation and hold yourself in the trance. But keep trying. You are on the road to success.

When you do succeed, you will find behind the dark curtain sights which are meaningful in terms of your problem. You may see people, houses, places where you have never been, words or sentences, symbols or other objects which have a meaning for you. To interpret these is difficult and requires imagination and keenness of understanding. This too necessitates much practice.

Very often, all that you can do is to describe what you see and allow the person whose life you are reading to make his own interpretation. The place you see may have a meaning for him but none for you. The face you see may be that of someone he knows intimately but whom you have never seen and of whom you can know nothing.

Sometimes the scenes in the crystal will change as you gaze. You should tell what you see and what is happening before your eyes. Don't add to it. Just be a reporter who is perfectly honest. In this way you will build up skill in seeing and describing and very often the other person will supply the missing information or the meaning.

Practice in crystal-gazing will give you a talent which can bring a great deal of entertainment to any group in which you happen to be. But if the purpose of the group is entertainment and fun, do not tell all you see in the crystal, especially if what you see is bad. This may cause more trouble than entertainment.

VIII

The Psychology of Fortune Telling

A GOOD TELLER of fortunes is a keen observer of people and their ways of thinking and acting. It requires imagination, ability to piece together a whole personality from bits of conversation, the art of asking a few leading questions which are not obvious to the one being questioned, and a talent for drawing pertinent conclusions from the way a person is dressed, what he says, and the like, to be successful.

The average person is interested in himself and his own problems. Many of these problems result from personality characteristics which are more or less obvious to others but which escape him. Very often these facts can be used by a keen observer as the basis for talking about one's fortune.

But the entertaining fortune teller, one who is always ready to furnish fun at a party by telling the guests about themselves, must have a clever line of talk. He must begin the session by asking a few meaningless questions which put the inquirer at ease and allow him to act naturally. This type of question and a great deal of pleasant "patter" should be sandwiched in throughout the session so that the inquirer is kept at ease and is not fully aware of what is going on. This "patter" serves to make the inquirer interested and happy during the session.

But the heart of fortune telling is not the "patter" or meaningless questions. These are window dressing. You may learn something, or at least get a few hints during this part of the procedure. But you learn most from making careful observations of the inquirer. Look at his or her dress. Is it plain or gaudy? Does the person dress in style or does he show a lack of taste? Does the manner of dressing show wealth or a meager income? Is the person pleasing in dress and facial appearance, or just plain, or repelling? All of these matters are related to his life and are often results of personality characteristics which are meaningful.

Watch the person's manner. Is he possessed or nervous even after you have attempted to put him at ease? Is he quiet and relaxed or jumpy and uneasy? Is he attempting to put on a front, acting as though he did not care, or is he interested and anxious? These can be cues for you to follow.

Then, from time to time during the session, ask leading questions, questions based on what you have seen. His answers will give you hints for further questions. Sometimes the tone of voice used in answering your questions, the facial expressions, the bodily movements, will suggest to a keen observer facts which can be drawn out as the conversation proceeds.

Remember, the things found in the palm, in tea leaves, in cards, or in any other device which you may use are suggestive only. They have general meanings, but the important facts are to be found within these general meanings. And these latter are what you must discover by your own ingenuity. At times you must make shrewd guesses, a little at a time, and watch your inquirer's reactions. These will tell you a great deal, and you can move from them to other suggestions which will give you new cues. In this way you can fill in a picture which would otherwise be general and applicable to many people. Your inquirer is not vitally interested in the general factors, but in more specific things.

Let us take an example. Suppose your inquirer is a young lady of seventeen or thereabouts. She is nicely dressed and has a pleasant smile. Her hands are kept carefully and tastefully. She is pretty and has a soft vibrant voice when she speaks. From these few facts you can make many judgments. Without doubt, she is thinking of love. She possibly has many admirers. You deal out the cards after talking with her a few minutes and making certain observations to yourself. Then you see a young man in the cards. He is tall, dark, and handsome. A mere suggestion of this fact may bring a glow to her eyes. You have a cue. She knows someone who fits this description. You can afford to ask a few questions and let her dwell on the fact of the man for a moment. Her actions will reveal enough for you to go on to talk about him and his relationship to her.

This line of procedure applies regardless of the medium you are using. The medium will give you suggestions upon which you must build your case. What the inquirer does, even the most insignificant act, may be your cue. Use it. Work it for all that it is worth. It may lead to other cues and, with the help of your medium, you can construct an interesting and meaningful fortune.

The most important asset of a good fortune teller is ability to size up personalities. This requires a kind of sensitivity to personal moods and actions. It is highly possible that you will be looking directly at a person and yet be blind to actions which mean much. You cannot afford this blindness. It is like a curtain between you and the inquirer and will make anything that you do with your medium of little value. Some persons are gifted with a keen sensitivity to other persons and their moods. If you have even a little of this gift, develop it.

How can you develop it? That is easy. Obey your first impressions. Act upon the weakest "hunch" that you have. These are beginnings. As you make use of them, act as they direct, you will find yourself becoming keener. Your sensitivity will grow. It is just like the development of sensitivity in any field. The musician is sensitive to tone and the artist is sensitive to color because neither has ever refused to act when it seemed necessary. They have not tried to suppress the first drawings of sensitivity, but have taken hold of these early and vague beginnings and by constantly protecting them have developed them into full maturity.

A person enters your booth and immediately you sense that he is unhappy, or studious, or an energetic businessman. Follow these "hunches." Ask questions, not bold and obvious questions, but vague questions to confirm your "hunch." Then go on from there. At first you will make mistakes. Not every "hunch" is correct. But keep practicing. You will be surprised at the results even after a short time.

Having sensed the nature of the person you are dealing with and having sized up his interests and personal characteristics, emphasize in your fortune telling things in which he is interested. These will open doors for you to enter and explore further. Play on these interests, expand them, and watch his reactions.

There is one thing to remember. You are not a professional seer. There is a great mass of lore that has come to us from the ages. Many people have given their lives to the study of this lore. Others come from a long line of people who have developed fortune telling as a racial occupation. The gypsies are such a people. But you are primarily an entertainer. You want to tell fortunes for fun.

Therefore, look for good things. If you find some evil in the cards, in the hand, or elsewhere, play it down or overlook it altogether. You may cause trouble and do more harm than good. And you may be mistaken. Then look for the good. Look for health, wealth, prosperity, happiness. Play these up and you will be a popular person at the party or other gathering. People like to hear the good and not the bad. You, as an entertainer, should play on this like. It will make everybody happier, and a good time will be had by all.

. . . .other best selling
NEWCASTLE books
you won't want to miss. . . .